FAULKNER'S IMPERIALISM

Southern Literary Studies

FAULKNER'S IMPERIALISM

Space, Place,
and the
Materiality
of Myth

TAYLOR HAGOOD

Louisiana State University Press)(Baton Rouge, Louisiana

Published by Louisiana State University Press
Copyright © 2008 by Louisiana State University Press
All rights reserved
Manufactured in the United States of America
Louisiana Paperback Edition, 2018

Designer: Tammi deGeneres
Typefaces: Sabon, Myriad Pro

Library of Congress Cataloging-in-Publication Data

Hagood, Taylor, 1975–
  Faulkner's imperialism : space, place, and the materiality of myth / Taylor Hagood.
    p. cm. — (Southern literary studies)
  Includes bibliographical references and index.
  ISBN 978-0-8071-3344-6 (cloth: alk. paper) — ISBN 978-0-8071-6996-4 (pbk. : alk paper)
  1. Faulkner, William, 1897–1962—Criticism and interpretation. 2. Imperialism in literature.
  3. Space in literature. 4. Place (Philosophy) in literature. 5. Myth in literature. I. Title.
  PS3511.A86Z78425 2008
  813'.52—dc22
                  2008001891

Parts of the discussion of whiteness in chapter 1 and elsewhere first appeared in "Negotiating the Marble Bonds of Whiteness: Hybridity and Imperial Impulse in Faulkner," *Faulkner Journal* 22.1–2 (2006–7): 24–38 (© 2007 by the University of Central Florida; reprinted with permission). A portion of the discussion of *Pylon* in chapter 2 first appeared in "Media, Ideology, and the Role of Literature in *Pylon*," *Faulkner Journal* 21.1–2 (2005–6): 107–19 (© 2006 by the University of Central Florida; reprinted with permission). Some of the material on cotton in chapter 3 appeared in "Taking 'Money Right out of an American's Pockets': Faulkner's South and the International Cotton Market," *European Journal of American Culture* 26 (2007): 83–95 (© Intellect Ltd. 2007; reprinted with permission). And a version of chapter 4 was published as "Faulkner's 'Fabulous Immeasurable Camelots': *Absalom, Absalom!* and *Le Morte Darthur*," in *Southern Literary Journal* 34.2 (2002): 45–63 (© 2002 by the *Southern Literary Journal* and the University of North Carolina at Chapel Hill Department of English; reprinted with permission).

The paper in this book meets the guidelines for permanence and durability of the Committee on Production Guidelines for Book Longevity of the Council on Library Resources. ∞

To Raymond, Lucy, and Libby Hagood,
Phoebe Lee Mohundro Brown,
Marsha L. Dutton,
David Noble,
and
Carl B. Jarrell

CONTENTS

ACKNOWLEDGMENTS
ix

INTRODUCTION
The Passive Recalcitrance of Topography
Space, Place, Myth, Imperialism, and Cosmos
1

CHAPTER ONE
Here Pan's Sharp Hoofed Feet Have Pressed
Arcadian Place and the Roar of the Present
33

CHAPTER TWO
A Tearing of Endless Silk
New Orleans and the Exotic Frame of Revelry
71

CHAPTER THREE
Sold into Egypt
The Raiding of Mythic Place
119

CHAPTER FOUR
Fabulous Immeasurable Camelots and Carcassonnes
The Quest of Imperialism

153

CONCLUSION
Rapacity Does Not Fail
Mythic Place, Imperial Space, and *A Fable*

185

NOTES

201

WORKS CITED

219

INDEX

239

ACKNOWLEDGMENTS

Heading the list of individuals who have been important to the process of writing this book is Joseph R. Urgo, whose support in the roles of department chair, dissertation director, and mentor have been crucial; he thinks big and has encouraged me to do so as well. Of no less importance to me have been Campbell McCool and the McCool family, who honored me as the inaugural recipient of the Frances Bell McCool Dissertation Fellowship in Faulkner Studies, which made it possible for me to complete a solid first draft of this book; thanks are also due to Donald M. Kartiganer and Jay Watson for their parts in granting me the fellowship and for encouraging me as a fledgling Faulknerian. I thank Alfred J. López, Annette Trefzer, and Charles Reagan Wilson for their valuable feedback on early drafts of this work, and I thank the staff of the University of Mississippi's John Davis Williams Library Department of Archives and Special Collections. I also thank Tommy Covington, of the Ripley (Mississippi) Public Library, for allowing me access to Faulkner material and for suggesting research directions.

Special thanks are due to Joan Wylie Hall, who chaired the panel on which I presented my first conference paper, at the 1999 Southern Writers, Southern Writing Conference, the material of which was the kernel of this book. She has remained a supportive friend and did the particular favor of introducing me to John Easterly, executive editor at Louisiana State University Press. I cannot imagine a better person to work with than John: he has been open and helpful at each step in the publication process, and it has been a great privilege to work with him. I am also grateful to Fred Hobson, the Southern Literary Studies series editor, who also served as one of the readers, and to the anonymous reader whose comments were so helpful in revising this volume. And my thanks to Joanne Allen and all the people at Louisiana State University Press for their part in producing this book.

Several friends and colleagues have provided support and feedback along the way. Christopher B. Bundrick, Mary Faraci, Randall J. Jasmine, Ashley Craig Lancaster, Crystal Lorimor, Travis Montgomery, Suzanne Penuel, and David Ramm have been to me as family (Suzanne was of special help in gathering last-minute bibliographic information). Several Faulkner scholars, including Edwin T. Arnold, Deborah Clarke, Thadious Davis, Susan V. Donaldson, Anne Goodwyn Jones, Barbara Ladd, Peter Lurie, John Matthews, Noel Polk, Evelyn Jaffe Schreiber, Theresa Towner, Dawn Truoard, and Michael Zeitlin graciously admitted me to their presence. I am equally grateful to Suman Basuroy, Steve Blakemore, Robert DeMott, Ben Fisher, Ann Fisher-Wirth, Andrew Furman, Warren Kelly, Colby Kullman, John Lowe, Douglas McGetchin, and Kathryn B. McKee. My thanks to Laura Cade, who has generously offered intellectual and emotional support. Thanks to Julia Davis for believing in this book and "blessing" it. The members of my graduate seminar on Faulkner provided helpful insights, and the following students have been particularly inspiring: Heather Everly, Deryck Lance, Melissa Loucks, Victoria Swanson, Dana Webster, and Matthew Wohlgemuth.

To a few I want to state my deepest gratitude. First, to Carl B. Jarrell, coal miner turned philosopher and creative writer, who befriended me and generously encouraged me until his death. To Marsha L. Dutton, who believed in me from the beginning of my graduate career and who continues as mentor and friend. To David Noble, who believed in me from the beginning of my undergraduate career. And to my mother, father, sister, and grandmother, whose kindness exceeds elaboration.

FAULKNER'S IMPERIALISM

INTRODUCTION

The Passive Recalcitrance of Topography
Space, Place, Myth, Imperialism, and Cosmos

[T]hings always tell several stories; they tell about their own making, they tell about the historical circumstances under which they were made, and if they are real things, they also reveal truth.
—Christian Norberg-Schulz, *Genius Loci*

It would not be too much to say that myth is the secret opening through which the inexhaustible energies of the cosmos pour into human cultural manifestations.
—Joseph Campbell, *The Hero with a Thousand Faces*

William Faulkner begins *The Unvanquished* with a scene in which the young Bayard Sartoris and his slave companion, Ringo Strother, construct a map to represent the siege of Vicksburg. "Behind the smokehouse that summer," Bayard narrates, "Ringo and I had a living map. Although Vicksburg was just a handful of chips from the woodpile and the River a trench scraped into the packed earth with the point of a hoe, it (river, city, and terrain) lived, possessing even in miniature that ponderable though passive recalcitrance of topography which outweighs artillery, against which the most brilliant of victories and the most tragic of defeats are but the loud noises of a moment" (3).

Like many of Faulkner's passages, this compact overture contains a matrix of axioms that constitutes the mapping of place, space, and power in the Faulknerian cosmos.[1] The scene is striking, first, for its displacement, a fundamental problem in the mythic nature of Yoknapatawpha and practically the rest of Faulkner's created world: Bayard and his enslaved shadow "brother" construct a parallel miniature that is displaced from the "real" place it reproduces, and this event revolutionizes their lives in terms of their relations to each other "behind" rather than in the front of the smokehouse. The location of their activity informs the activity itself as something already past, already profane, for the "the rear is profane," Yi-Fu Tuan writes. "Maintenance men and janitors enter through service doors at the back and move along the 'guts' of [a] building, while executives and their secretaries enter by the front door" (40–41). In this scene in *The Unvanquished* the position "behind" is thrice stressed: (1) Bayard and Ringo are positioned behind the "Big House"; (2) they are behind the smokehouse, which is part of the behind of the Big House; and (3) since it is narrated in the past tense, they are positioned behind the present time of narration.

From their position "in back of" and therefore on the periphery of time, space, and maturity, Bayard and Ringo give to local habitation the name of airy nothing. This playground re-creates Vicksburg, a town already defeated and thus a space that is a narrative, a mythologized place they use to define their space. Neither Bayard nor Ringo has seen Vicksburg, as Ringo's uncle, Loosh, reveals when he tells them that Bayard's father is actually in Corinth, "[a]nother un you aint know" (5). The place/narrative they do know is "the pattern of recapitulant mimic furious victory [held between them] like a cloth, a shield between ourselves and reality, between us and fact and doom" (4). And they naturally create their microcosmic place/narrative according to the rules of their macrocosm, rules that dictate that Bayard be the Confederate General Pemberton twice to Ringo's once and depend on a sense of fraternity (however fallacious) in which the two of them "first [. . .] join forces and spend [themselves] against a common enemy, time, before [they] could engender between [them] the pattern of recapitulant mimic furious victory" (4). Despite the narratives and rules they construct, however, Bayard and Ringo nevertheless discover "that ponderable though passive recalcitrance of topography" that refuses finally to conform to the myth that would order it.[2] The myth is an imperial one, whether it be the boys' colonizing of the yard or the Unionists' defeating the Confederate rebels or the African American Loosh's destroying the boys' model of Vicksburg when he "with his hand [. . . sweeps] the chips flat" (5). But the land will not be imperialized, and throughout his oeuvre Faulkner and his characters rhapsodize over the land's being finally "the unvanquished," making the final impotence of myth's imperialism one of the great mythic tenets of Faulkner's mythic world.

This passage is significant because it offers, if not a germ of apocrypha, at least a cell of the Faulknerian cosmological organism, complete with DNA, from which can be spawned the larger conceptualization of the fictional world of Faulkner's creation. Elements of his complex constitution of place and space appear here, interacting to create the paradoxical combination of motion and stasis that Richard P. Adams explains is fundamental to Faulkner's art. Tuan asserts that place "is a pause in movement. [. . .] The pause makes it possible for a locality to become a center of felt value" (138). And yet, encapsulated in Faulkner's place—his own tumultuous village and tortured boughs frozen on his own backward-gazing urn—is a dynamic interrelation of perspectives and conflict of powers. In a sense, these places in Faulkner's created world and indeed the world itself function much like Flem Snopes's "footprint," which according to V. K. Ratliff marks a pause, a stop along the way that proclaims, *"This is where I was when I moved again"* (*The Town* 26).

In this volume I reread William Faulkner's fictional relationship with and depiction of space by reconsidering myth and place in his cosmos as fictional elements that encode, exhibit, and serve imperial impulse. Rather than reading the roles of myth and place according to conventional myth criticism or typical place models used by Faulkner scholars, I examine the ways myth and place articulate both oppressive and subversive narratives of empire. Accordingly, I examine intertextuality on both a horizontal plane (William Faulkner's writings) and a vertical plane (writings by others stretching back to much earlier eras) by analyzing the ways various constituents create and negotiate space and place by operating within and generating textualities that interact with textualities from other locations temporally and (therefore) spatially. These intertextual spaces embody both oppressive narratives and their subversive counternarratives; these narrative spaces are protean in nature, and their relationships with one another are flexible and dynamic. They are the spaces that make up Faulkner's cosmos—the combination of the world of intertextuality in which he lived and the world he created.

Roland Barthes discusses the "inter-text," the interaction of texts and reading experiences, in *The Pleasure of the Text*. He observes that when reading

> a text cited by Stendhal (but not written by him) I find Proust in one minute detail. [. . .] I recognize that Proust's work, for myself at least, is *the* reference work, the general *mathesis*, the *mandala* of the entire literary cosmogony—as Mme de Sévigné's letters were for the narrator's grandmother, tales of chivalry for Don Quixote, etc.; this does

not mean that I am in any way a Proust "specialist": Proust is what comes to me, not what I summon up; not an "authority," simply a *circular memory*. Which is what the inter-text is: the impossibility of living outside the infinite text—whether this text be Proust or the daily newspaper or the television screen: the book creates the meaning, the meaning creates life. (35–36)

The Faulknerian cosmos is marked by disappearing edges, places where the work drifts into other texts and textualities, and the intensely personal aspect of Barthes's comments is noteworthy. Indeed, I as the author of this text am obliged to acknowledge my particular investment in the reading of Faulkner that follows, for its edges and endings are me, myself, just as they are a collection of narratives that are other readers of Faulkner, as well as Faulkner as a reader of others (and sometimes even himself). I wholeheartedly acknowledge that my own reading affects my peculiar engagement with Faulkner's work: my discussion of Faulkner, like any discussion, is embedded in and operates within the intertext, just as Faulkner's writing exists within and participates with other works in the slippery cosmos of textuality.

This examination of intertextuality does not amount to some academic game (although it very much is a game). The forging together and connecting of one textuality with others marks the dynamic of the creation of meaning. And William Faulkner is one of those writers whose work stands as a nerve center, a conduit. In explaining why his book *Faulkner the Storyteller* focuses solely on Faulkner's work, Blair Labatt seeks to analyze Faulkner's tactics of plot construction by "finding out how a 'great writer' (the phrase was once respectable) actually *makes* [plots]. Instead of a general study, let alone a poetics, with examples from Faulkner, this [book] became preeminently an empirical description of plots that attempted to give practical value to terminology, which assumed that the abstractions had no significance outside their unique working in unique texts" (x–xi). *Central* may be substituted for *great* as a description of Faulkner's work to stress the fact that it occupies a central place in world literature. However much Faulkner's stature in academe and the literary world are the result of cold-war politics, his work has also influenced writers who would write against empowered perspectives and traditions. A major figure in places as far away as France and Japan and a prime influence on such writers as diverse as Gabriel García Márquez and Toni Morrison, Faulkner is ubiquitous in the intertext. And his presence is difficult to quantify. Clearly speaking from a codified position of empowerment and obviously privileging that perspective, Faulkner also articulated (both intentionally and unintentionally) the perspectives of the unempowered.

If Faulkner is such an influential presence in the matrix of intertextuality, then it seems particularly important to make a statement on the whole of his work. Such a project has rarely been undertaken since early studies by Olga Vickery, Cleanth Brooks, and others. The majority of Faulkner scholarship has canonized certain texts and groups of texts or worked to recuperate others; this book seeks to accomplish neither. While my reading sees Faulkner's works in a different alignment from those schematizations recognized by past scholars, I do not suggest a new schematization of Faulkner's career. Instead, I seek to consider a certain way the texts fit together and speak to one another; rather than evaluating them individually as good or bad, I focus on their interconnections in relation to other texts. My reading is slippery, flexible, and not entirely consistent in accordance with Faulkner's slipperiness, flexibility, and inconsistency. While I propose a model of reading Faulkner's work in terms of what I call mythic place and imperial space, I am not interested in applying that rubric in some rote way that simply proves the model. The model is simply a tool of investigation and interrogation—a magnifying glass, a polygraph, fingerprint powder—but a tool that also knows that it is a tool. My hope is that the material and the tool, which is itself material, will produce a reading that can help make and see the meaning of the Faulknerian cosmos for a world that has taken that cosmos as one of its keystones.

This book thus focuses on Faulkner's entire etching on the jailhouse window; it wants to give Kilroy a thorough going-over. It recognizes the multivocality not only of Faulkner's texts but of the various Faulkners themselves, and it discusses what those voices together or separately say because the Faulknerian cosmos is one of the pillars, the props, of contemporary writing and thought, to be visited and revisited and examined for what it has said and continues to say. However, in attempting to discuss the whole of Faulkner's work, I do not aim to discuss every word he wrote. Examining these textualities requires a gestural effort that is both tremendously ambitious and inexorably doomed (in Faulknerian fashion) to failure. It is an investigation that must stop somewhere, for the world and its proliferation of textualities cannot be contained in a single glimpse or comprehended by a single mind. In a sense, then, my effort is therefore unabashedly personal, and deliberately so in hopes of inspiring others to undertake such a project so that collectively perhaps the vastness of intertextuality as channeled through space and place can be approached. Recognizing that I cannot produce a reading that does not exclude, let me say, à la Whitman, that I sing and embrace both exclusion and inclusion.

The text that follows is also messy, in part in the hope that Faulkner's own messiness might be preserved, denounced, and celebrated. For at the same time that I acknowledge the ways I am implicated in the text, I also seek to approach Faulkner's work on its own terms, dreadfully naive as that sounds. Labatt laments that few "postmodern critics have adequately distinguished whether they are talking about novels [Faulkner] wanted to write, or novels they believe him to have written without understanding what he was doing, or simply novels they think should have been written" (xiii). This concern has been sounded before in Faulkner criticism, from Brooks's warning against "symbol-mongering" (*William Faulkner* 9) to Walter Slatoff's insistence, as he defends the exclusions implicit in his thesis, that "most novels, especially those of Faulkner, are so rich and varied that seekers will usually find in them what they are looking for" (2). I hope that my own efforts lie somewhere in between an empirical description and symbol-mongering, as I hope to have produced, or at least initiated, a discussion that arises out of and depends upon the specificity of Faulkner's texts but also freely acknowledges theoretical and literary influences on Faulkner and even on my own reading.

Thus, this book undertakes to rearrange the Faulkner Rubik's Cube. That project may begin by reexamining two fundamental elements of Faulkner's work: place and myth. Discussions of these two elements have been staples of Faulkner criticism. Until recently, with few exceptions, scholars have tended to focus on Faulkner's southern spaces. Likewise, discussions of Faulkner's myth have often focused on the aesthetic significance of his use or development of a given myth, situating his "mythic method" in relation to those of other modernists rather than reading his use of myth as a means of addressing complex political situations whose constituents employ myth to further their designs.

The starting point of these myth/place examinations of Faulkner's work is Malcolm Cowley's landmark introduction to *The Portable Faulkner*. The significance of this essay in resuscitating Faulkner's literary reputation is undeniable. Although Lawrence H. Schwartz has rightly problematized the sometimes grandiose claims of this document's impact, the fact remains that it and the volume it introduces were major factors in the status-boosting that led to Faulkner's winning the Nobel Prize and being considered one of the United States' "greatest" writers. Two paragraphs into his introduction, Cowley identifies the two-pronged thrust of Faulkner's fiction as he sees it: "There in Oxford, Faulkner performed a labor of imagination that has not been equaled in our time, and a *double* labor: first, to invent a Mississippi county that was like a mythical kingdom, but was complete and living in all its details; second, to make his story of Yoknapatawpha County stand as a parable or legend of all the Deep South" (viii, emphasis mine).

Joseph R. Urgo has shown the ways *The Portable Faulkner* imposed order on what was actually apocrypha, and Faulkner's correspondence with Cowley reveals how erroneous was the latter's assertion that Faulkner's "work has become a myth or legend of the South" (xx).[3] But the problems with Cowley's project are not the immediate issue; rather, the influences of his observations on other critical approaches to Faulkner are important to consider. Schwartz writes that one of Cowley's goals was "to end critical neglect and to offer a base from which to confront the entirety of Faulkner's work, stressing the coherent design that tied together the Yoknapatawpha novels and stories; and he hoped to force a serious reconsideration by other critics" (25). In this endeavor Cowley succeeded almost too well, as critics initially worked simply to elucidate the inchoate points he had already made by mining the parallels that he suggested existed between the mythic Yoknapatawpha County and the real Lafayette County.[4]

Those Cowley-initiated scholarly efforts are significant for the political ideologies they reflect, namely, their insistence on privileging the local over the whole, or, more metaphorically, the individual over the mass of society. Cleanth Brooks, for example, argues from the very beginning of *William Faulkner: The Yoknapatawpha Country* that the great writer's great theme was that of agrarian opposition to modern industrial "man," a theme that in *I'll Take My Stand* he and the other Twelve Southerners saw as being exemplified in the South but also as a larger trait of the non-mechanized regions of the United States. Furthermore, as Schwartz argues, Faulkner's rise in prominence "coincided with United States political and economic hegemony at the end of [World War II]. With that rise in power and position came, given the devastation in Europe, preeminence in culture. [. . .] Faulkner became universalized as an emblem of the freedom of the individual under capitalism, as a chronicler of the plight of man in the modern world [. . . exemplifying] the same values that Western intellectuals saw in capitalism which made it morally superior to communism" (4).

Scholars thus understood Faulkner and the South as exceptional for a specific political reason: they represented the individual and the individual's values in the face of an opposing socialistic system. What is odd in this line of thought is that a place so exotic and exceptional as a fictional county in Mississippi (which requires reams of paper to explain because of its *difference*) should so easily stand for even such a larger imagined community as the South, much less the entire United States—that, as Schwartz further notes, Faulkner should come "to represent American literary modernism" (4).

Recent theorists have begun to rethink the nature of space in the South and have thus opened the door to a reconsideration of Faulkner's treatment of it. An early example of this rethinking was Michael Kreyling's *Inventing Southern Literature,* which used Benedict Anderson's concept of the "imagined community" to describe the nature of southern space and literature. This idea quickly caught on as it seemed to move closer to the heart of describing a region that is not a separate nation nor even all that different from the rest of the United States in terms of a set of concrete quantifiable distinguishing traits, yet is very "different" indeed. In his foreword to Suzanne Jones and Sharon Monteith's *South to a New Place* Richard Gray further develops the spatial conception Kreyling introduced by observing that the "South is an imagined community made up of a multiplicity of communities, similarly imaged" (xxiii). In the essays in that volume and in much scholarly thinking since, the monolithic notion of "the South" signifying the white aristocracy with its conspicuously patriarchal hegemony has been usefully fragmented, and southern space has come to be understood as plural in nature.[5]

But recognizing the fragmentedness of southern space has not been the only reevaluation of the place(s) of the South; accompanying this change has been a new understanding of the placement of southern U.S. spaces on the globe. Drawing on the work of postcolonial theorists and especially following the lead of Edouard Glissant's seminal *Faulkner, Mississippi,* scholars of southern literature and culture have recognized the U.S. South as a liminal space situated between and participating simultaneously in the cultures of the global North and the global South.[6] These developments in thinking about southern U.S. spaces are important because they introduce a move toward precise thought about literary depictions of the often oversimplified phenomenon (always more imaginary than geographical) called "the South." Understanding southern space as fragmented demands reassessment and avoidance of the positing of large generic southern "themes," meant to offer easy explanations of southern experience.

The purpose of this volume is not just to discuss Faulkner in terms of a fragmented South but also to consider his work in a fragmented world. Although some scholars have recently begun to consider Faulkner's space on a microscopic level, it is important to move beyond South-versus-North paradigms and focus on all spaces within Faulkner's created cosmos, considering their interrelationships in a more holistic and precise way.[7] Of course, such constructs as U.S. North and South, global North and South, and others cannot be ignored; perhaps, however, they might be considered not so much as fixed constructs but rather as *strategies* of performance and definition. In *Outline of a Theory of Practice,* Pierre Bourdieu explains the dynamics of the *habitus* as a performance of environment that mystifies its strategies of behavior into "rules" in order to police or expand its imagined borders. Bourdieu acknowledges the protean nature of what seem to be constructs of behavior and meaning within imagined communities. These observations do not render geography utterly bereft of meaning, as the *habitus* can very much attach itself to a given geographical space; rather, they permit a close examination of shifts and overlappings of space and environment, as well as the complexities of definition and performance within given spaces.[8]

The strategies that contribute to the maintenance of *habitus* register, on the minutest level, an imperial impulse. Whether the imagined community is a vast empire or a negligible hamlet, its professed rules of performance and interaction are elements to be enforced and even imposed, marked out according to boundaries that, however indistinct, are of paramount importance to maintaining stability and power. Wesley A. Kort describes the phenomenon of what I call "imperial impulse" when he writes that when "we think of space, especially social space, in an abstract way, great harm can be done. The imperialist colonial enterprise is inconceivable apart from such ingrained habits of mind. Newly occupied lands become vulnerable to planning imposed on them by minds conditioned by abstract ways of viewing places. Particular places and the relations of their inhabitants to them could simply be subsumed by rational categories that could legitimize economic and political agendas" (9).

The spaces "created" by imperially conditioned "ingrained habits of the mind" and perpetuated by their respective strategies of performance might be called *imperial spaces*. Whether used by groups to build powerful political, military, or economic empires or imagined by individuals to demarcate personal domestic, religious, or aesthetic domains, imperial space connotes a dynamic of power, a center whose purlieu always represents a colonizable possibility. These spaces, these strategies, are imperial precisely because they are the viaducts through which the larger cultural-imperial designs that define them are channeled: the macrocosm is present in the microcosm. It is important to heed Alfred J. López's warning not "to forget how far and in what diverse forms the discourses of imperialism have trafficked through the centuries" (3); nor should we forget the ways in which these discourses have made themselves invisible.

This understanding of space in terms of strategies driven by imperial impulse is based on models of spatiality and empowerment elucidated by postcolonial theorists. Although these writers recognize broad global political configurations of center and periphery and warn against easy constructs of victim and victimizer that would promote dubious and deceptive political agenda, they also follow Gramsci's lead in paying attention to individual colonial and postcolonial situations—individual imperial configurations. While the power of Western hegemony is everywhere evident and the plight of the oppressed East has been examined and documented, it is equally important to understand that the dynamics of center and periphery are finally arbitrary and can reassert themselves in multiple configurations and that the oppressor's situation is just as complicated as that of the diasporic oppressed. Reconsidering Faulkner's spaces in terms of strategies of performance that register imperial impulses requires a different model of reading the narratives in the Faulknerian cosmos. Instead of reading them as part of a lengthy discourse on the expansion of the South around the globe or on the dynamics of a dualistic realm in which the South is pitted against the rest of the world, attention may be paid to minute constitutions of space and the ways they wield performative strategies to enact imperial impulses. This reading of Faulkner's space would seek to achieve an ultimate fragmentation, free even from largely inert models of southern spaces and invested, instead, in dynamic assertions and reassertions of spaces according to multiple and conflicting imperial designs. This reading seeks to identify configurations of center and periphery heretofore unrecognized and to analyze the protean shifts of those configurations and the dynamics of empowerment they register, enforce, and encode. This reading reads Faulknerian space as imperial space, bathed in the machinations of power and control.

The strategies of constituting and perpetuating spaces are enacted within language by means of narrative, which infuses spaces with dynamic abstractions of empowerment. J. E. Malpas notes this relationship between narrative, power, and the constitution of space, writing that "we understand a place and a landscape through historical and personal narratives that are marked out within it and that give that place a particular unity and establish a particular set of possibilities within it" (186). Narrative clearly operates in the construction of imagined communities; it also pervades the most tactile, material incarnations of space. Indeed, narrative can dictate the material administration of power. Faulkner himself acknowledged this nesting of material within narrative in his address "To the Graduating Class, University High School, 1951":

> What threatens us today is fear. Not the atom bomb, nor even fear of it, because if the bomb fell on Oxford tonight, all it could do would be to kill us, which is nothing, since in doing that, it will have robbed itself of its only power over us: which is fear of it, the being afraid of it. Our danger is the forces in the world today which are trying to use man's fear to rob him of his individuality, his soul, the economies or ideologies or political systems, communist or socialist or democratic, whatever they wish to call themselves, the tyrants and the politicians. (*Essays* 122–23)

According to Faulkner, it is narrative, not the material incarnation of power itself, that holds the spirit of humankind in thrall. And narrative, with all of its power, is inescapable, because, as Spivak notes, "we cannot but narrate" (*Postcolonial Critic* 19).[9]

It is in the centrality—indeed the inescapability—of narrative that myth emerges as the critical factor in the constitution and maintenance of imperial space, for myth is a heterogeneous economy of narrative in which any and all groups can participate.[10] In her essay "Can the Subaltern Speak?" Spivak argues that the oppressed periphery is constantly caught in the paradoxical and debilitating space between subject and object position; the subaltern cannot speak because doing so requires appropriating the language of the oppressor, which by nature alienates the oppressed from his or her own language. Yet, the language of myth is inherently heterogeneous, an open space in which the values of the center and margin can be voiced simultaneously and with equal narrative if not equal political authority. Joseph Campbell himself asserts in *The Hero with a Thousand Faces* that "when scrutinized in terms not of what it is but of how it functions, of how it has served mankind in the past, of how it may serve today, mythology shows itself to be as amenable to life itself as to the obsessions and requirements of the individual, the race, the age" (382). Although Campbell drew on the works of Freud, Jung, Rank, and others to cast myth as the language of archetypal expression, this passage is striking in its delineation of the relationship between myth and materiality and the pragmatic flexibility of narrative in a socially constructed world. Indeed, while such theorists as Bruce Lincoln and Richard Slotkin show the role of myth in creating the hegemony of imperialistic powers, Henry A. Murray suggests that myth might also function to articulate the desires of oppressed peoples: "[I]t may be said that the creative imaginations which participate in the formation of a *vital* myth must be those of people—often alienated and withdrawn people—who have *experienced,* in their 'depths' and on their own pulses, one or more of the unsolved critical situations with which humanity at large or members of their own society are confronted. In other words, suffering in 'representative men' may be one of the necessary determinants of an adequate response to challenge" (32).

This appropriation or wielding of myth by the periphery is part of what Michel de Certeau calls the *"ways of using* products imposed by a dominant economic order" (xiii). Certeau cites the example of the Spanish colonizing of New World Natives, pointing out that "[s]ubmissive, and even consenting to their subjection, the Indians nevertheless often *made* of the rituals, representations, and laws imposed on them something quite different from what their conquerors had in mind; they subverted them not by rejecting or altering them, but by using them with respect to ends and references foreign to the system they had no choice but to accept" (xiii).[11]

In Faulkner's writing, myth is wedded to space and place. Like discussions of Faulkner's place since and even before Cowley's introduction to *The Portable Faulkner,* myth has been a mainstay of Faulkner criticism, with critics' understandings of myth in Faulkner's work generally taking two forms. One focuses on the mythology of the South both as appropriated and as generated by Faulkner and appears in many of the early critical treatments of Faulkner already noted, beginning with George Marion O'Donnell's essay "Faulkner's Mythology" and proceeding through the introduction by Cowley to Coughlan, Ward, Kerr, and so on. The second, which focuses on the role ancient myth plays in informing Faulkner's narratives, may be found in such book-length treatments as Richard P. Adams's *Faulkner: Myth and Motion,* Lynn Levins's *Faulkner's Heroic Design,* and Joan M. Serafin's *Faulkner's Use of the Classics,* as well as in countless observations in such texts as André Bleikasten's *The Ink of Melancholy,* John T. Matthews's *The Play of Faulkner's Language,* and Lennart Björk's "Ancient Myth and the Moral Framework of Faulkner's *Absalom, Absalom!*" Faulkner's use of Hebraic, Greek, Roman, and other narratives to articulate his own themes has been shown again and again and has been viewed in the context of the "mythic method" of other modernists, such as Joyce and Eliot.

In addition to these approaches to Faulkner's use of myth, another reading of myth and Faulknerian place complements a reading of his cosmological space as fragmented and imperial. In his helpful and succinct essay, "Definitions of Myth," Murray notes that "[a] single mythic image in the mind, in a poem, or depicted in a painting (e.g., Axis Mundi, Tree of Knowledge, Angel, Virgin Mary) is, in my terminology, a *part* of a myth (*mythic object, mythic character, mythic symbol,* or *moment* of a myth), a part which is very commonly sufficient to bring the complete mythic event to the consciousness of those who are familiar with it" (13). An additional synecdochal "part" that can be added to Murray's catalog is *mythic place,* a place (city, region, etc.) of mythic significance such as Troy or Camelot. This mythic place gains particular empirical power when it is used to describe physical (geographical, topographical, architectural) space; such naming was a part of European imperial projects in the New World, and it is part of Faulkner's project of creating a cosmos of his own.

Faulkner's fragments of imperial space may be isolated and analyzed as mythic places, sites of narrative informed by their mythic significance. Jefferson, Mississippi, signifies as a narrative, anchoring the dynamic strategies of center and periphery that are the abstract imperial space in the poetics of control and subversion encoded in that narrative; the mythic place specifies the fragment of imperial space, giving specificity to the abstraction, or more accurately, the specific narrative engendering the abstract dynamic. The newly created place comes into existence already fraught with the complexities of center and periphery because myth itself contains its own heterogeneity both horizontally (within its own story) and vertically, these mythic places being in fact composed of multiple mythic places since myth draws on preexisting mythic material. Roland Barthes explains this when he notes that myth as a language transforms the sign of "la langue" into the signifier of the signification: "The signifier of myth [which is "the final term of the linguistic system," has a meaning that] is *already* complete, it postulates a kind of knowledge, a past, a memory, a comparative order of facts, ideas, decisions" (*Mythologies* 117). The historical conditions that created the fundamental threads of which myth is woven are suppressed (although, as Barthes also notes, not completely obliterated), which results in myth's seeming ahistoricism. This alleged ahistoricism of myth lends itself to the illusion of (or rather facilitates it as strategic) universality, which allows myth to be transferred from one epoch, with its material situation, to a radically different one. Still, as Claude Lévi-Strauss notes, when the myth-making *bricoleur* uses these stock mythic units to construct a *bricolage,* these preexisting elements bear the traces of their former signification. In their newly ordered form they "serve as extension[s], in the other as material. But the possibilities always remain limited by the particular history of each piece and by those of its features which are already determined by the use for which it was originally intended of the modifications it has undergone for other purposes" (19).

Thus, Faulkner's mythic places are a collection of myths and conform in their structure to what Michel Foucault calls "heterotopias." In his essay "Of Other Spaces" Foucault notes that unlike utopias, which have no real place, heterotopias are "real places—places that do exist and that are formed in the very founding of society—which are something like counter-sites, a kind of effectively enacted utopia in which the real sites, all the other real sites that can be found within the culture, are simultaneously represented, contested, and invented" (24). Engaging in what he labels "heterotopology," Foucault describes the "rules" of heterotopias, noting that they tend to be sites of either crisis or behavioral deviation or both; that their functions can change as civilizations develop; that they can contain multiple and contradictory sites; that they are connected with "slices of time [. . . that] might be termed [. . .] heterochronies" (26); that they "presuppose a system of opening and closing that both isolates them and makes them penetrable" (26); and that they function either as illusory or compensatory spaces, exposing themselves and all other real spaces as illusory or providing other ordered spaces, respectively.

Implicit in Foucault's argument is that these heterotopias are generated either by or in contradistinction to imperial narratives; they are "plots" of ground composed of multiple plots, or narratives. In Faulkner's cosmos, mythic places are plots made up of stacks of plots, something like a stack of transparencies on an overhead projector (if I may be permitted to make an analogy utilizing outmoded equipment, and not for the last time). The layers of the stack are transparent and indistinguishable save for the single space of opacity, the portion of the transparency meant to add to the composite picture created by the entire stack. This opaque space renders each layer visible at the same time that it is otherwise invisible; it is the trace of the past signifying of mythic layers that Lévi-Strauss describes. And the reader may peel back the layers of myth that accrete to define the mythic place and thereby analyze the traces of historical significance in each layer and the way that signification is modified as narratives/places are stacked on top of one another. Joseph A. Kestner has, along with others, especially Gérard Genette, noted this sort of palimpsestic layering in literature, stressing that "all the works by one author may be analyzed in their relation to one another. In this latter instance, each work is conceived as a single plane read as a transparency to another work" (50). Kestner's further comments are perhaps worth quoting in full, especially in light of the keystone status of Faulkner's cosmos, its influence on later writer in the intertext, which Margaret Donavan Baeur has recently shown. Kestner writes that a

> particularly distinguished application of the theory of line as several superimposed planes occurs in Cervantes's *Don Quixote*. These planes constitute a palimpsest which includes not only past romances, as ur-texts over which Cervantes wrote, but also potential texts which were written after Cervantes's own text. This is to say that the novel *Don Quixote* then becomes the ur-text over which such works as *Joseph Andrews* (1742), *The Female Quixote* (1752), and *The Spiritual Quixote* (1772) will be written. There is only one central image in *Don Quixote,* and that is the mirror. This mirror implies that *Don Quixote* contains within itself not only texts preceding it but also those succeeding. The text embodies its past as well as its future. *Don Quixote* cannot stand alone. (50–51)

Faulkner depicts the creation of such a mythic place in *Requiem for a Nun,* the prose parts of which trace the building up of layers of Jefferson and Yoknapatawpha County. In this novel-play the term *trace* takes on significant connective meaning because just as the Natchez Trace connects various parts of Faulkner's landscape and exists throughout successive epochs, another connective "trace" appears in the jailor's daughter's name, which she scratches on a window in the jail, "a fragile and workless scratching almost depthless in a sheet of old barely transparent glass, and (all you had to do was look at it a while; all you have to do now is remember it) there is the clear undistanced voice as though out of the delicate antenna-skeins of radio, further than empress's throne, than splendid insatiation, even than matriarch's peaceful rocking chair, across the vast instantaneous intervention, from the long long time ago: *'Listen, stranger; this was myself: this was I'*" (648–49).

Multiple groups appropriate the linguistic-narrative currency of myth to "speak" within several spatial configurations of mythic place and imperial space. On one hand, configurations of center and periphery may align themselves according to different mythic places in which one mythic place stands as the center in relation to another peripheral mythic place. On the other hand, a single mythic place contains its own center-periphery paradigms, which are, again, both horizontal—across a single mythic layer—and vertical—extending from one mythic layer to another. Hence the oppressor can also be oppressed, or the oppressed can be the oppressor, within different hierarchies of sociopolitical structures, so that the oppressor (representative of a cultural center) in one configuration of center and periphery can be the oppressed (representative of a cultural periphery) in another such configuration.

It is this protean quality, the quality of flexibility in the power dynamics of Faulkner's mythic places (as it is in all space and places), that makes them so complex, intriguing, and important in understanding his attempt to render the struggles of and against imperial impulse in society. Faulkner resists simple or politically safe identifications of centered and peripheral groups, and such overlapping and shifting configurations of oppressor and oppressed find succinct expression in his "Address to the Graduating Class of Pine Manor Junior College." Explaining that only "man can put his final signature to the job" of "finishing" the world, Faulkner notes that it is "man's high destiny and proof of his immortality too, that his is the choice between ending the world, effacing it from the long annal of time and space, and completing it" (*Essays* 135). He offers as his illustration for the hope of humanity's success in "completing" the project of the world the "splendid dark" angel "who possessed the arrogance and pride to demand with, and the temerity to object with, and the ambition to substitute with—not only to decline to accept a condition just because it was a fact, but to want to substitute another condition in its place" (137). Faulkner suggests that

> God used the dark spirit too. [. . .] He already presaw the long roster of the ambition's ruthless avatars—Genghis and Caesar and William and Hitler and Barca and Stalin and Bonaparte and Huey Long. But He used more—not only the ambition and the ruthlessness and the arrogance to show man what to revolt against, but also the temerity to revolt and the will to change what one does not like. Because He presaw the long roster of the other avatars of that rebellious and uncompromising pride also, the long roster of names longer and more enduring than those of the tyrants and oppressors. They are the long annal of the men and women who have anguished over man's condition and who have held up to us not only the mirror of our follies and greeds and lusts and fears, but have reminded us constantly of the tremendous shape of our godhead too—the godhead and immortality which we cannot repudiate even if we dared, since we cannot rid ourselves of it but only it can rid itself of us—the philosophers and artists, the articulate and grieving who have reminded us always of our capacity for honor and courage and compassion and pity and sacrifice. (137–38)

In other words, the oppressor and the oppressed are cut from the same marble block, the same oak trunk, the same slice of air, and "He used that split part of the dark proud one's character to remind us of our heritage of free will and decision" (138).

The dark angel is a figure of ambivalence and liminality, one that directs attention to the centrality of hybridity in Faulkner's fiction. Faulkner's cosmos is replete with ambivalence not only in characters but also in spaces, as the center-periphery configurations of and within mythic places and layers overlap and shift, always in motion, always becoming, always exposing ways in which their mythic economy allows articulations of both the oppressors and the oppressed. The hybrid and subversive nature of the linguistic currency of myth is expressly Faulknerian, or rather it is instrumental in creating the trope of hybridity so central to Faulkner's art, as Thadious M. Davis argues in *Games of Property*. John T. Irwin has shown the centrality of psychological doubling in Faulkner's work in his classic *Doubling and Incest/Repetition and Revenge,* and Keith Cartwright has explained how the creolism of the United States, particularly that of the South, serves as an all-encompassing element of figuration in Faulkner's work and in U.S. writing in general. That Faulkner evokes the half-human, half-deity figure of Christ time and again attests to his fascination with the perspective of hybridity, whether in terms of race, gender, class, region, or any other formulation in which one can be "in-between."

To pause for summary: the spatial-political model being developed here is one that posits named (narrativized) spaces as imperial in that they are organized as plots that may be referred to as mythic places because their linguistically constructed existence lies within the rhetoric of imperial impulse even when they are not overtly part of an imperial project. For example, Sutpen's Hundred is a plot of ground, but it is also a "plot," a narrative defined in the context of the establishment of a dynasty. Within that imperial plot, however, lie anti-imperial narratives, which find expression in the same mythic plot that affirms the imperial drive. These antiplots exist partially because there are other voices within that space—Clytie, Rosa, Charles Bon, and so on—but also because the voice of the owner/generator of the imperial narrative is itself hybrid: Thomas Sutpen is himself *both* poor white and aristocratic patriarch and colonizer; indeed, his very body can serve as a mythic place containing multiple myth-informed perspectives. The task therefore is to identify the multiple mythic places of Faulkner's imperial space and analyze the ways the oppressors and the oppressed not only of those spaces but among them articulate their respective desires. At the same time that the narratives of the Compsons, the Sartorises, and the McCaslins must be reexamined in terms of the imperial impulses they encode, so, as Annette Trefzer urges, "the recovery of silenced ethnic presences in Faulkner's work—African, Arabic, Jewish, Chinese, Polish, Caribbean, Caucasian, Native American, and others—will reveal the unbounded openness of his texts as well as insights into how American culture is never merely present but always produced" (68).[12]

This interaction of mythic place and imperial space might be further shown by examining a concrete example of one of Faulkner's mythic places, noting in the process his manner of fragmenting space and the imperialism implicit in that fragmentation. He describes Yoknapatawpha County in two similar but strikingly different ways. The first appears in his 1953 essay "A Note on Sherwood Anderson," in which he writes that he learned from Anderson "that to be an American and a writer, one does not necessarily have to pay lip-service to any conventional American image such as his and Dreiser's own aching Indiana or Ohio or Iowa corn or Sandburg's stockyards or Mark Twain's frog" (*Essays* 8). Instead, "[y]ou had only to remember what you were." Faulkner goes on to "quote" Anderson:

> "You have to have somewhere to start from: then you begin to learn," he told me. "It dont matter where it was, just so you remember it and aint ashamed of it. Because one place to start from is just as important as any other. You're a country boy; all you know is that little patch up there in Mississippi where you started from. But that's all right too. It's America too: pull it out, as little and unknown as it is, and the whole thing will collapse, like when you prize a brick out of a wall." (8)

Here Faulkner "interrupts" this semifictitious dialogue with the comment, "Not a cemented, plastered wall," to which Anderson replies, "America aint cemented and plastered yet. They're still building it. That's why a man with ink in his veins not only still can but sometimes has still got to keep on moving around in it, keeping moving around and listening and looking and learning" (8). The regions of the United States constitute a brick wall, or different patches, all of which have at least ostensibly equal importance in the overall collage that is the United States. Anderson/Faulkner's figuration suggests a collection of centers that are simultaneously peripheries. As one keeps "moving around" from one brick/patch to another, one discovers in the parts some essence of the whole.

Faulkner employs slightly different language in his 1955 interview with Jean Stein Vanden Heuvel. Responding to the question, "What happened to you between *Soldiers' Pay* and *Sartoris*—that is what caused you to begin the Yoknapatawpha saga?" Faulkner answers:

> Beginning with *Sartoris* I discovered that my own little postage stamp of native soil was worth writing about and that I would never live long enough to exhaust it, and by sublimating the actual into apocryphal I would have complete liberty to use whatever talent I might have to its absolute top. It opened up a gold mine of other people, so I created a cosmos of my own. I can move these people around like God, not only in space but in time too. The fact that I have moved my characters around in time successfully, at least in my own estimation, proves to me my own theory that time is a fluid condition which has no existence except in the momentary avatars of individual people. There is no such

thing as *was*—only *is*. If *was* existed there would be no grief or sorrow. I like to think of the world I created as being a kind of key-stone in the Universe; that, as small as that keystone is, if it were ever taken away, the universe itself would collapse. My last book will be the Doomsday Book, the Golden Book, of Yoknapatawpha County. Then I shall break the pencil and I'll have to stop. (Meriwether and Millgate 255)

Here, the "patch" has transformed into a "postage stamp." Besides being a sort of cruel joke on himself—he *did* wind up "at the beck and call of every son-of-a-bitch who's got two cents to buy a stamp"[13]—his reference to a stamp represents a very different type of authority. The stamp must be juxtaposed with narratives—a name and an address—on what is otherwise the tabula rasa, the blank envelope, to legitimize and legalize that item's mission with the codified approval of centralized government. Faulkner understands this "postage stamp" as being infused with authority that is both spatial and temporal. It is in this temporal dimension that myth operates, for mythic places are finally those "momentary avatars" of compressed time and space that articulate desire. Faulkner's mythic places are complex, for while they are frozen moments in time, those moments contain the geological strata of their history, the traces of the stacks of transparent/opaque mythic layers that constitute them.

Faulkner's role in creating these mythic places is threefold, corresponding to three stages of myth development. Philip Wheelwright suggests "a theory of three main ways in which 'myth' has been and may legitimately be, conceived. [. . .] *primary* myth, *romantic* myth, and *consummatory* myth" (96). Richard Slotkin, who applies these three stages of myth development to the evolution of the myth of the American West, offers a gloss of Wheelwright's argument, noting that

> [t]he primary stage is that in which the "mythopoeic mode of consciousness" predominates both in activity of the myth-maker and in the perceptions of his audience. Through repetition of the formulas or repeated use of the artifacts of this primary myth, however, a convention of form is established and identified with the content of the primary myth. In this romantic stage, the attainment of an original experience of mythopoeic insight into the nature of reality becomes less important than fulfilling the social obligations established for the myth and for the priests who keep and ritualize it. [. . .] In highly sophisticated cultures, such as that of modern Europe and the West, artists and thinkers become aware of this corruption of the modes of belief

and expression and attempt to overcome it, either by reachieving the mythopoeic, spontaneous element in artistic perception and creation or by critically separating the "gold" archetypal myth from the "dross" of particular traditions. This consummatory stage is marked by a conscious attempt to [in Wheelwright's words] "recapture the lost innocence of the mythopoeic attitude by transcending the narrative, logical and linguistic forms which romantic mythologizing accepts and utilizes." (*Regeneration* 12–13)

Faulkner employs, enacts, and critiques all three of these stages of myth development in his creation of mythic places. His materials include Egyptian, Hebraic, Christian, Greek, Roman, British, and other ancient narratives; the myths of America, whether those of Native, African, or European Americans; and even his own stories and characters, which he recycles. Working with these mythic materials, Faulkner fulfills the roles of primary, romantic, and consummatory mythmaker himself either simultaneously or at different points in his career.

A particularly fecund site for modeling a reading that analyzes Faulkner's treatment of space, place, and imperialism is his essay "Mississippi." In this semifictional, pseudobiographical work published originally in *Holiday* magazine, Faulkner presents a portrait of his native state that exemplifies the dynamics of mythic place and imperial space.[14] Only two pages after an advertisement announcing that "Every Road Leads to Scenic Thrills and Romance in Old Virginia," setting the tone for a Moonlight-and-Magnolia-esque myth-romance, the magazine announces in large type: "THE MAGAZINE STORY OF THE YEAR: With great pride Holiday presents a memorable article about his native state by the Nobel-Prize-winning author, William Faulkner. Here is William Faulkner's own account of his own South, his people and his country; a moving tribute by one who has loved his land and has written about it more brilliantly than any other living American" (33). Positioned on the page beside this bit of trump-sounding is an introductory column by "the distinguished critic, Malcolm Cowley," above which is affixed a photograph of Faulkner standing in front of his home, Rowan Oak. He might be what Spivak calls a "native informant." Yet, facing right and wearing an almost threatening expression, not only is he looking in the direction of conservatism but his countenance gives off a defensive signal rather at odds with the inviting cedar-lined walk up to the house. It looks almost as if he is caught in the picture by accident or as if the image of his face has been pasted onto the background of the plantation house. Or perhaps he is standing aside, making room for you, if "you" are a nonsoutherner, to make your way up to the house, sit down and smoke a pipe or sip some bourbon, and read some Dos Passos or Wolfe or whatever other failure should interest you; but remember that this will be a somber affair (you do not even know yet that you will be having supper in stony silence) and that in just one step the Master can be in front of instead of beside the path, barring your way to his civilization.

Or barring your way into his private world, which he assembled only one of the largest oeuvres of any writer precisely for you to see. The picture calls to mind the 1952 *Omnibus* television program "William Faulkner of Oxford," which Noel Polk describes as a "very successful effort to edit Faulkner, to normalize him [. . .]" ("Polysyllabic" 299). Polk's description of the program could just as easily describe the photograph in *Holiday*: "[T]he film rather consciously *mainstreams* [Faulkner] into, makes him acceptable to, a culture and a world whose Chamber of Commerce values he had subjected to the intense scrutiny of his critical eye, and which he would continue to reject in his fiction and his personal life, even if not in his public pronouncements and postures" (299).[15] In the television program, the camera is not just to the side but all the way behind Faulkner as he greets Phil Mullen at the door, leads him inside, and says, "Look, Phil. I don't see what my private life, the inside of my house, or my family have to do with my writing." But he acquiesces, saying, "All right. Do your story. But no pictures." To which Mullen replies that Faulkner had "let the Oxford High School paper print [his] picture, by golly." "Yes," Faulkner says, "but my daughter was the editor of that paper, by golly." As Polk notes, Faulkner is "a farmer who looks deep into the heart of life, writes about it, and doesn't want his picture taken" (299).

The most arresting item on the page in *Holiday*—the photograph of Faulkner—is significant because Faulkner-as-portrait/Faulkner-as-icon is somehow secondary, relegated as he is to the bottom left corner of the photograph, to the larger matter of time (myth) and space. He stands in a liminal position, halfway between the beginning of the road to his place and the road to everyone outside that place, having even allowed a picture to be taken, whatever disapproval may lurk about his expression. In fact, he seems to be looking in the distance, waiting for "you," the heavy-pulsed summer traveler reading *Holiday* to plan a trip to Mississippi. But even when you reach him—the Virgil who will guide you down to his domain or perhaps the driver who will conduct you to Dracula's castle—you still must make your way through time down the pathway of black cedars and white columns to the dark door of the house, which thus emerges as "the place." In other words, when one reaches the point where Faulkner stands, he or she is not quite "there" yet. Time and space must still be negotiated to reach Faulkner's "place." Hence the article.

Indeed, Malcolm Cowley writes, "[h]ere is William Faulkner's tour of his native state, through space and history and his own life story" (33). Cowley prepares the reader for the experience, offering orienting signposts to aid the would-be traveler who is about to encounter a complex and ambivalent space. Jefferson "isn't a town to be found on any map," Cowley notes, "except those that Faulkner himself has drawn. [. . .] But Jefferson also resembles the real town of Oxford" (33). At the same time, "in Faulkner's Mississippi tour, there is a mingling of names taken from life with names taken from his novels"; there are those like "Ben and Caroline, [who] have also appeared in his novels, but [who] were real persons and here they are given the names they bore in life" (33). Again, Faulkner stands in-between, the native who knows the outlander; in the essay itself he is alternately "the boy," "the young man," "the middle-aged," "William," "Bill," "Mr. Bill," and "Memmy" according to different narrative-spatial configurations.

Turn the page, and you have passed through the dark door of Rowan Oak and into a bizarre world that seems the foreboding opposite of Faulkner's pristine mansion. Here, in a photograph on the other side of the leaf, stands Windsor ruins, a decayed Mississippi antebellum plantation "Big House" quite a distance from Oxford, no longer white but a burnt amber against a backdrop of dead leaves and bland sky and reflected even more darkly in pond water beside "the once proud, five storied mansion" (34). The reader familiar with Faulkner's work now recognizes the not-so-attractive world in which Quentin Compson might descend into the waters to greet his Little Sister Death. Now you are inside, and the Civil War–era cannon in the photograph on the next page, which guards the portal through which you have just passed, points away from you (again to the right); you stand behind it in the dark shade of a tree and the monstrous darkness of Windsor ruins. And then Faulkner's sonorous voice begins with what might seem an absurd statement: "Mississippi begins in the lobby of a Memphis, Tennessee, hotel and extends south to the Gulf of Mexico" (35). It is an odd opening, for however porous the state's borders may seem in the assertion that they extend across the Tennessee state line, Faulkner goes on to show that the reader has actually entered a closed realm.

In the Mississippi of "Mississippi," space is partly fragmented into "little towns concentric about the ghosts of the horses and mules once tethered to the hitch-rail enclosing the county courthouse" (34). These towns are mythic places with mythic-imperially significant names such as "Hattiesburg, and Laurel, and Meridian, and Canton: and [then there are] towns deriving by name from farther away than Ohio" (never mind China) (42). These antetypes are "farther away" not just in space but also in time (the two dimensions Cowley identified): "Kosciusko named after a Polish general who thought that people should be free who wanted to be; and Egypt because there was corn there when it was nowhere else in the bad lean times of the old war which the old women had still never surrendered; and Philadelphia where the Neshoba Indians whose name the county bears still remain for the simple reason that they did not mind living in peace with other people, no matter what their color or politics" (42). Here are the quintessential Faulknerian mythic places, all signifying narratives of imperialism by reaching past the present and even the recent past to access ancient mythic-imperial spatial layers. The contexts of the American as well as the Polish revolution lie underneath the implied layer of the South's struggle for "Independence" in the reference to Kosciusko. The story of Joseph's divinely informed wisdom and the Israelites' future enslavement are inherent in the place of Egypt as Faulkner focuses on the unreconstructed white aristocratic "old women" who would see themselves as suffering under the imperial thumb of the northern states after the Civil War. And here is the "City of Brotherly Love," with its name's Greek etymology, symbolizing an imperializing myth of industriousness as devised by Benjamin Franklin, who, fair-minded as he strove to be, nevertheless represented the imperializing hegemony of the Founding Fathers, which would invade the Natives' land with the narrative-dream of national space.

But towns are not the only units of space in the essay; Faulkner also fragments and identifies rural spaces with narratives of imperialism. There is "Jones County which old Newt Knight, its principal proprietor and first citizen or denizen, whichever you liked, seceded from the Confederacy in 1862, establishing still a third republic within the boundaries of the United States" (42). Then there is "Sullivan's Hollow: a long narrow glen where a few clans or families with North Ireland and Highland names feuded and slew one another in pre-Culloden fashion too" (42). And then there is the Delta, invaded by "that Mexican cotton seed which someone had given the Natchez doctor[, which] was clearing the land fast now [. . .], deswamping the whole vast flat alluvial delta-shaped sweep of land along the Big River [. . .] so that the steamboats carrying the baled cotton to Memphis or New Orleans seemed to crawl along the sky itself [. . .] on its way to the Liverpool mill" (36). Faulkner operates in the capacities of primary, romantic, and consummatory mythmaker/mythologist. Identifying the components of the mythic place he describes, he challenges myths in a consummatory fashion by laying bare the machinations of mythically constituted spaces, explaining why certain spaces bear the names/narratives of Kosciusko, Egypt, Philadelphia, Jones County, Sullivan Hollow, or the Delta. Paying constant attention to the role of cotton, lumber, and other economic as well as cultural and political campaigns, he presents the imperial motives and experiences that create these places. For instance, after noting the role of cotton in producing the Delta, Faulkner relates the mythic story of "a pre-Snopes, one of the tall men actually, a giant of a man in fact" (36). A "dedicated lay Baptist preacher but furious not with a furious unsleeping dream of paradise nor even for universal Order with an upper-case O, but for simple civic security," this fellow went into the wilds of Mississippi "alone, and talked not of gospel nor God nor even virtue, but simply selected the biggest and boldest and by appearance, anyway, the most villainous there and said to him: 'I'll fight you. If you lick me, you take what money I have. If I lick you, I baptize you into my church'" (36). At length, he "battered and mauled and gouged that one into sanctity and civic virtue then challenged the next biggest and most villainous and then the next; and the following Sunday baptized the entire settlement in the river," where, Faulkner reminds us, "the cotton wagons now cross[ed over] on Wylie's hand-powered ferry [. . .] peacefully and unchallenged on to Memphis until the railroad came and took the bales away [. . .]" (36). Here Faulkner highlights imperial impulses by equating the evangelical and economic imperialistic drives.

At the same time, Faulkner acts as a romantic mythmaker by perpetuating rather than deconstructing the mythic significance of those places, an endeavor particularly appropriate for an audience planning to pack its tent and cooler in a station wagon to set out for summer fun. Even though he states that he hates Mississippi's racism, the state is still "his native land; he was born of it and his bones will sleep in it; loving it even while hating some of it" because in the end "you don't love because: you love despite; not for the virtues, but despite the faults" (46). The knowing reader sees these lines as glosses on several moments in Faulkner's work, the most conspicuous being Quentin Compson's impassioned insistence regarding the South, "I dont. I dont! I dont hate it! I dont hate it!" (*Absalom, Absalom!* 303). Faulkner also revisits the opening scene of *The Unvanquished,* described earlier. He reframes the fraternal relationship between the black and white boy so that they are the sons of a Mammy rather than an Ole Miss; here, the Mammy is "a matriarch with a score of descendents [. . .], one of them a boy too [. . .] born in the same week with the white child and both bearing the same (the white child's grandsire's) name" (36). These two boys

> suckled at the same black breast and [were] sleeping and eating together and playing together the game which was the most important thing the white child knew at the time since at four and five and six his world was still a female world and he had heard nothing else that he could remember: with empty spools and chips and sticks and a scraped trench filled with well water for the River, playing over again in miniature the War, the old irremediable battles—Shiloh and Vicksburg, and Brice's Crossroads which was not far from where the child (both of them) had been born, the boy because he was white arrogating to himself the right to be the Confederate General—Pemberton or Johnston or Forrest—twice to the black child's once, else, lacking that once in three, the black one would not play at all. (36)

In this rendition of the mapmaking scene Faulkner adds to the materials of the map as described in *The Unvanquished* "spools," which suggests the production of thread and implies the presence of cotton. Because of the implied economic context of the essay, this addition functions as a consummatory act to signify the imperialistic drives as well as the residue of the Civil War in order to deromanticize the previously created myth. But this addition, along with the altered matriarchal genesis of the fraternal relationship, also suggests a retelling that conforms to the romantic stage of myth development.

But this retelling is also part of the overall "telling" of the myths of Yoknapatawpha, making this essay a furtherance of Faulkner's primary mythmaking project. Bayard and Ringo are not a part of this story; instead it is William Faulkner the fictionalized/mythologized character himself and his African American counterpart, also named William, who build a map, not while the Civil War is being fought (as Bayard and Ringo do), but after that time—behind that time. Here again, "William" is both white and black, and while the white William controls the game and its rules, the black William nevertheless can enforce his own empowerment by simply refusing "to play at all." By embracing the mythology of the game of reenactment, the black William can become white and thereby "speak," empowering himself with an identity of whiteness. In fact, the white aristocratic narrative of empowerment and the black antinarrative remain in tense relation throughout the essay, with Mammy reminding William throughout his life "not to forget you owe her eighty-nine dollars." Meanwhile, the reader sees a photograph of an African American couple on the lawn of Alcorn Agricultural and Mechanical College (now Alcorn State University), with the white columns of a campus building in the distance behind them, that pictures an eerily plantationlike arrangement (44). And opposite that picture spreads the image of a black convict, hoe in hand, sitting on the bottom step of "a Confederate monument in front of the Washington County Courthouse" with his chin on his wrist, a pose reminiscent of *The Thinker* (45).

African Americans are not the only group to speak against the imperial narrative. As is often the case in Faulkner, there are the aristocratic women who denounce what they see as northern aggression and colonization: "the indomitable, the undefeated, who never surrendered, refusing to allow the Yankee *minie* balls to be dug out of portico column or mantelpiece or lintel, who seventy years later would get up and walk out of *Gone with the Wind* as soon as Sherman's name was mentioned [. . .]" (36). Moreover, there are the Natives, who "in the beginning [. . .] crept with their simple artifacts, and built the mounds" but now, "except for looking occasionally out from behind the face of a white man or a Negro," had vanished (35). Yet, these natives speak not only from submerged mythic-imperial layers of the space of white and black faces but also in the names of mythic place, indeed in the overall place Faulkner describes: Mississippi. Ultimately, Faulkner makes it clear that the spaces he identifies are the composite product of successive imperializing projects, each part of which plays the roles of both oppressor and oppressed:

> In the beginning, the obsolescent, dispossessed tomorrow by the already obsolete: the wild Muskhogean—Chickasaw and Choctaw and Natchez and Pascagoula—looked down from the tall Mississippi

bluffs at a Chippeway canoe containing three Frenchmen—and had barely time to whirl and look behind him at a thousand Spaniards come overland from the Atlantic Ocean, and for a little while longer had the privilege of watching an ebb-flux-ebb-flux of alien nationalities as rapid as the magician's spill and evanishment of inconstant cards: the Frenchman for a second, then the Spaniard for perhaps two, then the Frenchman for another two and then Spaniard again and then the Frenchman again for the last half-breath before the Anglo-Saxons, who would come to stay, to endure [. . .]. (35)

Faulkner sees himself as part of this last wave of colonization, but he recognizes that it and "he too [are] obsolete" (35). His group is the one that has invaded "without avarice or compassion or forethought either: felling a tree which took two hundred years to grow, to extract from it a bear or a capful of wild honey" (35). And his group is particularly ruthless because it can and does change "the whole face of Mississippi" (35) by transforming "what he remembered as dense river-bottom jungle and rich farmland [into] an artificial lake twenty-five miles long," upon which, regardless of whatever disapproval he may have, he does not hesitate to put a sailboat as he witnesses what might seem the taming even of topography's recalcitrance (44). Of course, though manipulated, the land remains, although in the end his group would leave the ground altogether, as when he "watched John Moissant land a bicycle-wheeled aileronless (you warped the whole wing tip to bank it or hold it level) Bleirot monoplane on the infield of the Memphis race track and knew forever that someday he too would have to fly alone" (46); the race track here implies horses and the cavalry the airplane would replace in the business of imperialization. Indeed, the essay closes with an image of the liminal, a photograph of black land and house juxtaposed with the nearly white (with a touch of red) horizon of sunset mediated by a strip of gray clouds; above all stretches a mixture of white-gray-black wind-chopped clouds smeared into bands across the darkening night sky (the next frontier) and the caption "A shadowy fragment of life between the land and sunset sky, a cabin rises from a cottonfield between the Yalobusha and Tallahatchie Rivers" (47). Such is the world, the cosmos, of William Faulkner, a world characterized by the traumas and triumphs of imperial impulses and their resulting fragmentation, hybridity, and liminality.

Faulkner's "cosmos" is itself a dialectic of two realms. First, it is the collection of mythic places/imperial spaces that make up his overall created fictional world. This cosmos is the one he ostensibly speaks of to Jean Stein Vanden Heuvel, the world of Yoknapatawpha as well as other places on the Faulknerian globe, such as New Orleans, New Haven, and Europe. The second realm of Faulkner's cosmos is the world in which he lived, which includes the past and present (and arguably even the future as articulated by the past and present) of the historical, geographical, literary, economic, social, cultural, and political worlds in which he lived. This cosmos consists of a plethora of narratives: writings before and contemporary with Faulkner, advertising forms, historical documents, and everything and everyone else that contributes to the creation of culture, from architecture and agriculture to big-game hunters and baseball stars. These two forms of cosmos emerge as interdependent, defining and modifying each other, so that Faulkner acting alternately as primary, romantic, and consummatory mythmaker creates, draws on, and critiques mythic-imperial matter (space and place). For practical purposes, the "real" cosmos that Faulkner the historical person inhabited and breathed in can only be hinted at, being too vast and at last irrecoverable in full, while the other—Faulkner's "fictional" cosmos—can be scrutinized as a closed and fully analyzable space. Thus, in this volume the focus will be, not on these two cosmos's separateness, but on their points of intersection and conversation, for it is in that liminal space of hybridity that Faulkner's mythic-imperial body of work dwells.[16]

Finally, and again, foremost attention here rests on the ways this fragmented and liminal cosmos facilitates speaking, whether oppressively or subversively. The constant shifting of spatiality continually redefines the position of the subject and so perpetuates a hybridity of speech appropriation according to varying situations and levels of empowerment and disempowerment. For it is in examination of the mythic place and imperial space of Faulkner's cosmos that there can be found the significance of the human's "puny inexhaustible voice," which Cowley saw fit to let Faulkner himself explain by concluding *The Portable Faulkner* with the Nobel Prize address. In this speech, place and time are omnipresent, for "when the last ding-dong of doom has clanged and faded from the last worthless rock hanging tideless in the last red and dying evening," not only will the puny inexhaustible voice still be talking, it will "prevail," moving forward in time by "reminding him of the courage and honor and hope and pride and compassion and pity and sacrifice which have been the glory of his past"

(724). This voice speaks in and from a place mythically defined within a framework of spatial imperialism, and it is this voice that both makes and unmakes the meaning and unmeaning of the narratives of history.

The configurations of mythic place and imperial space dealt with in the chapters that follow are arranged in a cumulative order. Chapter 1 applies the model of mythic-imperial spatiality presented in this introduction to a reading of a prevalent mythic layer in Faulkner's writing—Greek and Roman mythology—examining the political implications of such myths in Faulkner's fictional world by showing how they define racially hybrid spaces that are ostensibly designed to articulate white, aristocratic, patriarchal narratives of imperial control but in fact carry within their very dreams of Arcady the presence and the anti-imperial narrative of the Other. I turn in chapter 2 to a real place and its fictional analogues in Faulkner's writing by examining the mythic-imperial layers that inform the narratives of the space of New Orleans, a city that contains multiple layers of imperial design, which designate a space of racial and cultural amalgamation that Faulkner uses to dramatize the constant struggle between the oppressor and the oppressed. Chapter 3 deals with both a purely literary mythic place and an actual physical place by examining the role of ancient Egypt as embodied in the Egypt-informed constructed place of the Mississippi Delta, which is modeled on the Nile Delta in Egypt. Plantation owners evoke the imperial power of ancient Egypt to confirm their own cultural ascendancy, while African Americans use the biblical narratives of the Israelites enslaved in Egypt to speak against the power that controls them. And chapter 4 engages the U.S. South's cavalier myth by rereading the imperial nature of the Arthurian legend that underpins it. Where the Greco-Roman mythic layer underlies practically all of Faulkner's cosmos and New Orleans represents a specific Faulknerian space, and while the Egypt-informed Mississippi Delta stands as a hybrid of the two, the Arthurian legend's prime space of Camelot, with its Christian inflections, marks a second type of hybrid spatiality that, unlike the Mississippi Delta, emerges as portable in Faulkner's cosmos. Attention is given in this chapter not only to the ways that the nostalgia of that myth masks racial oppression in Faulkner's South but also to the ways that poor whites appropriate those myths to advance their own imperial designs.

After examining four ways in which Faulkner combines myth, imperialism, and spatiality, the book closes by focusing on a text that combines them all, the novel he referred to as his "magnum-o": *A Fable*. With its large spatial scope, *A Fable* contains multiple mythic-imperial spatial configurations that Faulkner works with throughout the rest of his oeuvre. At the same time that Greco-Roman, Egyptian, and Arthurian myths haunt the experiences of soldiers in the trenches of France, Faulkner returns in the very core of the narrative to the spaces of the Mississippi Delta and New Orleans. In so doing, he creates a rhapsody on the inexpugnable voice of the imperialist and the equally inexhaustible cries of the narratives of subversion.

CHAPTER ONE

Here Pan's Sharp Hoofed Feet Have Pressed
Arcadian Place and the Roar of the Present

[H]ere would be the community house built to look like the Coliseum and the community garage yonder made to look like it was a Acropolis, and how the grape vine would be grubbed up entire and the hillside terraced to make a outdoors theatre where they could act in one another's plays; and how the meadow would be a lake with one of them Roman barges towed back and forth on it by a gas engine, with mattresses and things for them to lay down on while they et.

—"Black Music"

A strain of Greek and Roman mythology of tragic and pastoral poetics runs throughout Faulkner's writing, from his earliest forays into poetry on through to *The Reivers*. Many critics have noted these aspects of this presence, particularly in such an explicit case as that of the evocation of Agamemnon's tragedy in *Absalom, Absalom!* These elements of the work have not, however, been considered in terms of their materiality—their peculiar articulations of imperialism and their specific indications of economic factors. Faulkner establishes plots of space informed by an Arcadian ethic and haunted by configurations and reconfigurations of pagan values. And he uses these places to tease out the conflicts of speech and speechlessness by evoking literal historical earth to expose the mythic layers of experience that define the mythic-imperial place and control its constituents.

Faulkner's use of Greek-Roman mythic place echoes the classical element in the colonizing project of American space, which Greek Revival architecture dominated. The classical revival began in England in the 1750s as a result of archaeological activities in Greece; it was an aspect of the larger British imperial project. As Talbot Hamlin notes, with the Revolution and the break from England, American leaders both borrowed from England's focus on classical antiquities and looked away from that influence to the superseding "inspiration of the ancient classic world of Greece and Rome" (3). The United States' interest in Greece and Rome was particularly strong, writes Hamlin, as part of "the enthusiasm which the whole Western World, and particularly the new republic, showed for the struggles of Greece during her wars of independence" (xvi–xvii). Classical influences can be found in architecture from the nineteenth century (especially buildings constructed between 1820 and 1860) up and down the East Coast, especially in Philadelphia, Boston, and New York. And this interest in Greece and Rome registered on two temporal levels as it focused on the glory of the two regions' ancient empires while also signaling the will to dominate the modern incarnation of these spaces, making the project hybrid in its attractions as well as in its style, for, as J. Mordaunt Crook notes, the Greek revival was actually a Romantic-classical hybrid that blended rationalistic balance and emotional asymmetry in style.[1]

With one of the most visible figures in this movement being the Virginian Thomas Jefferson, the southern states particularly embraced this form of architecture.[2] Jefferson thoroughly engaged and embraced classical art and culture, as is exemplified in his many projects, including his estate, Monticello. And southern architects such as Robert Cary Long and his son Robert Cary Long Jr. followed suit. Southern appropriations of this architectural style represented the establishing of a heritage of empowerment, for, as William T. Ruzicka explains, the "specific occurrence of Greek Revival architecture in the American South was not, as in the Northern states, a matter of style, but rather the particular response of a culture which understood itself to be a repetition and not an imitation, a recurrence rather than a recreation of ancient Greece, and fortuitously found the architectural style proper to its image" (6).

Greco-Roman mythic place constituted a large part of the setting of Faulkner's early work, especially his poetry. The pinnacle of his use of pagan mythic place in his early poetry is *The Marble Faun*, his first commercially published volume. The spaces in this long poem are foundational in their exemplification of Faulknerian mythic-imperial space. In fact, not only are the pagan-informed spaces that the faun negotiates and seeks to occupy significant but the very space of the marble faun's body manifests the poetics of hybridity—the cloudy boundaries and interchanges between center and periphery—in Faulkner's fiction. Scholars have discussed the Greek and Roman presence in Faulkner's early writing primarily in terms of aesthetics; however, Gary Lee Stonum also offers noteworthy insights into the *space* of Faulkner's early writing, in which Greco-Roman mythology marks an explicit presence, especially in *The Marble Faun*.[3] Stonum argues that the "chief task of Faulkner's poetry is to express a poetic landscape in such a way that it will point beyond itself to the absolute" (55). Faulkner, according to Stonum, yearns "for a transcendent state of arrested motion," as prescribed by Keats, Swinburne, and other poets whose work influenced his own (45). Stonum's argument posits a Faulkner seeking to negotiate motion as time with a sort of platonic eternity, and this assertion not only carries some truth but harkens back to the poetics of Hawthorne (a writer who, like Faulkner, was interested in marble fauns), whose symbolism John F. Lynen argues was influenced by a Puritan notion of time that by "sharp contrast between the present and eternity which its doctrine of grace fostered [. . .] accustomed the imagination to conceive experience in terms of purely present in relation to a total history or conspectus of all times" (304).

But Faulkner, even at this early stage of his development as a writer, does not ignore the evidence of labor and hegemony in the material he describes. Although Phil Stone asserts in the beginning of his preface to *The Marble Faun* that the poems therein are "primarily the poems of youth and a simple heart" (6), the reader may be jarred by the uncanny pragmatism in Faulkner's own comment mentioned by Stone at the end of the preface:

> On one of our long walks through the hills, I remarked that I thought the main trouble with Amy Lowell and her gang of drum-beaters was their eternal damned self-consciousness, that they always had one eye on the ball and the other eye on the grandstand. To which the author of these poems replied that his personal trouble as a poet seemed to be that he had one eye on the ball and the other eye on Babe Ruth. Surely there must be possibilities inherent in a mind so shrewdly and humorously honest. (8)

Stone would later find out about the possibilities of Faulkner's mind when the writer slipped out from under his own colonizing efforts, but what is significant about the statement mentioned above is that Faulkner stated the politics of Stone's criticism even more explicitly than Stone. Stone's denouncement of poets for their concern about audience, fortune, and fame belies his own obvious bid for literary recognition as founder, developer, and owner of what he expected to be a famous poet. But Faulkner opts to emulate not just the home crowd (the literary world) but an actual icon generated by media located in the nation's cultural center. Babe Ruth was a Yankee, the quintessential northerner and prime representative of a baseball team that represented the culturally centered place (New York) that made Faulkner's own native place peripheral. For Faulkner to overtake Babe Ruth is for the periphery to overtake the preeminence of the center.

Faulkner would bring up Babe Ruth again in a very revealing economic context. In *The Sound and the Fury* Jason Compson spends April 6 losing money on cotton to "that New York crowd" (227). In a conversation with "a drummer," Jason explains that "[c]otton is a speculator's crop. [. . .] Let [a farmer] make a big crop and it won't be worth picking; let him make a small crop and he won't have enough to gin. And what for? so a bunch of dam eastern jews [. . .]" can rob him of it (191). After bemoaning the fact that the "country suckers" of Jefferson (including himself) continually ingratiate themselves with New Yorkers to be "taken," he finds himself at the drugstore on the square trying to cure his headache only to be addressed by a person named Mac, who ventures, "I reckon you've got your money on the Yankees this year" (252). To which Jason replies, "I wouldn't bet on any team that fellow Ruth played on [. . . e]ven if I knew it was going to win [. . .] I can name you a dozen men in either league who're more valuable than he is" (252). Mac asks him what he has "against Ruth," and Jason retorts, "Nothing. [. . .] I haven't got any thing against him. I don't even like to look at his picture" (252). Jason lashes out at the icon of Ruth, the mythology of Ruth, precisely because it represents his sense of being oppressed by the "eastern sharks" economically—his experience of being positioned as a peripheral figure, when he is accustomed to occupying the empowered center of Jefferson, Mississippi.[4]

Faulkner's comment to Stone about his poetic aspirations signals a similar awareness of the reality of the production of art. Throughout life, Faulkner would make many conflicting comments about the various forms of remuneration for artistic production; these ranged from his proclamation in his Nobel Prize acceptance speech that he wrote "not for glory and least of all for profit" to his (in)famous statement that *Sanctuary* was a "cheap idea" that was "deliberately conceived to make money."[5] In fact, his sense of irony cut both ways in regard to the purpose and payment for art: he could joke that he wrote so he would not have to work, but he could also defend himself against deprecating comments about writing or himself as a writer, as evidenced in his encounter with the actor Clark Gable.[6] Whatever the case, irony, with its ability to amplify the otherwise inaudible sound of the subversive narrative, was a staple of Faulkner's artistic endeavors from the beginning. In fact, critics have tended to allow themselves to get so caught up in the seductive descriptions of what Stonum calls Faulkner's "poetic realm of absolute time" that they sometimes have seen him as simply a romantic and forgotten his ever-present sense of irony. Even though in real-life encounters Faulkner consistently undercut the most desperately romantic and gestural statements he made in his fiction—such as his substitution of "Between Scotch and nothing, I'll take Scotch" for "Between grief and nothing, I'll take grief"—scholars and biographers have seemed unable to resist the temptation to cast the young man as a romantic.[7] Of course, he invited such description by posing as such, but the point is that he *was posing.* While he was a nattily dressed poet who may have been hurt somewhat by a classmate's ridiculing his poetry when he was a student at the University of Mississippi, he also (along with two other young men) created the "Bluebird Insurance Company," a fictitious institution meant to insure students against difficult professors.[8]

It seems more than plausible, then, that the relentless albeit slippery irony so characteristic of and effective in Faulkner's later work already exists in the incipient stages of his career. The bluebird incident suggests that even in its inchoate form, Faulkner's style demands the perspective of a fourteenth blackbird in order to be understood. Just as the rhetoric of *The Hamlet* must not be mistaken as simply epic in style but rather understood as a negotiation of epic and mock-epic form attenuated to achieve maximum tragicomic effect, such a text as *The Marble Faun* should be analyzed for the ways its romantic forms operate against themselves. Indeed, in another early work, *Mayday,* the irony is explicit, as the narrator introduces elements that subvert the heroic and chivalric style in which the story is written. *The Marble Faun* may not contain the same self-deprecation as that found in *Mayday,* but certain ambivalences may exist that have gone unnoticed. At the very least, its "romanticism" is certainly much more grounded in materiality than has generally been thought.

Perhaps the best way to begin an examination of the ambivalence of Faulkner's romanticism would be to reconsider the imagery of the urn provided by John Keats's "Ode on a Grecian Urn." Many scholars note the urn as a central image of Faulkner's notion of arrested motion. But it is important to remember that Faulkner's eye was on the icon as icon, and he was not one to ignore the traces of production present in art, nor was he one to read without a keen sense of context. There is every reason to believe that Faulkner read not just "Ode on a Grecian Urn" but also "On Seeing the Elgin Marbles" or "On First Looking into Chapman's Homer," both of which treat imperialism as a theme. The power of the British Empire is implicit in the ownership of the Greek sculptures, and Keats describes the culturally binding thread of colonization inherent in translating a text and equating the experience of reading that text with Cortez's march across the New World to discover the Pacific (erroneous though the reference may be).[9] Even if Faulkner had not read these poems, though, it is not likely that the implications of empire and the problems of speech within systems of oppression in "Ode on a Grecian Urn" escaped him. Just as the spools in the rewritten scene of the Civil War battlefield map in "Mississippi" represent traces of the imperial/economic motives of war, so the Grecian urn bears the traces of empire. The urn "speaks," not just in the image on its exterior, which negotiates Apollonian and Dionysian forms of expression, but in its value as a product, a vessel containing the silenced remains of an individual, representing affluence or importance in Greek society and the power of a British empire that might own such an artifact. Furthermore, as a product—as a thing—the urn is both Self and Other, emblematic of the British (and ancient Greek) center as well as of the periphery of the Mediterranean space of Greece.[10]

The speaker in *The Marble Faun* is also a product; carved of marble, the faun signifies and bears the traces of empire. Note the faun's comment about Pan:

> Here Pan's sharp hoofed feet have pressed
> His message on the chilly crest,
> Saying—Follow where I lead,
> For all the world springs to my reed.
>
> (13)

Pan and the faun represent the epoch of Greece's cultural predominance, an epoch now passed of which the faun is a relic, for he observes that the "whole world breathes and calls to me / Who marble-bound must ever be" (12). This statement evokes the Keatsian motif of the "unravished bride of quiet": at one point the faun attends the coaxing notes of a blackbird's song that echoes the alluring melody of the nightingale, which tempts him to enter a world of motion and excitement. This realm is the mythological one of paganism, full of sexual freedom and Bacchic pleasure; the faun signifies not only Greek and Roman myth but also the sophistication and political power of the cultures that generate them. But it is not the ancient Greek empire alone that is represented in the poem: Faulkner's evocation of Keatsian themes implies the presence of the British Empire in the faun as well as in the marbles around it.

Faulkner infuses the poem with yet another context by placing the faun and the other marbles in a garden. Scholars tend to discuss his early work as being uninformed by region, especially the South, designating his first fictional efforts as his initiation into regional writing that addresses contemporary "real-world" settings and situations. But note the faun's description of its garden environment:

> Why cannot we always be
> Left steeped in this immensity
> Of softly stirring peaceful gray
> That follows on the dying day?
> Here I can drug my prisoned woe
> In the night wind's sigh and flow,
> But now we, who would dream at night,
> Are awakened by the light
> Of paper lanterns, in whose glow
> Fantastically to and fro
> Pass, in a loud extravagance
> And reft of grace, yet called a dance,
> Dancers in a blatant crowd
> To brass horns horrible and loud.
> (46)

The faun is entrapped in a garden set in the jazz age—the dancers are likely swinging to a *southern-influenced* tune (perhaps "Charleston"), for this garden is not far from the Keats-informed jazz world of F. Scott Fitzgerald in *This Side of Paradise* or of Gatsby's garden in *The Great Gatsby* (although published a year later than *The Marble Faun*), in which Nick says, "There was music [. . .]. In his blue garden men and girls came and went like moths among the whisperings and the champagne and the stars" (43). This setting can be read as a southern place, and although

Faulkner does not assign the garden to any nation or region, it signifies American/U.S. prosperity, articulated in the rhythms of southern African American musical expression, rhythms that are expressly Dionysian.

This Dionysian element is important to note because the faun bears *racial* implications. Half man and half goat, the faun evokes the dark Other, whether Native, African, or Latin American. It is important to remember that by the Middle Ages the chief of the goat-men, Pan, had been reworked in Christian iconography as Satan. The sexual freedom, revelry, and drunkenness that the goat god signified in pagan culture became redefined as sins in Christianity. As Jeffrey Burton Russell argues, this new "symbolism was intended to show the Devil as deprived of beauty, harmony, reality, and structure [. . .]. Among the common bestial characteristics given [him] were tails, animal ears, goatees, claws, and paws [. . .]" (131), and demons "were blacks, who were popularly associated with shadow and the privation of light" (49). Such conflations of Satan, goats, and blackness informed New World definitions of the Other, whether the red Natives of the new land or the black imported slaves.[11] A direct influence of the racial signification of the faun might be cited, as has already been suggested, in Hawthorne's *The Marble Faun*. The clash of pagan Greco-Roman and Christian layers of myth in terms of place is everywhere evident in the novel, as Hawthorne shows the painful encroachment of the Christian-influenced Rome's drab monastic reconfiguration of Roman buildings and materials taken from those buildings. Donatello emerges as the dynamic trace of the pagan layer, for he is the marble faun who, unlike Faulkner's model, is free initially from the bonds of Christian guilt and immobility; indeed, the sculptor Henry cannot seem to capture Donatello in his art. As the novel progresses, however, Donatello becomes ensnared in that Christian guilt when he murders Miriam's tormenter, and the book closes with the faun confined in a dungeon for his crime. Although the novel is set in Italy, Nancy Bentley and Anna C. Brickhouse have noted the American-informed constructs of race that inform Hawthorne's depiction of Donatello.

Faulkner's marble faun therefore represents a body that registers a complex set of racial and cultural signifiers. It symbolizes the Nietzschean intersection of Apollonian and Dionysian forms of artistic expression that Stonum evokes. At the same time, it manifests certain U.S.- and southern U.S.-informed elements: as a statue of a creature from Greek narrative, the faun may be seen as an extension of Greek Revival architecture. And the half-goat status of the faun makes the creature at least half "Negro."[12] What is particularly problematic about the faun's racial construction, though, is that it is a "Negro" that passes; carved of white marble, the faun may in fact be viewed as a "counterfeit Other" and thus stands as the precursor of Joe Christmas and Charles Bon, whom Faulkner investigates in much more specific and detailed cultural terms.[13]

Configured according to these mixed signifiers, the faun emerges as a liminal figure caught between "centers" and even constituting his own "center." Throughout the poem, the faun expresses the ontological problems of his positioning:

> [. . .] I
> Am prisoner to dream and sigh
> For things I know, yet cannot know
> 'Twixt sky above and earth below.
> (12)

The faun imagines the vivacity of Dionysian experience, and yet the very act of that imagining and its very "marble-bound" existence render it an Apollonian creation that must converse with Apollonian forms. In terms of racial constructs, the faun must negotiate its stiff and fixed whiteness with its loose and fluid "blackness"; indeed, continually expressing his desire to be like "the snake" and therefore Satan in the garden, the faun ultimately finds himself stuck between Greek and Christian figurations. In fact, even though, as scholars have noted, *The Marble Faun* contains no explicit cultural setting, it critiques the very problems of southern pastoral, which Lucinda MacKethan calls "the dream of Arcady." For the faun accentuates a fundamental paradox in the mythic conception of southern pastoral agrarianism as promulgated originally and most famously by Thomas Jefferson. Specifically, the model of pastoralism set forth in the U.S. South's aristocratic ideal is based on *Greek pastoral,* and yet that Greek pastoral champions a pagan world of Dionysian values inhabited by satyrs and nymphs. In other words, the very model of pastoralism operates within a system of values and figurations that characterize the racial constructs that the aristocratic South possesses and whose objects the aristocratic white South abhors. Miscegenation therefore exists within the very construct of agrarian whiteness the South promotes.

But again the cultural context is not just a southern one: as a piece of carven material, the faun simply *cannot* speak verbally (however much he "speaks" as a signifying object) and is therefore as an icon nothing less than a permutation of Kawliga, the wooden cigar-store Indian. In fact, the same goat-demon racial implications imputed to black people in the New World also devolved upon Native Americans, who were represented as satanic figures and upon whom the iconography of the goat was also grafted. The faun is therefore also part Native American and suffers the commodification of the Native as icon, reduced to a prop set up in a garden, embodying the oxymoron *noble savage*.[14] Taciturn and inscrutable yet wild and virile, the marble faun and the wooden Indian are both products of the imperialist mythologies that drove the expansion of the United States westward across the North American continent, as Richard Slotkin has shown. It is therefore not surprising that the faun should want to make his way into the wilderness—he seeks to flee the paper lanterns, blaring horns, and other manifestations of the oppressor who would control him and keep him forever locked in as a decoration, sapped of his cultural presence and power.

Faulkner explores the figure of the cigar-store Indian most thoroughly in Darl's descriptions of Jewel in *As I Lay Dying*. In a novel full of lumber, Darl's first description of his brother appears in his first monologue. "Still staring straight ahead," Darl says of Jewel, "his pale eyes like wood set into his wooden face, he crosses the floor in four strides with the rigid gravity of a cigar store Indian dressed in patched overalls and endued with life from the hips down" (4). Jewel is literally the Other in the Bundren family, the son, not of Anse, but of Reverend Whitfield. Silent like the static Native American statue and the marble faun, Jewel shows particular hatred for Cash's sawing and hammering on the coffin while his mother is dying; in fact, Jewel would have himself and his mother "on a high hill and me rolling the rocks down the hill at their faces, picking them up and throwing them down the hill faces and teeth and all by God until she was quiet and not that goddamn adze going One lick less. One lick less and we could be quiet" (15). His mother believes "that words are no good; that words dont ever fit even what they are trying to say at" (171), and Jewel hardly speaks in the novel, his single monologue being even shorter than his mother's and his speaking elsewhere in the novel primarily cursing. He is the silent and silenced wooden Indian, the iconic incarnation of the colonized subject.

And yet, returning to *The Marble Faun,* there is a fundamental paradox in the faun's response to the blaring jazz music in the garden. Just as Joe Christmas in *Light in August* is repelled by African Americans even as he would at times claim to be African American himself, so the faun balks at the very Dionysian scene that would seem to appeal to him. It is true that the jazzy party about which the faun complains does represent modernity, and certainly the ideal he hopes for is quiet*er* than what he experiences. But the reason the faun hates the party held in his garden is because the presumably white affluent partygoers have actually appropriated the very Dionysian poetics and values that the faun represents and then have morphed those values and poetics to suit their own ends. In other words, the vital rhythms and subversive potentialities of the blues are rendered as harmless novelties tailored to the desires of the empowered, just as W. C. Handy's "St. Louis Blues" would be whitened and transformed into an anthem of the state in Glen Miller's "St. Louis Blues March." The problems of "speaking" for the faun and later for Joe Christmas arise when the language and figuration that they would employ as tools of subversion are drained of their subversive power: Christmas will not have his turn with a black woman when it means affirming white empowerment over the black female body, while he accepts it as his due to sacrifice his own body to lynching and mutilation as a sort of cultural rape in retribution for cultural myths of African American male sexuality because that sacrifice uses his racial "speech" in the subversive manner that he sees as its peculiar value.

Several different and conflicting layers thus constitute the mythic place of the garden in which the faun dwells and of which he is an integral part. The faun is both Satan lurking in the garden and Pan stuck in the garden yearning for the freedom of the wilderness. He represents Greek and British empire and yet is also the African American and Native American resisting the enslavement or imperialization of Europeans and their encroachment on the American wilderness. As a marble figure in a formal garden the statue is a sign of affluence, yet it is also a sign of the impoverishment of signification: it speaks a narrative that it deplores, and it cannot speak the narrative it would. The garden, therefore, is Eden, Arcadia, London, Charleston, slave quarters, and wilderness simultaneously, and the faun itself both the quietly speaking imperialist and the loudly silent imperialized.

Faulkner released the faun from his marble bonds in his 1926 story "Black Music."[15] In this story Faulkner makes concrete the elements of empire and place implicit in *The Marble Faun*. The story's play with center and periphery is signaled most immediately by its being a frame narrative, a device that U.S. local colorists had employed for very specific purposes since the Civil War and Reconstruction. Elizabeth Ammons and Valerie Rohy note that local color "remains a paradoxical genre, an example of both the marginal and the central, deviance and social discipline, diversity and the imperative to nationalistic unity" (xxviii). Local-color writing operated within a configuration of center-periphery in which such cosmopolitan centers as New York City, Chicago, and Boston represented political and cultural empowerment, while regions such as the South or the Midwest represented the cultural periphery. These writers thus negotiated a balance between fulfilling national unity and creating spaces of resistance for the individual regions they wrote about, thereby enacting a doubleness in which they stressed the individualness of the regions while also bringing them into the national discussion. The tool of choice was the frame narrative, which actually *centered* the peripheral figure by having a cosmopolitan narrator relinquish narrative control to a peripheral representative. This frame was Faulkner's regionalist inheritance, and he would incorporate it into more than one of his works.

The frame of "Black Music" is set in Rincon, a location vaguely situated in the Caribbean. A port "less large even than one swaybacked tanker looming above the steel docks of the Universal Oil Company" (799), Rincon is securely located in the global South and bears the signs of industrialization and imperialism, as the Universal Oil Company is a thinly disguised Standard Oil Company, John Davison Rockefeller's economic empire, which was roundly attacked for its ruthless tactics.[16] The narrator is an outsider to this peripheral location and thus echoes local-color frame narrators by representing the cultural-political center, which is interested in collecting the peculiar details of the periphery. Perhaps he is a Universal Oil Company boss who indulges his curiosity about the locals during his off time. The frame actually contains two narratives: the first is told by someone who represents an ambiguous "they," possibly workers in the company, as they are self-professedly "white"; the second narrative is told by a mysterious ex-draughtsman named Wilfred Midgleston, whose coming to Rincon was precipitated by an experience in which he believed himself to have been transformed into a faun.

The first frame introduces the second and is significant because of its racialization of Midgleston. The racial overtones of the story are suggested by the title, which echoes that of Sherwood Anderson's *Dark Laughter,* a novel that operates on the concept of African Americans as Dionysian, which Thadious M. Davis has shown influenced Faulkner's own early depictions of blacks.[17] The narrator of the first framed story asserts that Midgleston "came from the States" and is "a white man," yet after "sponging on us white men" until they "got tired of it he took to sponging on these Spigs. And a white man has got pretty low when he's got so stingy with his stealings that he will live with Spiggotties before he'll dig up his own money and live like a white man" (799–801). Midgleston is not completely white but rather hybrid. The speaker himself is somewhat shady, having apparently stolen money and run away to Rincon to hide out, and he possesses some disdain for the frame narrator, who is not one of the "down-at-heel compatriots [of this] informant," who were "men a little soiled and usually unshaven" and "unavoidable in the cantinas and coffee shops, loud, violent, maintaining the superiority of the white race and their own sense of injustice and of outrage among the grave white teeth, the dark, courteous, fatal, speculative alien faces" of Rincon's natives (802).

After hearing this narrative about why Midgleston is in Rincon, the frame narrator finally catches up with the man himself. He buys him a meal and persuades him to tell his story. Midgleston begins by assuring the narrator that his reason for being in the port "ain't what you think. [. . .] I never stole any money" (804). Instead, he is there and will not return home because he "done something. [. . .] Something that ain't in the lot and plan for mortal human man to do. [. . .] At one time in my life I was a farn" (805). When the narrator asks what a "farn" is, Midgleston answers:

> A Farn. Don't you remember in the old books where they would drink the red grape wine, how now and then them rich Roman and Greek senators would up and decide to tear up a old grape vineyard or a wood away off somewheres the gods used, and build a summer house to hold their frolics where the police wouldn't hear them, and how the gods wouldn't hear them, and how the gods wouldn't like it about them married women running around nekkid, and so the woods god named— named— [. . .] Pan. And he would send them little fellows that was half a goat to scare them out— (805)

At this point, the narrator realizes that Midgleston is talking about a *faun,* and Midgleston notes that "the Bible says that them little men were myths. But I know they ain't [. . .]. Because for one day in my life I was a farn" (805). Here, pagan and Christian mythic layers collide, the trace of the older layer showing through in the presence of the hybrid goat-human creatures.

Midgleston then proceeds to describe a heterotopic mythic place in the construction of which he participates. On a "tract [of land consisting] of a meadow, a southern hillside where grapes grew, and a woodland" in Virginia, a Mrs. Van Dyming decrees a pleasure dome (806). This plot of ground has a layered history: first, a New Englander used the land to grow grapes, but he moved away when a ram among his herd of goats rammed into and broke his leg. Then an "I-talian" man began to "gather the grapes and make wine out of them" (806); after "doctoring" the wine and getting rich from its sale, he died when his truck full of grapes wrecked. The narrator quite naturally observes, "I don't see how that reflected on the place," to which Midgleston replies that the neighbors were superstitious and would not live on the land "maybe [. . .] because they were not anything but country folks" (807). Finally, the Van Dymings, a rich couple from "Park Avenue," purchase the land for a small price and plan to transform the place into a Greco-Roman replica.

> [Mrs. Van Dyming] would stand there, with them other rich Park Avenue folks, showing them how here would be the community house built to look like the Coliseum and the community garage yonder made to look like it was a Acropolis, and how the grape vine would be grubbed up entire and the hillside terraced to make a outdoors theatre where they could act in one another's plays; and how the meadow would be a lake with one of them Roman barges towed back and forth on it by a gas engine, with mattresses and things for them to lay down on while they et. (807)

The Van Dymings are constructing their own Monticello, but while the Jeffersonian imperial impulses are strong, the passive recalcitrance of topography ultimately thwarts the Van Dymings' plans.[18] The Van Dymings are doomed to fail—doomed in the Greek sense—precisely because their imperial project ignores the traces of its historical moment. In Midgleston's depiction of the situation, the country people have a proper fear and practiced avoidance of hubris, although it is unlikely that they would be able to explain the connections between their own superstitions and those of the Greeks. Meanwhile, the Van Dymings, particularly Mrs. Van

Dyming, celebrate the trappings—the art, the architecture, the drama—of ancient Greece but fail to understand the power of the elements of Greek tragedy that accompany those trappings and so fail to recognize hubris and fate as powerful and inevitable forces. For, as Midgleston makes clear, "they [the gods] used me. [. . .] just as they used that ram on that New England fellow, and that storm on that I-talian" to dismantle the Van Dymings' project (809). Stated another way, the Van Dymings embrace the perspective of empowerment in the imperializing Greco-Roman myth, while the country people and Midgleston recognize the subversive subtext of the layers that make up that mythic place.

The gods "use" Midgleston when his boss, an architect, sends him to the Van Dymings' place with the blueprint for the theater to be built on the property. On the way, he sees from the train

> animals inside a fence [. . .] when all of a sudden it felt like I had been thrown off the earth. I could see the bank and the fence go whirling away. And then I saw it. And just as I saw it, it was like it had kind of exploded inside my head. [. . .] I saw a face. In the air, looking at me across that white fence on top of the bank. It was not a man's face because it had horns, and it was not a goat's face because it had a beard and it was looking at me with eyes like a man and its mouth was open like it was saying something to me when it exploded inside my head. (811)

Some men on the train revive him with whiskey, and when he arrives at his destination and steps off the train, "it was all green, the light was, and the mountains," and he exclaims, "Let her rip" (812). He then goes and buys a "a tin [whistle], with holes in it," and as he makes his way to the Van Dymings he begins to undress (812–13).

When Midgleston arrives at the Van Dymings' place, he unchains a bull that is kept in the pasture and then begins chasing Mrs. Van Dyming around the yard in a scene that recreates the frieze on Keats's Grecian urn. Where Keats's image uses pottery for its raw material—its canvas—and where the raw material for the faun in Faulkner's earlier poem is marble, Faulkner uses paper, a canvas for him to paint his story on that is endowed with authority (in the form of currency, written law, and so on). When Midgleston tells his story, he produces an old newspaper "yellow with age, the broken seams glued carefully with strips of soiled cloth," upon which is written the narrative of his encounter with Mrs. Van Dyming (814). The headline reads, "MANIAC AT LARGE IN VIRGINIA MOUNTAINS: PROMI-

NENT NEW YORK SOCIETY WOMAN ATTACKED IN OWN GARDEN," followed by, "Mrs. Carleton Van Dyming Of New York and Newport Attacked By Half Nude Madman And Maddened Bull In Garden Of Her Summer Lodge" (814–15). There are "pictures and diagrams" and a story in Mrs. Van Dyming's own words about how she had expected the draughtsman but instead had encountered a maniac who chased her with a long knife (presumably the whistle—who knows who is lying?). The narrative ends with her standing against a tree, terrified, while the bull circles her and Midgleston raises the "knife" to his lips to blow, at which point she faints, thus creating a tableau in which, as on the Keatsian urn, the constituents never actually meet and touch and, as in another Keats poem, "Ode to a Nightingale," the question comes, "Do I wake or sleep?" The gods' use of Midgleston was successful, as the article goes on to note that immediately after the encounter the Van Dymings moved away and sold their land.

"Black Music" closes with Midgleston showing the frame narrator another clipping, one announcing that "Wilfred Middleton, New York Architect, Disappears From Millionaire's Country House: POSSE SEEKS BODY OF ARCHITECT BELIEVED SLAIN BY MADMAN IN VIRGINIA MOUNTAINS" (819). The narrator rightly notes that the paper misspelled Midgleston's name, at which point Midgleston produces a letter reprinted in the *New York Times*. The letter, written by Midgleston and sent from New Orleans, notes that the "name is Midgleston not Middleton. Would thank you to correct this error in local and metropolitan columns as the press a weapon of good and evil into every American home" (820). Midgleston explains that he made this correction for his wife's sake, as she was concerned about what the people on Park Avenue thought. Furthermore, he had sent the clippings to her but was not sure they had reached her because she had "moved to Park Avenue when the insurance was paid [. . . and] was married to a young fellow" (821). As with the marble faun and Spivak's subaltern, once Midgleston leaves the silent empowerment of the center to speak from within the periphery, his voice may grow louder, but it becomes less intelligible.

This closing evokes another "legend," Washington Irving's "Legend of Sleepy Hollow," in which Ichabod Crane encounters a headless (instead of a goat-headed) horseman and moves away from the superstitious hollow dispossessed of the woman he had hoped to marry. Irving's story suggests an anti-imperial narrative ethic: Crane is an empire builder, "a native of Connecticut, a State which supplies the Union with pioneers for the mind as well as for the forest" (33), who not only would participate in the intellectual colonization of the periphery but would also marry Katrina Van Tassel and with "a whole family of children mounted on the top of a wagon loaded with household trumpery, with pots and kettles dangling beneath [. . . set] out for Kentucky, Tennessee, or the Lord knows where" (39). As Midgleston is sent to the Van Dyming estate, Crane is summoned to the impressive Van Tassel abode by a messenger from the gods, "a negro, in towcloth jacket and trousers, a round-crowned fragment of a hat, like the cap of Mercury" (43). Although both Crane and Midgleston make their way into the periphery with imperial blueprints, they are overtaken by the periphery's superstitions and finally bereft of their ascendant status. Neither succeeds in his imperializing mission.

Again, although "Black Music" is not explicitly "southern" in the conventional sense, the narrative of imperialism and the larger context of the oppression of the global South infuse it with very recognizable southern themes. Trapped by the industrial-material center of New York/Park Avenue, Midgleston moves steadily southward through Virginia to New Orleans and then to Rincon. As he treks further south he grows "darker," from the less-than-white hybridity of being a faun to the not-exactly-white status he maintains in Rincon. Again there is a flaw in the Jeffersonian pastoral, this time because Monticello is being rebuilt with New York money, the superfluity of industrial capitalism. But even the deviations—or revisions—of the Jeffersonian ideal are a southern theme, particularly for southern local colorists of the post-Reconstruction era. As Wayne Mixon has shown, after the Civil War southerners who would work to reestablish the South's glory worked to resuscitate the Old South agrarian ideal by appropriating the value system of industrial capitalism, which characterized the nation's cultural center. For example, the title character of Thomas Nelson Page's *Gordon Keith* becomes a successful frontier town builder and then a businessman in New York City and uses his earnings to buy back and restore to its former glory his ancestral plantation, Elphinstone.

The irony of the story is that while the faun Midgleston has been loosed, he ostensibly is enclosed in the frame narrative. Although from the center originally, Midgleston becomes Other (indeed, with a different name), a shadow of himself, and thereby becomes the colonized subject of the periphery. He speaks in a slight dialect, his most conspicuous marker being his mispronunciation of *faun* as *farn,* which very nearly becomes *farm,* which is striking not only because of its Jeffersonian overtones and claim for Midgleston's attainment of autochthony but also in relation to Faulkner's likening Sherwood Anderson to a "corn field with a tongue in it." Still, while the frame narrative would seem to contain this faux faun, it is not the frame narrator but Midgleston who closes the story.

Of course, Midgleston's pronunciation of *faun* as *farn* also suggests a southern colloquial pronunciation of *foreign,* and in this respect Midgleston anticipates another marble faun figure, a person who "runs" and is designated as a "foreigner," Joe Christmas. Connected by name to the hybrid figure Christ, Christmas and the people he encounters throughout *Light in August* suggest that he may be white trash, Hispanic, African American, Italian, and above all, a "foreigner." Still, he passes as "just white"—the dietitian herself realizes that he *"will look just like a pea in a pan full of coffee beans"* (495) when he is removed to an all-black orphanage. Actually, Christmas is one of a host of hybrid white-Others in the novel; for example, Joanna Burden is a white woman who is also "a foreigner whose people moved in from the North during Reconstruction. A Yankee, a lover of Negroes, about whom in the town there is still talk [. . .] that lingers about her and about the place: something dark and outlandish and threatful" (432). And even though Gail Hightower is a white man, he is also a foreigner whose skin is the slightly off-white "color of flour sacking" (456); when he leaves his congregation amid newspaper photographers after his wife's death, his face hidden behind a hymn book "looked like the face of Satan in old prints" (448). Christmas too has "the face of Satan" (549); he is recognized as "the devil! It's Satan himself" (637), the incarnation of the goat-informed black beast rapist who is nevertheless a figure of whiteness, a figure whose racial instability makes him all the more threatening as he struggles to negotiate the white to almost-white shades of his skin color while alternately embracing and rejecting the perspective and experience of the Other. Like Midgleston, he spends his life running both from and toward himself, trapped in silent futility as he wields a fluid sense of identity to try and negotiate the fixed forms of societal identity labeling.

The figure of the fleeing faun appears also in *Soldiers' Pay.* Where *The Marble Faun* and "Black Music" seem to celebrate the Dionysian values the faun represents, Januarius Jones, the satyr of *Soldiers' Pay,* seems the most villainous of the novel's characters. Indeed, Jones is displaced in terms of mythic place; he is Pan entrapped in a world of Christianity, just as much a soldier without a war as the injured veteran Joe Gilligan. Vile and licentious, ugly and overweight, secretive and conniving, Jones has no seductive powers and is the antithesis of the open, exuberant, and attractive ideal of the Greco-Roman goat-man. Jones first appears, appropriately enough, in a garden setting. "[L]ately a fellow of Latin in a small college," he encounters the rector, Mahon, in the Episcopal church yard while leaning "upon a gate of iron grill-work breaking a levee of green and embryonically starred honeysuckle, watching April busy in a hyacinth bed" (56). "Jones's face [is] a round mirror before which fauns and nymphs might have wantoned when the world was young" (58); his eyes, "clear and yellow, obscene and old in sin as a goat's" (67), are likened to a goat's throughout the novel, and his greatest power lies in his gaze.

But as may be expected, Jones is a strange and paradoxical Other, like Midgleston one of Faulkner's expressly southern fictional counterfeit Others. As Davis has noted, with the exception of Mammy Callie, the African Americans of *Soldiers' Pay* merely form a backdrop to the actions of the white characters. So Faulkner makes Jones into the "black beast" would-be rapist even though he is one of the whitest of all the characters.[19] Jones first attempts to seduce Cecily Saunders and then tries his luck with Margaret Powers; although Cecily permits him to kiss her, both women repel him, leaving him to chase the maid, Emmy: "Suddenly Emmy came around the corner of the house running and darting up the steps and through the entrance, swift in the dusk. [. . .] then they saw Jones, like a fat satyr, leaping after her, hopelessly distanced" (286). Like Midgleston and Mrs. Van Dyming, Jones and Emmy reenact the image on the Grecian urn.

But again, the pagan Jones-as-faun is abhorrent in the novel, reworked (like Joe Christmas) as Satan and a force of evil rather than (like Midgleston) Pan and a force of joy. Much like Joe Christmas, "Jones, who had no mother that he could name and who might have claimed any number of possible fathers" (230) and who "grew up in a Catholic orphanage" (231), cannot be sure who or what he is. He stands outside of the overarching codes of Christianity, occupying an older and other pagan space that is nevertheless defined by Christian iconography. He explains his relationship with Catholicism by telling a story from his childhood:

> At our church they gave prizes for attendance and knowing the lesson, and my card bore forty-one stars, when it disappeared. [. . .] My father had used it to enter a one-dollar bet on a race-horse. When I

> went to my father's place of business to prevail on him to return home, as was my custom, just as I passed through the swinging doors, one of his business associates there was saying, "Whose card is this?" I recognized my forty-one stars immediately, and claimed it, collecting twenty-one dollars, by the way. Since then I have been a firm believer in Christianity. (231)

Clearly, Janaurius Jones, "born of whom he knew not and cared not, becoming Jones alphabetically, January through a conjunction of calendar and biology, Januarius through the perverse conjunction of his own star and the compulsion of food and clothing" (56), is a figure caught in the intersection of systems, a part of a transparent layer of Greek-Roman myth overlaid by another Christian layer bearing the traces of that layer and yet vilifying its core values.

There are other woodland/pastoral characters in the novel. The first of these is Emmy, the Mahons' maid and the nymph of *Soldiers' Pay*. Faulkner describes her at one point as "raising garments to a line with formal gestures, like a Greek masque" (250). She is clearly not at home in town but rather in the periphery of the country, specifically in the woods, where she encounters the novel's other faun, Donald Mahon. Emmy informs Margaret that she and Donald carried on an Arcadian-inflected affair before he left to fight in the war:

> Sometimes he used to walk home from school with me. He wouldn't never have a hat or a coat, and his face was like—it was like he ought to live in the woods. You know, not like he ought to went to school or had to dress up. And so you never did know when you'd see him. He'd come in school at almost any time and folks would see him way out in the country at night. Sometimes he'd sleep in folks' houses in the country and sometime niggers would find him asleep in sand ditches. (125)

Emmy explains that she and Donald would swim together in the afternoons. At length, her father discovered that she "liked Donald," and he told Donald "not to come fooling around there no more," and he made Emmy "swear [she] wouldn't never see Donald again" (126). Emmy did not see him for some time, and in the meantime it was rumored that Donald was engaged to Cecily, but one night he came to Emmy and they ran away from the house to the woods to swim. Unlike Januarius Jones, who cannot quite catch Emmy, Donald could run with her; in fact, she says that "all of a sudden Donald ran on ahead of me. I can keep up with

Donald when I want to" (127). That night Donald made love to her, and they spent the night in the woods, much like the lovers in *A Midsummer Night's Dream* (another lovefest in Arcadia). Although Donald is never explicitly described as a faun, he clearly fills that role much more effectively than Jones. Donald's hair, now dulled, "had once been so wild, so soft" (166), and when Emmy remembers him, she recalls that "he was beautiful, with his body all brown and quick" (274). His loving her makes "her feel beautiful, too," lifting her from her own poor-white status, in which she had "to wear coarse dresses and shoes," to the status of the "girls who wore silk and thin leather"; while she had to walk "home to where work awaited her [. . .] other girls were riding in cars or having ice-cream or talking to boys and dancing with him" (274). Indeed, although Jones wants to claim her as his "Cinderella" (133), it is Donald who offers her a fairy-tale life of upward mobility.

In the triangle of Donald-Emmy-Jones, Faulkner more sharply employs the Brom Bones–Katrina Van Tassel–Ichabod Crane situation in Irving's tale. While in "Black Music" the triumphant lover merely shows up to claim his prize after Midgleston has gone, in *Soldiers' Pay* two fauns lay claim to the hand of a single nymph. Regarding such a situation, John Faulkner claims that his brother told him "that any story must have a conflict in it. You set it up, then solve it. He said the best conflict, the one people like to read about the most, is two men trying to get in bed with the same woman" (191). However suspect John Faulkner's assertions may be, his brother Bill does employ this triangular dynamic in a compelling compilation of mythic place as the Georgia woods become the forest of Arcadia and the woods of Sleepy Hollow.

The problem with Januarius Jones is that he is not entirely a creature of the forest; he is also a creature of the garden, although he fails in that place as well. At the same time that he stands outside of the Christian system that would vilify him, he is one of the modern dancers in the marble faun's garden. He tells Emmy, "You don't seem to have any golden hair [like Cinderella's], but then you might jazz your hair up a little, too. Ah, this restless young generation [of which, of course, Jones is a part]! Wanting to jazz up everything, not only their complexions, but the shapes of their behinds as well" (134). But when a jazzy dance *is* held on a lawn in Charlestown (Charleston?), despite being one who upholds the jazz values of modernity, Jones is just as inadequate in the garden jazz dance as he is in the forest.

This dance scene, which takes place in chapter 5 of the novel, depicts one epoch's nudging aside another and the two coexisting uneasily. The main constituents of the event are the soldiers and the noncombatants. The soldiers' time of attraction, the time when they could command the attention of all the female dancers simply because of their uniforms, has passed. Now, at this dance, they are like "people who are brought together by invitation yet are not quite certain of themselves and of the spirit of the invitation; in this case the eternal country boys of one national mental state, lost in the comparative metropolitan atmosphere of one diametrically opposed to it. To feel provincial: finding that a certain conventional state of behaviour has become inexplicably obsolete overnight" (198). This striking passage renders a temporal tableau of the shifting and relative nature of Faulkner's configurations of center-periphery; his fiction operates on comparative metropoles and peripheries. The soldiers, who are the marble statues in the garden, are also metaphorically the "country boys," not a part of the center that is "Charlestown, [which] like numberless other towns throughout the south, had been built around a circle of tethered horses and mules" (112). There is one hybrid character who can negotiate these two groups—the androgynous Margaret Powers. Although Margaret reflects that "I'm not a man" (265), she also acknowledges that in Joe Gilligan's eyes she "just happened to be the first woman you ever knew doing something you thought only a man would do" (161), and later she asks him, "What kind of fellows do you think we ought to have been, Joe?" (303). Indeed, throughout the novel Margaret Powers is surprisingly the most em*powered* character, single-handedly orchestrating Donald Mahon's short-lived future. In the dance, however, she is all "woman," young and pretty enough for the young women to be jealous of her and the noncombatants to desire her, yet clearly able to relate to and be a member of the peripheral group, the soldiers.

Overall, the crisis of place in the novel is that of displacement and misplacement. Nothing—and no one—is where it belongs spatially or temporally. In fact, time and space have run out. The narrative of Emmy's youth has passed away with Donald's memory; Donald's virile, faunlike personality has ceased to exist altogether, and he is now a static, silent figure; Margaret has outlasted one husband and winds up outliving another; Jones the faun's values are part of another system of morality; and the soldiers have outlasted the war. Certain characters do seem to show promise of negotiating or at least enduring the new epoch: Rector Mahon, though broken, maintains a degree of optimism about the future, which he also instills in Gilligan, who cannot secure the affections of Margaret; and Julian Lowe seems to make out all right in the dances at his home in California. But Cecily and her husband George leave town and get married in Atlanta, Margaret leaves on a train, and a general sense of the inadequacy of place pervades the novel. The problem of place and time may be understood in terms of the conflicts inherent in the mythic place of the novel's setting. The layers of narrative feud: Christian iconography effaces pagan iconography; the jazz narrative of the modern epoch roars into the silence and death of World War I.[20] And just as "Black Music" ends with a fleeing Midgleston, so *Soldiers' Pay* closes with Januarius Jones fleeing the grasp of Joe Gilligan, who would thrash him for his advances toward Emmy.

Again, Faulkner makes the themes of region and race that are implicit in the garden dance in *The Marble Faun* explicit in *Soldiers' Pay*. Where the dancers in the earlier volume might be swinging to the "Charleston" rhythms of African origin, the dancers in the author's first novel are in Charlestown, Georgia, dancing to the tunes of a "Negro" band and doing steps that one character describes as "jumping around—like monkeys" (166). And Faulkner adds another layer of narrative to the image of the marble statue: in addition to the marble faun as cigar-store Indian, Faulkner notes the presence in Charlestown of "a stone shaft bearing a Confederate soldier shading his marble eyes forever in eternal rigid vigilance" (112). This statue is one among countless others erected in towns and cities throughout the South; in one sense this figure encodes the same iconography as the cigar-store Indian, a fossilized sign of the United States' imperial drive. Indeed, this statue is part of a square with a courthouse that is "a simple utilitarian edifice of brick and sixteen beautiful Ionic columns" and elms beneath which "on scarred and carved wood benches and chairs the city fathers [. . .] in black string ties or faded brushed grey and bronze meaningless medals of the Confederate States of America [. . .] slept or whittled away the long drowsy days [. . .]" (112). Like the pagan world that furnished the model of Ionic columns, the faun/cigar-store Indian/Confederate soldier are traces of opacity that show through the layers of transparent narrative that define the place of Charlestown.

At the same time, though, the statue of the Confederate soldier represents postwar southern white aristocratic New South hegemony driven by the United Daughters of the Confederacy. For the statue of the Confederate soldier keys into a culture of the glorification of defeat, a spirit of religious-like zeal that fuels a reformation of southern culture and empowerment, a reconfiguration built on the making of whiteness and the creating of a new economic and cultural empire. This hegemony in the form of the marble statue appears in the statue of Colonel John Sartoris, described at the end of *Flags in the Dust:* "He stood on a stone pedestal, in his frock coat and bareheaded, one leg slightly advanced and one hand resting lightly on the stone pylon beside him. His head was lifted a little in that gesture of haughty arrogance which repeated itself generation after generation with a fateful fidelity, his back to the world and his carven eyes gazing out across the valley where his railroad ran and beyond it the blue changeless hills, and beyond that" (427–28). This statue represents New South success (the building of railroads, the advancing of southern civilization), and the Old South's demise was the phoenixlike birth of this New South's growing glory. Still, even this image is problematic, for by the time of the action in *Flags in the Dust* and *Soldiers' Pay,* as Charles Reagan Wilson writes, a "romantic view of the Confederate heroes [had] eventually made them into marble men, their human struggles forgotten by the modern world" (*Judgment* 162).

But as scholars have often noted, in *Soldiers' Pay* Faulkner fails fully to constitute southern space, to root it in culture and history in a way compelling enough to register it as a tactile and significant location. That is, with the exception of the reference here to the Confederacy, Faulkner leaves out the narrative of the South; or perhaps more accurately, he does not fully realize it, for the marginalization of African Americans is present, and the rules of patriarchy are everywhere evident in Cecily's ordeal (as well as in her manipulations of her situation). While these elements appear, Faulkner does not exploit their potential for the conflicts arising from the imperializing impulse. Indeed, as many readers have recognized, the ostensibly "southern" space of the novel simply does not emerge as solidly constituted; instead, the mythical Charlestown might be any town in the United States. It is rather as an "American" space that the forces of imperialism come closest to realization in the novel's setting. Although there are some slight regional variations, primarily in a few gestures in dialect differences, the reader does not encounter great difficulty moving from New York through Ohio and then to Georgia as the novel progresses. One does not get the sense that any great aunts plan to walk out of a theater because Sherman's name is mentioned in a film. A vague sense of the United States as a victorious power hangs about the pages of the novel: when Gilligan reads Gibbon's *History of Rome* to Donald, describing the activity as "[busting] up a few more minor empires" (279), he might be thinking that he and Donald had been engaged in a similar activity. But overall there prevails the implication that the United States has thwarted the ruthless Huns, that somehow the young and roguish globally peripheral place that is the United States as a nation has resisted the older European enemy rather than working to establish its own imperial project. Still, this notion is only thinly evident at best, hinted at but not a compelling part of the narrative. And at times even any opposition between the United States and Europe collapses, such as when Sergeant Madden, flying over France, "seeing the intermittent silver smugness of rain spaced forever with poplars like an eternal frieze giving way upon vistas fallow and fecund," thinks of Green, who "had been a college instructor and [. . .] could explain to you where Alexander and Napoleon and Grant made their mistakes" (177). Clearly, at this point Faulkner is comfortable importing a narrative of U.S. imperialism (from a southern perspective) into a European context and collapsing time into a larger mythic place. Indeed, the Americans (even the southerners) in Europe have little trouble speaking as subalterns; one even manages to scream "You got us killed" before shooting Dick Powers in the face (179).

Nevertheless, the problem of speech does stand as a crisis of control in the novel. Latin emerges as a language of empire: it is the language of Rome and Caesar, and it is the language of Januarius Jones. Joe Gilligan cannot speak it, nor can he read English particularly well when reading to Donald; Jones, on the other hand, encodes his language with pagan phrases, placing himself above Emmy and Joe. Emmy is herself a poor white, as is borne out in her speech, which is tinged with dialect and poor grammar. The one character who cannot speak in any way that is meaningful within the fabric of the communication around him is Donald. Like the marble faun, he is stuck in his mind, remembering a moment of flight and a (perhaps half-imagined) crash. Still, Donald speaks in a manner like that of the marble faun and the Grecian urn: he speaks with the scar on his head, the trace of the struggle for imperial control that created the icon that he is.[21] As usual, language is power, but the most effective wielder of that power is Margaret *Powers,* a hybrid figure whose speaking registers the control of the center even as the periphery struggles to speak in the way that Spivak warns about. Even though Jones employs language in his seductions, those attempts fail, and even his effort to blackmail Cecily ultimately falls flat.

While the elements of speech and imperial impulse do not intersect in a fully clarified portrait in *Soldiers' Pay*, they play a central role in *The Hamlet*. This work was conceived in the vein of imperialism, having been initiated in the uncompleted *Father Abraham,* which develops the story of the single son whose progeny would be made into a great nation, invading and possessing the Promised Land. Here too the image of the faun is central; in an apparent moment of musing, Faulkner even sketched an image of Pan on the back of one of the manuscript pages of *Father Abraham* that closely resembles the one he drew for *Mayday*.[22] In *The Hamlet,* the goat emerges as a unit of currency as Faulkner explores both the satanic and the Dionysiac aspects of the goat-man, while the nymph reappears as goddess in an Arcadian setting fraught with the crises of an invading capitalistic system manipulated and attenuated to the point that its every loophole is exploited to fullest effect.

Flem Snopes is certainly the god of goats, and being Pan-like, he is a presatanic figure literally able to out-Satan Satan. V. K. Ratliff may be the longstanding champion of Yoknapatawpha County and the shrewdest of traders, but it is Flem Snopes who literally gets his goats on his way to becoming emperor of the hamlet. After being sick and therefore absent from Frenchman's Bend for a time, Ratliff returns to the village with a plan to make money,

> in his pocket a contract to sell fifty goats to a Northerner who had recently established a goat-ranch in the western part of the county. It was actually a subcontract which he had purchased at the rate of twenty-five cents a goat from the original contractor who held his from the Northerner at seventy-five cents a goat and was about to fail to complete. Ratliff bought the subcontract because he happened to know of a herd of some fifty-odd goats in a little-travelled section near Frenchman's Bend village which the original contractor had failed to find and which Ratliff was confident he could acquire by offering to halve his profit with the owner of them. (793)

Ratliff, however, makes the mistake of telling about his plan to buy goats from Ben Quick in the presence of Flem Snopes, who heads him off in the game.

Particularly revealing is Ratliff's discourse on the Northern goat rancher. When one of the anonymous porch sitters of the hamlet questions the whole concept of goat ranching, Ratliff replies, "You never heard of a goat-rancher. Because wouldn't nobody in this country think of it. It would take a Northerner to do that" (804). Ratliff explains that the Northerner was proceeding successfully until he "run out of goats" (804); such a situation arose, Ratliff notes, because he was a Northerner and "[t]hey does things different from us. If a fellow in this country was to set up a goat-ranch, he would do it purely and simply because he had too many goats already" (804). "But a Northerner don't do it that way," Ratliff continues. "When he does something he does it with a organised syndicate and a book of printed rules and a gold-filled diploma from the Secretary of State at Jackson saying for all men to know by these presents, greetings, that them twenty-thousand goats or whatever it is, is goats. He dont start off with goats or a piece of land either. He starts off with a piece of paper and a pencil and measures it all down setting in the library—so many goats to so many acres and so much fence to hold them" (804). Proceeding thus, the goat rancher was doing well until "he found he had done run out of goats," at which point he "combed the country up and down and backwards and forwards to find the right number of goats to keep that gold diploma from telling him to his face he was lying" (79). The project thus failed: "now it aint a goat-ranch; it's a insolvency" (805).

The Northerner might be a representative of the West-Yoknapatawpha Company, come to colonize and exploit the Mississippi periphery with a goat farm. Coming from the cultural center of the North—Ratliff suggests that he could be from "Massachusetts or Boston or Ohio" or even from "Boston, Maine"—the goat rancher "come all the way down to Mississippi with his hand grip bulging with greenback money and bought him two thousand acres" (804). As Ratliff shows (and as Midgleston demonstrates in "Black Music"), a sign of centeredness and empowerment is paper, whether it be bills or golden-sealed diplomas. And the colonizer comes with a plan to define the "hill-gully and rabbit grass land" (804). These goats might be thought of metaphorically as African American slaves, or perhaps in the case of Quick's herd, Native Americans. The goat rancher himself compares roughly with Paul Rainey, of Cleveland, Ohio, a coal magnate's son and big-game hunter who built a sprawling mansion and ranch near Cotton Plant, just south of Blue Mountain and about ten miles south of Ripley, Mississippi. Faulkner writes of him in *The Reivers* that he "liked our country enough—or anyway our bear and deer and panther enough—to use some of the Wall Street money to own enough Mississippi land for him and his friends to hunt them in: a hound man primarily, who took his pack of bear hounds to Africa to see what they would do on lion or vice versa" (859). Rainey is one of the "northern millionaires" (859), like "Horace Lytle and George Peyton as magical among bird-dog people as Babe Ruth and Ty Cobb among baseball aficionados" (881).[23]

In other words, to the likes of the Northerner, Mississippi equals Africa, a global South space to colonize and exploit. Faulkner evokes more than just the U.S. South, noting that when Ratliff reaches Columbia, Tennessee (South America?), "after the first amazed moment or so, he looked about him with something of the happy surmise of the first white hunter blundering into the idyllic solitude of a virgin African vale teeming with ivory" (781). Indeed, running the gin in Frenchman's Bend (the site of another production of white material largely produced by nonwhite hands and nonwhite sweat), Will Varner and Flem Snopes "resembled the white trader and his native parrot-taught headman in an African outpost" (786). Frenchman's Bend is named for the "tremendous pre–Civil War plantation" built by a colonizing foreigner labeled "the Frenchman," his name now "forgotten, his pride but a legend about the land he had wrested from the jungle and tamed as a monument to that appellation which those who came after him [. . .] could not even read, let alone pronounce" (731–32).

However, Ratliff discovers that paper is not something manipulated by northerners only when he goes to get the fifty goats from Flem, who has bought them from Quick before him. Ratliff plans to buffalo Flem with the notes he received from Flem's cousin Mink; when Flem asks for seventy-five cents per goat rather than twenty-five, Ratliff produces a note for ten dollars given to him by Mink in payment for a sewing machine, signing Flem's name as well as his own. "You figure this note is worth fifty goats," Flem says and then burns the subcontract for the goats (809–10). Then Ratliff hands him another note given to him by Mink, for "ten dollars with interest, payable on demand one year after date of execution, to *Isaac Snopes or bearer,* and signed *Flem Snopes*" (801). Realizing that Ratliff "want[s] to collect this too" (810), Flem shows Ike to Ratliff so that he can see Ike's condition and says, "That was Isaac Snopes. [. . .] I'm his guardian. Do you want to see the papers?" (811). Ratliff replies, "So if I pay him his ten dollars myself, you will take charge of it as his guardian. And if I collect the ten dollars from you, you will have the note to sell again. And that will make three times it has been collected"; then he burns the note (811). Even though Ratliff has claimed, "I be dog if I had hardly got outen bed [from illness] before Him or somebody had done sent me a sheep just like He done to save Isaac in the Book. He sent me a goat-rancher" (803–4), Isaac in fact proves to be the instrument of Ratliff's failure in his project.

Flem, in the meantime, is the new Frenchman, perhaps not foreign enough to be considered European but definitely a colonizing outlander, his home being a faraway place, nothing less than Hell itself. Indeed, the novel's constantly repeated expletive "Hell Fire" and Ratliff's having been taken in the goat deal informs his vision of Flem swindling Satan. Once again, Flem utilizes the power of paper in Ratliff's imagined scene, as Satan's minions inform him that they *"cant do nothing with [Flem . . .]. He says he dont want no more and no less than his legal interest according to what the banking and civil laws states in black and white is hisn"* (870). Son of a barn burner, Flem is utterly unperturbed by Satan, whom he cheats not only out of his soul but out of Hell itself. As Satan, whom Ratliff refers to as "The Prince," fades from power amid *"bright, crown-shaped flames,"* he yells, *"Take Paradise! [. . .] Take it! Take it!"* (873). As the goat god, Pan, Flem actually precedes Satan as icon. Note, too, the hybridity of written law—"in black and white"—and Flem's comfort with such a medium; the Prince learned how to use his pitchfork "on Chinees and Dagoes and Polynesians, until his arms would get strong enough to handle his share of white folks" (871), but Flem, descendant of the marble faun, is neither and both white and nonwhite.

Ratliff's vision of Flem in Hell represents a radical stripping away of the transparent geological layers of mythic place, a project that is manifested literally in his final encounter with Flem Snopes in the novel. Ratliff develops a scheme to buy the Frenchman's place from Flem for the purpose of digging up money allegedly buried in the ground; this myth of the Frenchman's place is all that is left of the Frenchman's "dream and his pride now dust with the lost dust of anonymous bones, his legend but the stubborn tale of the money he buried somewhere about the place when Grant overran the country on his way to Vicksburg" (732). Along with two companions, Ratliff has been watching Flem dig for the money every night, and having found the money before him, they plan to outdo him. When Flem asks Ratliff why he wants the land, Ratliff responds with irony, "To start a goat-ranch" (1063). Once Flem and his compatriots buy the land, they discover that Flem has swindled them, tricking them into thinking antebellum money was buried there, when in fact Flem actually buried postwar-minted money for them to find, so that they in their scheming suffer from his own scheme.

Flem understands the importance of manipulating the ambiguity of mythic place. As the other two novels in the Snopes trilogy illustrate, he constructs and manipulates a narrative of respectability in his efforts to secure his ascendant position in Yoknapatawpha society. He shows uncanny awareness of the myths that have arisen around and about him, many of which are driven by Ratliff, who like Ichabod Crane "retail[ed] from house to house the news of his four counties with the ubiquity of a newspaper and carrying personal messages from mouth to mouth about weddings and funerals and the preserving of vegetables and fruit with the reliability of a postal service" (741). Understanding Ratliff's propensity to narrativize/mythologize, Flem manages to shift the opaque spot of the mythic layer of which he is a part in the successive stages of ownership of the Frenchman's place. In other words, he rearranges his own mythic plot so that another mythic layer seems to supersede his own; he does this by literally digging down to another layer of time and space. Of course, though it bears the traces of past significance, a myth is finally an immediate thing invested in the present layer of signification, as Ratliff discovers when he realizes that the coins Flem buried were all minted after the Civil War. In his efforts to be a primary and romantic mythologist, Ratliff makes the grave mistake of forgetting that Flem is never anything but a consummatory mythologist, forever playing with mythic layers, and that the only hope of "beating" Flem lies in constant critical thinking about accepted modes of thought and meaning.

As goat god, Flem must have his goddess, and her name is Eula. With "eyes like cloudy hothouse grapes" (738), Eula Varner emerges as a figure whose "entire appearance suggested some symbology out of the old Dionysic times—honey in sunlight and bursting grapes, the writhen bleeding of the crushed fecundated vine beneath the hard rapacious trampling goat-hoof" (817). Like the marble faun, "[s]he seemed to be not a living integer of her contemporary scene, but rather to exist in a teeming vacuum in which her days followed one another as though behind sound-proof glass, where she seemed to listen in sullen bemusement, with a weary wisdom heired of all mammalian maturity, to the enlarging of her own organs" (817). Rather than "behind" she might be "within" the pane of sound-proof glass, the mythic layer of earthy pagan celebration that is her peculiar transcendent epoch. She maintains the doubleness that characterizes the faun, for there "was one Eula Varner who supplied blood and nourishment to the buttocks and legs and breasts; there was the other Eula Varner who merely inhabited them, who went where they went because it was less trouble to do so" (822). She is Emmy reborn, a nymph turned goddess, the product of "one blind seed of the spendthrift Olympian ejaculation" (867). In fact, she is the daughter of a faun, a man who even in old age regularly meets a woman in a "sylvan Pan-hallowed retreat" for lusty fornication during which he "would not even remove his hat" (861).

Eula is also Katrina Van Tassel, the object of the Frenchman's Bend pedagogue Labove's affection. Obsessed with his voluptuous student, Labove spends each day after school "wallowing" his face on the bench where she sits until one day she comes back, having forgot her book satchel, and asks him, "What are you doing down there?" (841). Labove then attacks her while "whispering his jumble of fragmentary Greek and Latin verse and American-Mississippi obscenity" in a manner that runs the gamut of mythic layers represented in his relation to Eula (842). She finally overcomes him, telling him, "Stop pawing me. [. . .] You old headless horseman Ichabod Crane" (843). Already described as having "legs haired-over like those of a faun" (839), Labove is Januarius Jones, the failed faun, who like Crane, Midgleston, and Jones then flees. As for Eula, this moment represents one of her few efforts to speak; and in this effort she successfully throws off the patriarchal-imperial mythic layers represented in Labove's attempted rape of her.

The majority of Eula's speaking takes place in *The Town,* a novel in which Faulkner continues his examination of monuments and hybridity.[24] She talks with Gavin Stevens throughout the time of her affair with Manfred De Spain, and Flem continues to play with the narrative of their scandalous affair, milking it for the most gain possible. Her greatest act of speech/disruption is her taking of her own life. Yet even that act is undone when Gavin erects what Ratliff calls Flem's "colyum" to her (Ratliff suspects that it was Flem's idea all along), "standing in the middle of that new one-grave lot, [. . .] looking—the stone, the marble—whiter than white itself in the warm October sun against the bright yellow and red and dark red hickories and sumacs and gums and oaks" (311). The monument bears a "marble medallion face [. . .] that never looked like Eula a-tall you thought at first, never looked like nobody nowhere you thought at first, until you were wrong because it never looked like all women because what it looked like was one woman that ever man that was lucky enough to have been a man would say, 'Yes, that's her [. . .]'" (311–12). On this phallic monument representing Flem's ultimate control over Eula's body (and even obliteration of it, since it does not resemble her) and registering his final imperialization of Jefferson, Flem (according to Ratliff) offers the following ironic myth/narrative:

EULA VARNER SNOPES
1889   1927
A VIRTUOUS WIFE IS A CROWN TO HER HUSBAND
HER CHILDREN RISE AND CALL HER BLESSED
(312)

This bit of mythmaking obfuscates the reality of her trysts with lovers before marrying Flem as well as her relationship with De Spain, transforming her into a stereotypical dutiful wife and rendering Flem the object of sympathy and respectability. Stated another way, Eula as a signifier transforms from a dynamic Dionysian narrative to a static Apollonian monument, an altogether different narrative.[25] Faulkner continues to develop this Eula-as-statuary presence in *The Mansion* when Ratliff speaks of the creation of the Eula grave marker in pagan-Arcadian terms, noting "that-ere financial Midsummer Night's Dream masque or rondeau that Linda and that Oxford lawyer composed betwixt them that had Linda's signature on it," and then proceeds to explain that it was actually Gavin who "was now busy over the headstone Flem had decided on. Because it would have to be made in Italy" (463).

Charles Mallison makes the Keatsian context even more visible when he tells the story of Tug Nightingale, who emerges as a type of marble faun. On one hand, Tug resembles his father, himself a sort of Confederate soldier statue, who believes that the world is flat and that Robert E. Lee betrayed the Confederacy and so "set his intractable and contemptuous face against the juggernaut of history and science both that April day in 1865 and never flinched since" (499). Even though Tug can sit "quite still" with his hands "hanging quiet too between his knees," he nevertheless is a restless figure—a hybrid who appropriately enough exhibits affinity with mules—who actually leaves Jefferson to fight in Europe even at the expense of his father's disowning him. Like the nightingale in Keats's ode, Tug is literally tugged between Apollonian quiet stillness and Dionysian loud motion when Skeets McGowan teases that Tug might head east and yet return to Jefferson "looking at it right square across Miss Joanna Burden's mailbox" (498) having rounded the earth. Tug lashes out so vehemently at this cut that it "took all the barbers and customers and loafers too and finally the night marshal himself to immobilize Tug" (500). Using similar marble-faun imagery, Charles refers to young Bayard Sartoris as "the last Sartoris Mohican" (501), suggesting that the statue of Colonel John Sartoris might reference not just the Confederate soldier but also the cigar-store Indian.

Charles continues to develop this opposition between motion and stasis when he describes Linda Snopes Kohl and Gavin's relationship with her. Gavin sits in Apollonian stillness, watching young girls, who "had to be alive for him to notice them, and they had to be in motion to be alive, and the only moment of motion which caught his attention, his eye, was that one at which they entered puberty like the swirl of skirt or flow or turn of limb when entering, passing through a door" (508). But Linda, who is "stone deaf" (503), actually usurps and thereby "captures" Gavin by becoming herself even more the Apollonian as "the inviolate bride of silence" (514). Linda has become as a result of war what Gavin, possibly working in tandem with or under the orders of Flem, had made her mother into when he had the Italian sculptor carve Eula's tombstone, which itself stands ironically as one of what end up being Flem's "three monuments in Jefferson now: the water tank, the gravestone, and the mansion" (513). Both Eula and her daughter are reincarnations of Helen, traces of a pagan mythic-imperial layer.

In the Snopes trilogy, Flem is not only the Grecian god who can gain ultimate control of the Grecian goddess but also the chief of a tribe of goat-men. Eck Snopes proves to be an incredibly virile man, spawning children with the rapacity of a goat. And Ike Snopes, with his "pointed faun's ears" (811), enacts *The Hamlet*'s most explicit Keatsian-urn imagery when he leads his garlanded bovine lover into a sylvan setting of amorous promise. Autochthonous in the extreme, Ike experiences the reality "that dawn, light, is not decanted onto earth from the sky, but instead is from the earth itself suspired," that "dark in the blind dark of time's silt and rich refuse" lie "Troy's Helen and the nymphs and the snoring mitred bishops, the saviors and the victims and the kings" (898). These are the mythic layers in which are articulated the struggles of the oppressor and the oppressed; the irony of the passage lies in Ike's not having the capability to grasp the significance of these layers as a whole. Peter Alan Froehlich has noted the Bakhtinian quality of *The Hamlet,* and this mock-pastoral romance induces a carnivalesque atmosphere, in which laughter exposes the idiocy of Ratliff and others who should understand the intricacies of empowerment inherent in the constitution of place.

Actually, for a moment Ratliff does manage to wield to decisive effect the power of narrative, although Flem is notably absent when Ratliff does find success. Appalled at the Ike-and-the-cow show that Lump Snopes runs at Littlejohn's, Ratliff reminds I. O. Snopes that "[w]hen Caesar's wife goes up to Will Varner next month to get that ere school job again, and he aint pure as a marble monument, what do you think is going to happen?" (917). Realizing the importance to the Snopes imperial project of maintaining a positive myth of family respectability, I. O. catches Ratliff's meaning and replies that the "Snopes name has done held its head up too long in this country to have no such reproaches against it like stock-diddling" (918). When Ratliff charges I. O. "sixteen dollars and eighty cents" for the cow because Mrs. Littlejohn refuses to let Brother Whitfield and I. O. have the cow in order to cook and feed it to Ike, I. O. sets about conning Eck into paying for it because of the importance of the "Snopes name. Cant you understand that? That aint never been aspersed yet by no living man. That's got to be kept pure as a marble monument for your children to grow up under" (919–20).

Examination of the marble faun's descendants and the traces of empire in Grecian-urn imagery might conclude with a discussion of "The Bear" in *Go Down, Moses*. The action of the story is set in the Big Woods, harkening back to a mythic layer of pagan freedom signifying an era of the faun's freedom from marble bonds. But these are the last days and final square miles of this mythic layer, for civilization encroaches, the train speeds quickly and more quickly into the forest's shadows, and soon the wilderness will be something merely imagined, obliterated by the timber industry. The marble faun of this story is Sam Fathers, the hybrid figure who has already fled the garden and entered the forest but can no longer run and instead must perish with his moment of mythic significance into the stack of layers, hidden behind the opacity of the present yet still lurking in the signifying of space and time.

Sam Fathers is part of a mythic layer being steadily shoved aside by a new one. The son of a quadroon slave woman and the Native American chief Ikkemotubbe, Sam is white, black, and red. Although members of the McCaslin Edmonds family defer to him, recognizing that he is "a prince" (213) and son of "an Indian King" (282), Sam is also the cigar-store Indian, repeatedly described as "motionless," relegated to a romanticized icon representing the vanquished in the society of the vanquisher. Indeed, as McCaslin Edmonds tells Ike McCaslin in "The Old People," Sam was "[l]ike an old lion or a bear in a cage [. . .]. He was born in the cage and he has been in it all his life" (161). Appropriately enough, in "The Bear," Sam, the bear named Old Ben, and the dog named Lion all expire at the same time, all three marble figures toppling before the march of civilization into the wilderness.

And these three are not all. For example, there is the other part–Native American, Boon Hogganbeck, "the quarter Indian, grandson of a Chickasaw squaw, who on occasion resented with his hard and furious fists the intimation of one single drop of alien blood" and who even claimed at times "that his father had been the full-blood Chickasaw and even a chief and that even his mother had been only half white" (217–18). With a "huge gargoyle's face" (216) that "looked like somebody had found a walnut a little larger than a football and with a machinist's hammer had shaped features into it and then painted it, mostly red" (218), Boon also emerges as a wooden Indian. And it is he who combines with Ben and Lion and "[f]or an instant [. . .] almost resembled a piece of statuary: the clinging dog, the bear, the man astride its back" (231). When this piece of bricolage falls, it does so "all of a piece, as a tree falls," and at the same time the hunters discover "Sam Fathers lying motionless on his face in the trampled mud" (231).

Then there is Isaac McCaslin, the one through whom there should be the promise of a great nation. Whereas Ike Snopes can never beget a generation of cow-people from his own race of goat-men, Ike McCaslin sees himself as part of the frieze on the Grecian urn. Ike says about himself that he is "an Isaac born into a later life than Abraham's and repudiating immolation: fatherless and therefore safe declining the altar because maybe this time the exasperated Hand might not supply the kid" (271). The image of Abraham's hand frozen in place just before plunging into the bowels of Isaac historically prefigures the image on the urn. And McCaslin quotes "Ode on a Grecian Urn" to explain why Ike could not shoot the bear; the fact is that Ike is one of the marbles, the lone marble faun remaining after the iconoclastic purge of the new mythic layer. He is the liminal bridge—although not a racial hybrid, a hybrid of mythic place, a relic, a reminder.

In fact, Ike most clearly comprehends the nature of the plot of ground bearing the powerful weight of mythic place and imperial space. Throughout section 4 of "The Bear" Ike explains the rise and fall of empires, constantly pointing to the passive recalcitrance of topography, the fact that the land will not acquiesce, that it will not be vanquished or ruled by human ambition. Ike continually returns to his father's, uncle's, and grandfather's ledgers, which are arranged vertically on the papers on which they are written, with horizontal layers of time and space recording the mischances of the past, all of which inform the present that Ike furnishes in his own annotations. Through all of this probing and brooding, Ike maintains the conclusion that, as McCaslin states it, "this land is, indubitably, of and by itself cursed," to which Ike replies, "Cursed" (284). Faulkner follows this axiom with a brilliant definition for mythic place: "Cursed," McCaslin says,

> and again McCaslin merely lifted one hand, not even speaking and not even toward the ledgers: so that, as the stereopticon condenses into one instantaneous field the myriad minutia of its scope, so did that light and rapid gesture establish in the small cramped and cluttered twilit room not only the ledgers but the whole plantation in its mazed and intricate entirety—the land, the fields, and what they represented in terms of cotton ginned and sold, the men and women whom they fed and clothed and even paid a little cash money at Christmas-time in return for the labor which planted and raised and picked and ginned the cotton, the machinery and mules and gear with which they raised it and their cost and upkeep and replacement—that whole edifice intricate and complex and founded upon injustice and erected by ruthless rapacity and carried on even yet with at times downright savagery not only to the human beings but the valuable animals too [. . .]. (284–85)

Although the two images of a stereopticon are juxtaposed side by side, seen through the lenses, the two merge and mix into one mythic place, full of the detail and depth of the separate parts but fraught with the conflicts and characterized by the unities of their blending.

In "The Bear" and in *Go Down, Moses,* generally, Faulkner achieves one of his most impressive ménages of the shifting paradigm of center and periphery, oppressor and oppressed, for therein he most thoroughly acknowledges just how blurry the lines between white and black and red, rich and poor, Self and Other really are in southern society. The ledgers are described as "that chronicle which was a whole land in miniature, which multiplied and compounded the entire South," registering the struggle of the oppressor and the oppressed (which in this story are often indistinguishable), "that slow trickle of molasses and meal and meat, of shoes and straw hats and overalls, of plowlines and collars and heel bolts and buckheads and clevises, which returned each fall as cotton—

the two threads frail as truth and impalpable as equators yet cable-strong to bind for life them who made the cotton to the land their sweat fell on [. . .]" (280–81).

Again the presence of paper is significant: in this chronicle, the slaves speak through the pens of their owners, who, in turn, have set them free; conversely, as Ike insists, the owners themselves are not free but instead are enslaved by the very system of which they are a part. Carried out as a dialectic, the ledgers record a conversation between Carothers, Theophilus, Amodeus, Isaac, and even the slaves; there is a play in the language, a revisionist movement. Most importantly, the ledgers form a chronicle, a narrative, *the* narrative of one human encroaching on others only to have his encroachment superseded by yet others. Stressing the centrality of narrative, Ike notes the "Jew": "a pariah about the face of the Western earth which twenty centuries later was still taking revenge on him for the fairy tale with which he had conquered it" (278).

Although "The Bear" employs no goat imagery, it offers a most compact discourse on the themes set forth in *The Marble Faun*. The story closes with the impending destruction of the Big Woods. Again, the theme of the machine in the garden crops up, as "the little locomotive shrieked and began to move" into the forest, "dragging its length of train behind it so that it resembled a small dingy harmless snake vanishing into weeds" (304). Beneath these weeds, like Whitman in the closing lines of "Song of Myself," in the earth await Sam Fathers, Lion, and all the other marble fauns finally bound by material, bound in fact always by wood, marble, or clay, and finally, like Midgleston, framed in the narrative of their mythic moment. Trotting along behind this behemoth are the new race of fauns, soon to be snapping to a jazz beat, blaring into the silent wilderness the next wave of a doomed will to dominate and endure.

CHAPTER TWO

A Tearing of Endless Silk

New Orleans and the Exotic Frame of Revelry

Outside the window New Orleans, the vieux carré, brooded in a faintly tarnished languor like an aging yet still beautiful courtesan in a smokefilled room, avid yet weary too of ardent ways.

—*Mosquitoes*

The very name "New Orleans" brings to mind a Mardi Gras pageant moving through the streets at night: crowds of masqueraders, rearing horses, great decorated floats glowing with color and glittering with gold-leaf. Aboard the swaying cars are centaurs, mermaids, satyrs, gods and men, illuminated by flaring torches carried by strutting negroes robed in red.

—Lyle Saxon, *Fabulous New Orleans*

With the recent hurricane disasters in Louisiana, New Orleans has emerged in media as a site of competing ideologies about class, race, religion, government policy, and any number of other concerns. This is not the first time the city has found itself offered up as such a specimen. From its somewhat shady origins as part of a scheme to help fund the gambling debts of the Duke of Orleans through its many disasters brought on by war, fire, flood, and disease, the "Crescent City" has remained a space of slippery identities while containing a multiplicity of hegemonic forces that keep it continually in political, cultural, and economic flux. These past disasters have led to rebuildings of New Orleans in which new identities were formed and new imperial impulses made apparent. During the times when William Faulkner lived in the French Quarter, the city was taking in a new group of immigrants from Italy, and the ways these people worked to carve out lives and form identities in the skeleton of the town left by the vanishing Creoles find treatment in the sketches he wrote for the *New Orleans Times-Picayune*. New Orleans is thus a historical-political-geographical place that exemplifies the phenomenon of mythic place and imperial space. The city was conceived in the context of empire, and as various imperial forces gained control over it throughout its history, several layers of narrative accumulated to render a space rich in mythic-imperial signification. A brief outline of the history of New Orleans, as well as the themes of empire that characterize the city as a culturally signifying space, should prove helpful in orienting a discussion of Faulkner's use of the city as a repository from which to draw a plethora of fictional elements.

A narrative informed the very founding of New Orleans. The impetus that initially brought René Robert Cavalier, Sieur de La Salle; Pierre Le Moyne, Sieur de Iberville; and other French explorer-colonists to the present site of New Orleans was an imperially driven narrative, namely, the legend of gold in El Dorado.[1] Just as impressive, however, is the conjunction of practically unadulterated fiction and imperial impulse that characterized the joint (or, more accurately, contiguous and occasionally cooperative) efforts of the three individuals most instrumental in founding New Orleans: Iberville's brother, Jean Baptiste Le Moyne, Sieur de Bienville; Philippe, Duke of Orleans; and John Law. With Bienville struggling to establish a strategic outpost at the mouth of the Mississippi River and Philippe, who was in charge of the outlying regions of the empire, seeking a way to get France out of debt, Law, a renowned and infamous Scottish scoundrel and gambler, devised a plan to help all involved. This plan, referred to as the "Mississippi Bubble," elicited funds from France, asking citizens to become shareholders in the Louisiana colony to glean its alleged natural resources (gold, diamonds, etc.). Building on the El Dorado myth, Law initiated a P. T. Barnumesque campaign to market New Orleans. Curiously, this proposed city "was on the French maps six months before a single tree was felled. There was no specific location; John Law and his land-speculators merely wanted a point of reference in promoting their great treasure hunt" (Leavitt 23).

From this fictional beginning, New Orleans began to be built, and its construction proceeded in a layered manner that vividly replicates the layered construction of mythic place as employed by Faulkner. The first layer was created in the fury of French imperialism, and then Bienville continued to build the city with whatever funds, materials, and people he could obtain (many of the people were prisoners sent over from France). He formally laid out the city with the help of the engineer, Adrien de Pauger, and the chief engineer, Chevalier Le Blond de la Tour.[2] After several terms as "governor" of Louisiana, Bienville retired. He was succeeded by Pierre-Cavagnal de Rigaud, Marquis de Vaundreuil, who transformed the city into a sort of large and opulent ballroom, replete with dances, music, feasts, spirits, gambling, prostitution, and a government that achieved a brilliant level of corruption.

This first layer extended in time from the first decade of the eighteenth century until 1764, when the citizens of New Orleans were informed that Louis XV had made a gift of most of Louisiana, including the new city, to his Spanish cousin Charles III in 1762. The first governor of the Spanish regime was Don Antonia de Ulloa, who with the help of Don Alexander "Bloody" O'Reilly, successfully brought the city under rule. After fires in 1788 and 1794 practically destroyed the city, the Spanish rebuilt it in their own florid architectural style. Grace King best describes the mythic significance of this rebuilding; noting the phoenixlike rise of the new city from the old, she observes that "what lay in the ashes was, at best, but an irregular, ill-built, French town. What arose from them was a stately Spanish city, proportioned with grace and built with stolidity" (*New Orleans* 130).

New Orleans continued to be manipulated by imperial designs, however. At length, Napoleon Bonaparte regained Louisiana for France from Spain in the Treaty of San Ildefonso only to sell it to the United States for four cents an acre; appropriately enough in the context of Faulkner's fiction, this 1803 Louisiana Purchase took place under the administration of Thomas Jefferson. In 1861 New Orleans became part of the Confederate States of America, and then after the South's defeat in the Civil War it again became part of the United States. The result of all this changing of imperial hands was a rich and curious ménage, a multilayered space, each layer exhibiting a different moment of imperial splendor and blending with the others in ways that made the divisions among them at times indistinguishable. Indeed, the French Quarter was no longer "French" at all, but rather a space constructed by the Spanish and now a part of the United States with southern loyalties. Underneath all of this constructed mythic-imperial space was the foundation of the original inhabitants, the Choctaws, whom the Europeans described as the "ugliest" of all Indians, as well as the dirtiest, because "they were in the habit of standing directly in fire-smoke at night to drive off mosquitoes. When they emerged from the smoke, they were blackened head to toe" (Leavitt 13).

Indeed, New Orleans exhibited a racial/ethnic ménage as part of and in addition to its manifest moments of varying imperial control. Along with the French and Spanish Creoles and their slaves, there were at least ten thousand German immigrants in New Orleans, who had come seeking the riches promised by John Law's advertising campaign. The 1850s saw a tremendous influx of Irish, and a decade into the twentieth century Italians immigrants, primarily from Sicily, had populated a Vieux Carré largely abandoned by the Creoles. In addition to these groups were the *gens de couleur libre,* the mulattoes, the quadroons, the octoroons, and whatever Choctaws or other Native Americans remained. The result of this racial and ethnic amalgamation was a paradoxically mixed and yet segregated society. In fact, from the mid-1830s to the 1850s New Orleans was actually divided into three municipalities—a Creole First District, an Anglo-Saxon merchant Second District, and a German-French-mulatto Third District—with Canal Street as the neutral ground.

Additionally, New Orleans was a space of legendary opulence. It was called the "Queen City of the South" in the years just before the Civil War, when it was also the third largest city in the nation and boasted the largest cotton market in the world. With lavish opera houses and fine hotels, the city's richness in both capital and culture made it a premier metropolitan center in the United States. During Reconstruction the city suffered economically and from epidemics of yellow fever, but as Blotner notes, by the time of Faulkner's six-month residence in 1925, New Orleans was "one of the leading banking and shipping centers of the 'new South,' [. . . and] it was becoming the nation's second busiest port" (127). Moreover, it was the center of an arts rebirth in the South led by "[y]oung artists in revolt and champions of the arts," who "had responded vigorously to H. L. Mencken's kind of icon-smashing" (12).

This monetary, artistic, and cultural richness was juxtaposed with an equally strong legacy of corruption. Storyville, with its infamous *Blue Book,* advertising its various houses of prostitution, was known throughout the country, if not the world. Tending to political misdeeds from its inception, the city benefited immensely in the nineteenth century from the Louisiana lottery, known as the "Golden Octopus," which skimmed funds from across the nation to finance such institutions as the French Opera House. From the mid-1920s through the 1930s and beyond, Louisiana, including New Orleans, was beset by the rise of poor whites led by Huey Long, one of whose compatriots, Robert Maestri, became mayor of New Orleans. Maestri and others proceeded to bleed the city and the state in a vast scheme of fraud and embezzlement dubbed the "Louisiana Hayride" into the 1940s.

Characterized by this rich racial, cultural, artistic, economic, and moral amalgamation and set in a sultry, semitropical climate, New Orleans possessed a foreign aura—Mediterranean, "Oriental" even, and part of the global South. Stereotypical descriptions of New Orleans's inhabitants as spectacular slovens resemble Edward Said's description of the "Orient" as defined by Orientalists. Tracing the works of eighteenth-, nineteenth-, and twentieth-century Western scholars who studied the Eastern and Middle Eastern civilizations colonized by their respective countries, Said observed that the Orient was "a European invention, [. . .] a place of romance, exotic beings, haunting memories and landscapes, remarkable experiences," and that the purpose of the discipline of Orientalism was to "dominat[e], restructur[e], and hav[e] authority over the Orient. [. . .] The relationship between Occident and Orient is a relationship of power, of domination, of varying degrees of a complex hegemony" (1–5). King describes the city as "not a Puritan mother, nor a hardy Western pioneeress [. . . but] simply a Parisian" and notes that "[h]istorians describe how the names of Mississippi, Louisiana, New Orleans filled the cafés where the new Arabian luxury held enchanted sway over men's minds" (*New Orleans* 35). At the same time, the parallel of a Western force suppressing the rebelliousness of an Oriental space is perhaps best expressed by General Benjamin "Beast" Butler, the federal officer in charge of the city after it was conquered by the North:

> I do not feel I have erred in too much harshness . . . I might have smoked you to death in caverns as were the Covenanters of Scotland by a royal British general, or roasted you like the people of Algiers were roasted by the French; your wives and daughters might have been given over to the ravisher as were the dames of Spain in the Peninsular War, and your property turned over to indiscriminate plunder like that of the Chinese when the English captured their capital; you might have been blown from the mouths of canons as were the sepoys of Delhi . . . and kept within the rules of civilized war as practiced by the most polished and hypocritical capitals of Europe. But I have not so conducted! (qtd. in Leavitt 111–12)[3]

New Orleans, like other southern U.S. spaces, ultimately represents liminality and ambivalence, being simultaneously a major metropolis bearing the characteristics of and participating in the economic proclivities of the global North and yet strongly characteristic of and steeped in the peripheral culture and economy of the global South, a space in-between, fecund, multifaceted, paradoxical, and sweaty in the most expansive and limiting and positive and negative senses of these terms. Kirsten Silva Gruesz calls New Orleans "the capital of the (other) Nineteenth century," a place characterized by "liminality, [occupying a] strategic position in the midst of what [. . . Joseph] Roach calls [in *Cities of the Dead*] 'the circum-Caribbean'" (Gruesz 53). At the time of Faulkner's coming of age, the city was both foreign and familiar, avant-garde and backward, set at the dropping-off point of the nation and yet also at its gateway, isolated and peripheral and yet a cultural center and the object of regional and national attention. The "Crescent City"/"Queen City of the South," was a site of concentrated mythic place and imperial space ripe for fictional exploration and exploitation.

The rich and contradictory quality of the city had already found expression in the literary works of several writers. Along with William Wells Brown, Harriet Beecher Stowe had presented the mournful and horrifying images of the slave trade under the dome of the St. Louis Hotel in *Uncle Tom's Cabin*. Grace King had explored elements of female Creole life in *Balcony Stories,* while Kate Chopin had exposed the stifling qualities of Creole society and the potentially destructive consequences of "passing" in such works as *The Awakening* and "Désirée's Baby," respectively. George Washington Cable had offered a powerful portrait of the interactions between class, race, and gender, most significantly in *The Grandissimes*. And in *Fabulous New Orleans* Lyle Saxon, a friend of Faulkner's, had blended history and fiction in celebration of the city's carnival spirit. In fact, this distinctive carnivalesque quality greatly informs these works and the city's reputation. New Orleans emerged as the Bakhtinian ideal, the liminal, ambiguous space of carnival, of subversion; its Mardi Gras atmosphere "of popular-festive merriment and grotesque realism thrust down, turn[ed] over, push[ed] headfirst, transfer[red] top to bottom, and bottom to top, both in the literal sense of space, and in the metaphorical meaning of the image" (Bakhtin 370).[4]

This element of play and subversion characterized Faulkner's experience of New Orleans. Play, in fact, seems to have been the license New Orleans offered Faulkner; he writes in the foreword to *Sherwood Anderson and Other Famous Creoles* (a conspicuous project of playing) that the city "has a kind of ease, a kind of awareness of the unimportance of things that outlanders like myself [. . .] were taught to believe important" (25) and that it is a "pity" that humor "is not more prevalent in [American] art," as it is America's "one priceless universal trait" (26). In his letters to his mother during his stay in the city, Faulkner explained that although he spent a great deal of time writing, he also golfed, loafed, and talked to people in the French Quarter. And Blotner reports that Faulkner made at least one trip with Sherwood Anderson to Storyville (122). William Spratling mentions the playful aspect of Faulkner's stay in New Orleans by pointing out the presence of a BB gun in the final drawing in *Sherwood Anderson and Other Famous Creoles*:

> The BB gun on the wall was important and very useful on rainy days and against boredom. The scene here drawn is my attic apartment and from those windows high over St. Peters Street we could nip people on the street, silently and with ease, usually in the buttocks. On the wall was a list of points for hits on various types. For example, a Negro nun rated a very high score. Rarity value. I think most victims were more intrigued than resentful. At any rate this was before the epoch of race-agitation and had nothing to do with such. (Spratling and Faulkner, *Sherwood Anderson* 13)

This story about Faulkner's playing exposes a disturbing other side to the carnivalesque freedom ostensibly encouraged by carnival, for masked by the gaiety of the carnival spirit stands an oppressive hierarchy of control that limits subversion to something of a professed safety valve. Spratling's uneasy and slightly defensive suggestion that the episode preceded "the epoch of race-agitation" is remarkable in light of the fact that the William Nichols incident of 1867 (in which the African American Nichols was ejected from an all-white streetcar) spurred a series of demonstrations that prefigured the civil rights actions of the 1960s. The scene Spratling describes asserts a rigidly fixed hierarchy in which two white southern men sit on a balcony shooting at their racial "inferiors," literally positioned below them. The description eerily resembles Faulkner's Flem-and-Satan-in-Hell scene in *The Hamlet,* in which "the Prince" is extolled for his "crude youthful inventions with BB size lava and brimstone and such," with which he would practice "on Chinees and Dagoes and Polynesians, until his arms would get strong enough to handle his share of white folks" (871).

In fact, the spatiality of power in the history of New Orleans is a tricky thing to define. The city was originally a peripheral space in relation to

Paris, the home of castoffs and criminals from France. In the New World, the city quickly developed into a cosmopolitan center, its criminals now turned Creoles, the lower element transformed into the upper element, whiteness (unstable though it might be) gaining ascendancy over the "nonwhite" groups, whether German, African American, Irish, or Native American. With the Civil War and Reconstruction the white aristocrats themselves became disempowered by invading northern forces. By Faulkner's time the Creoles' glory had faded, and the new "Creoles" were the artists, concentrated around Jackson Square, in the Pontalba buildings (where Sherwood Anderson and Elizabeth Prall lived and where Faulkner stayed with them) or in Pirate's Alley (where Faulkner later lived with Spratling); on the streets were those same nonwhite elements, milling about as a moiling conglomerate mass, upon which the cultural elite gazed down and fired.

It is unclear how cognizant Faulkner was of the frame that kept the carnival aspect of New Orleans clamped into place until later in his career, but his writing shows an interest in those lower elements of French Quarter society and their struggles to define their space in the city. In one letter to his mother he offers the following account of going to

> Victor's for dinner. It's one of those old established restaurants that has changed hands several times. The present owner is an Italian, named Guido. I go there—a small place, mostly people he knows personally, who dine and talk, all for 50¢. Soup, fish, meat, salad, fruit and coffee. Last night his "waitress" told me her particular story, she's from Florida, about being married and deserted, and ect, as Ring Lardner says; and when everyone had gone, Guido came in and asked me to have a glass of wine with him. And he told me his story. His father, it seems, was a duke (since the Medici's a wop duke is not anything, you know) and his older brother inherited the title and dashed little else. So Guido comes to America—"grrrand contree, when I come. But now she ruin herself with prohibition." He'd get excited and lapse into Italian and French at a great rate. "Liberty, hell," he'd say, "man come in, eat—'Che spendo yo, Combein de?' that's all." I suggested to him that money is not such a bad thing, taken by and large. "Monee?" he says, completely dashing my theory, "Plus d'argent, moins d'argent; coma es'?" quoting a stanza of Dante, stuff about the simple heart, and living on acorns. (*Thinking of Home* 159–60)

Guido's jumbling of Italian and French mirrors the jumbling of architectural layers of New Orleans's construction as well as its successive moments of colonization, and this experience at Victor's seems to have informed one of the sketches Faulkner wrote for the *Times-Picayune*, entitled "Jealousy." The story tells of a restaurant owner named Antonio who suspects his wife of infidelity with the young waiter who works for him. The waiter is "a tall young Roman god" (*New Orleans Sketches* 34) roughly the same age as Antonio's wife, who "was still young, and pretty [. . . with] her dusky oval face, her red mouth and raven hair" (38–39). Antonio becomes so crazed with jealousy that he finally decides that he and his wife must go to a different city to live. Before leaving, however, the young waiter goes to buy Antonio's wife a gift, and Antonio accompanies him on his shopping trip to "a curio shop where such things were sold—an orderless jumble of pictures, vases, bric-a-brac, jewelry, firearms and brass" (40). Still tortured by jealousy, Antonio "groped behind him among a litter of ancient weapons," where he finds an "old pistol fitting snugly in [his] palm," and he "pretends" that it is "a modern, deadly machine" as he points it at the oblivious waiter and pulls the trigger (40).

A vivid example of the fact that the past is never dead, that it is so alive that it can bring death to the present, "Jealousy" dramatizes the role of narrative in the movement of colonization and the effects that can be wrought by the traces of past narratives. As a young man in Sicily, Antonio dreamed of the future, which he thought was realized in his coming to New Orleans but then destroyed in his fancied narrative of his wife's adultery. When he decides to relocate, "he became his normal self again"; although his relationship with the waiter is "still strained," Antonio is well on his way to moving on, to passing the past (39). But in the shop—itself characterized by bricolage—the traces of past narrative assert themselves and lead to murder. Indeed, the point of dreams/narratives is that they become entangled with past dreams in a deadly conglomeration of indistinguishable layers, for Antonio "stared at the starred sky stretching like taut silk above the walled well of the alley, watching the same stars at which he had gazed in faraway Sicily, in his youth, when he had been a boy and life was clear and fine and simple; and that lads would stare wondering upon long after he and his dream and his problem were quiet underground" (38). Antonio displaces his frustrations with his failed dreams by grafting the narrative of infidelity onto the person of his wife (it is not clear whether the waiter and she are involved; both deny having an affair).

Interestingly, the story opens with Antonio's wife sitting in the restaurant knitting and blaming Antonio for generating his own suspicions by placing her in a situation that would make her appear to be untrue to him—she knits together layers of narrative in an indistinguishable mass, the silk sky of stars and dreams that have grown confused and torturous in Antonio's mind.

In "Jealousy" the economic-political context of Italian immigration as one of successive moments in New Orleans history articulates Faulkner's sense of the power of mythic-imperial layers. Implicit in Antonio's move to New Orleans is the promise of a bright future, a wish upon a star, the desire for El Dorado. He would overspread himself—his own moment—on the former layers of French, Spanish, and "American" glory to transform himself into a "Creole." Much like Thomas Sutpen, though, Antonio cannot control the elements of respectability needed to realize a dream of prosperity. Before deciding to emigrate from New Orleans, Antonio confronts the waiter after spying the latter speaking intimately with his wife. The waiter stands before Antonio "like a swordsman," again denying any involvement with his employer's wife. When Antonio threatens to kill him, the waiter replies: "[Y]ou do not dare, save from behind. And what will the world say, if you do? Can you bear to have your wife call you coward?" (38). Casting this confrontation as a duel, the waiter evokes the New Orleans Creole *code duello* of the late eighteenth and early nineteenth centuries; the waiter uses the strategies of a former mythic layer here to define those of a new mythic layer. Indeed, Antonio does not dare kill the waiter, and it is the waiter who buys the restaurant from Antonio. It is only when Antonio can reconfigure the strategies of conduct according to his own moment that he can destroy his enemy, shooting him in the back with an object that is a relic from the very mythic layer his own narrative action replaces.

The problems of space, immigration, and layers of mythic-imperial narrative in the city play a significant role in another of the New Orleans sketches, "Mirrors of Chartres Street." The narrator in the story encounters a one-legged drunkard, another of Faulkner's goat-men, with "eyes wild and soft as a faun's" (*New Orleans Sketches* 15), who in Bakhtinian fashion possesses "an untrammelled spirit" (16). Although this man represents a pagan mythic layer, the narrator casts him as a figure in the empire of Christendom, describing his spirit as "the heaven-sent attribute for finding life good which enabled the Jews to give young Jesus of Nazareth with two stars in His eyes, sucking His mother's breast, and a fairy tale that has conquered the whole Western earth" (16). Upon encountering a policeman, the man draws an imaginary rectangle about himself and claims, "This is my room [. . .] now, how can you arrest me, huh?" (16). When the officer informs him that a police car is on its way and attempts to take the man into custody, the man screams, "Arrest me in my own room! Arrest me! Where's laws and justice? Ain't I a member of the greatest republic on earth? Ain't every laborer got his own home, and ain't this mine?" (17). Gaining the attention of bystanders, the man continues, "Listen, men. I was born an American citizen and I been a good citizen all my life. When America needs men, who's first to say 'America, take me'? I am, until the railroad cut off my leg. [. . .] ain't every laboring man got his own room, and ain't this mine?" (17). Presently, the police wagon comes and picks him up, and the entire scene leads the narrator to imagine "Caesar mounting his chariot among cast roses and the shouts of rabble, and driving along the Via Appia while beggars crept out to see and centurions clashed their shields in the light of golden pennons flapping across the dawn" (18).

Although the story is ironic, it also functions as an interrogation of space within the fabric of a mythic tapestry. Carvel Collins notes in his introduction to *New Orleans Sketches* that the story ironically subverts another *Times-Picayune* piece entitled "Mirrors of Washington," which depicted "people in national affairs" in its extravagant treatment of such a mundane event, making the story a kind of consummatory one (xxvii). The narrator may not be a person of "national affairs," but he is empowered and seemingly closer to the imperialist tradition of New Orleans, dressed in "tweeds which came from the Strand" (15) and watching the one-legged man's encounter with the policeman from "a railed balcony— Mendelssohn impervious in iron" (16). Here the narrator is Faulkner sitting on his balcony shooting BBs at passers-by; the disabled man, meanwhile, complicates the seemingly democratic space of New Orleans, questioning both its enclosing and its liberating qualities as he constructs his own centered mythic place in an empowering act of subversive speech. Unlike the marble faun, this faun seeks the security of being in one place rather than the dangers of mobility (indeed, it was the machine in the garden that impaired his mobility).

Several of the *Times-Picayune* pieces develop the image of New Orleans as an international center for the acquisition of wealth, a cosmopolitan space packed with gold-seekers, whose experiences expose the immigration and El Dorado myths as spurious. In "Home," Jean-Baptiste has come to "the Golden Land" from his home in southern France; only "a lilting provencal air" played on a saw can assuage "his hot Southern temperament" and prevent him from blowing up a building he has been paid to destroy. The hero of "Chance," the protagonist of "Cheest," and the "chentleman" of "Damon and Pythias Unlimited" all seek the instant money to be made at the New Orleans horse races even as they discover how tenuous possession of it must always be. And the very first of these sketches, "New Orleans," opens with a soliloquy of a "Wealthy Jew," who affirms:

> "I love three things: gold; marble and purple; splendor, solidity, color." The waves of Destiny, foaming out of the East where was cradled the infancy of the race of man, roaring over the face of the world. Let them roar: my race has ridden them. Upon the tides of history has my race ever put forth, bravely, mayhap foolhardily, as my ancient Phoenician ancestors breasted the uncharted fabulous seas with trading barques [. . .]. Oh ye mixed races, with your blood mingled and thinned and lost; with your dream grown tarnished and pointless, knowing not what ye desire! My people offered you a dream of peace that passeth understanding, and arid Syrian sands drank the blood of your young men; I flung a golden coin, and you purchased martyrdom of Death in Ahenobarbus' gardens; ye took Destiny from the hands of my people, and your sons and my sons lay together in the mud at Passchendaele and sleep side by side beneath foreign soil. Foreign? What soil is foreign to me? Your Alexanders and Caesars and Napoleons rise in blood and gold, shrieking briefly of home, and then are gone as waves hiss curling on the beach, and die. (3–4)

Despite its tacit stereotyping, this passage is interesting in its situation of New Orleans as a mythic-imperial configuration: Faulkner casts New Orleans as a modern-day Scythia. The "Golden Land" of New Orleans is no foreign soil but rather a re-creation of the cradle of humanity, the reincarnated land of the Scythians. Located in what is now southern Russia and on roughly the same latitude as southern France, Scythia was what the Orientalist William Jones posited as the center of civilization. This space was centered between global northern and global southern spaces as well as between the East and the West and so formed the perfect space of centeredness. As Bruce Lincoln notes, "[B]eing unconnected to any contemporary peoples of Europe, [the Scythians] could encompass all without privileging any" (81). Known for their exquisite gold adornments, the Scythians were defined in turn as barbarians and then as Aryans, particularly by Nietzsche and others operating on Jones's argument that the Scythians were the world's universal ancestors. New Orleans is a sort of Scythia in reverse, a space not of "universal" begetting but rather of "universal" devolving: races and nationalities converge on the opulent space of New Orleans in a primal hunt for the thing that first united them, gold.

Faulkner's depiction of New Orleans as Scythia finds its greatest expression in the person of Charles Bon in *Absalom, Absalom!* Bon's very body represents amalgamation, ambivalence, and liminality, while he also metaphorically embodies the space of New Orleans as he emerges in the text's multiple layers of narrative. Indeed, Mr. Compson calls Bon "a myth, a phantom: something which they [who talk about him in the novel] engendered whole themselves; some effluvium of Sutpen blood and character, as though as a man he did not exist at all" (82). Even before Quentin Compson and Shreve McCannon top off the mythic layers of the space of Bon's body with a narrative of it as racially mixed, Mr. Compson describes a body narrativized as Eastern-Western, Oriental-Occidental, peripheral-centered. On one hand, Mr. Compson's description of Bon conforms to the elements of what Said calls "latent Orientalism," which may be termed as the fixed conception of the Orient's and its inhabitants' essence. This latent Orientalism produced the essentialized Oriental as bearing the following marks: "sensuality," a "tendency to despotism," "eccentricity," "silent indifference," "feminine impenetrability," and "supine malleability" (206–7). Indeed, Mr. Compson envisions Bon "presented formally" to Henry Sutpen at the University of Mississippi, "reclining in a flowered, almost feminised gown, in a sunny window in his chambers" (76). To highlight Bon's sensuality, Compson imagines him "lounging [. . .] in the outlandish and almost feminine garments of his sybaritic privacy" (76), acquiring "a name for prowess among women while at the University" (78). And as if to drive home the peculiarly Oriental nature of this romanticization, Mr. Compson observes that Henry must surely see Bon as "a hero out of some adolescent Arabian Nights who had stumbled upon (or rather, had thrust upon him) a talisman or touchstone" (76), whose very name and those with whom he comes in contact seem "now merely initials or nicknames out of some now incomprehensible affection which sound to us like Sanskrit or Choctaw" (80).

However, at the same time that Mr. Compson depicts Charles Bon as an Oriental, he also defines him as one of the empowered, a Western cosmopolitan. Although in one breath he presents Bon as an adolescent hero from the Arabian Nights, in another he characterizes the New Orleans native as a culturally superior metropolitan. "[Charles Bon] is the curious one to me," says Mr. Compson. "He came into that isolated puritan country household almost like Sutpen himself came into Jefferson: apparently complete, without background or past or childhood" (74). In Mr. Compson's imagination, Bon contemplates Henry and Thomas Sutpen "from behind [a] barrier of sophistication" (74). Mr. Compson even imagines an alternative scenario in which Henry meets Bon that differs greatly from the one that presents Bon as a lounging Oriental: he suggests that Henry first saw Bon "riding perhaps through the grove at the University or on the one or two horses which he kept there or perhaps crossing the campus on foot in the slightly Frenchified cloak and hat which he wore" (76). In these images, Mr. Compson presents a sophisticated, colonizing, Western Bon, the "youthful Roman consul making the Grand Tour of his day among the barbarian hordes which his grandfather conquered" (74). This Bon is the one whose sophisticated letters to Judith Sutpen are "the metropolitan gallant's idle and delicate flattering" (102). This Bon is an imperialist, a Westerner.

Above all, Mr. Compson sees Bon as "a man a little older than his actual years and enclosed and surrounded by a sort of Scythian glitter" (74). Bon's body reflects the body of New Orleans and the body of Scythia and is therefore in-between, a space composed of mythic layers, a body both imperializing and imperialized. Mr. Compson describes New Orleans as being, like Bon's body, a place where "the architecture [is] a little curious, a little femininely flamboyant and therefore to Henry opulent, sensuous, sinful" (87).[5] Bon thus emerges as another descendant of the marble faun; he is a counterfeit Other, a white man made black. At various moments throughout the text he is hero, villain, and victim, spoken for rather than speaking except for his one vehicle of unfettered speech in his letter to Judith, written with New England–manufactured stove polish on paper with *"the best of French watermarks dated seventy years ago, salvaged (stolen if you will) from the gutted mansion of a ruined aristocrat"* (102), an artifact itself characterized thus by hybridity, which Bon himself recognizes as he closes by writing,

> *I cannot say when to expect me. Because what IS is something else again because it was not even alive then. And since because within*

this sheet of paper you now hold the best of the old South which is dead, and the words you read were written upon it with the best (each box [of stove polish] said, the very best) of the new North which has conquered and which therefore, whether it likes it or not, will have to survive, I now believe that you and I are, strangely enough, included among those who are doomed to live. (104)

The tone of the comments is difficult to read: On one hand, a "black" Bon-as-trickster might conceivably parrot such patriarchal values as part of an ongoing effort to mask his own racial ambiguity. On the other hand, however, his very assertion that the South's defeat forever obliterates purity of race or culture suggests his investment in the poetics of white southern patriarchy, making Shreve and Quentin's "blackening" of him a remarkable obliteration of "facts."

In other words, the white southern male narrators in the novel—the Compson men—make Charles Bon, along with Thomas Sutpen, the center of the novel's tragic machinations by making these two men, both representative of the white southern aristocratic patriarchy, the hybrid Others and the tragic victims of the very things their social, economic, and racial status enact. The less-white nature of Sutpen's poor whiteness has been noted, but the strong context of hybridity and empire in the moment of Sutpen's loss of innocence deserves further explication. The description of this moment comes from Quentin's grandfather via Quentin himself; it is the moment when Sutpen discovers that there is a "difference not only between white men and black ones, but [. . .] between white men and white men" (183). The great epiphany comes for Sutpen when

> he stood there before that white door with the monkey nigger barring it and looking down at him in his patched made-over jeans clothes and no shoes and I dont reckon he had even ever experimented with a comb because that would be one of the things that his sisters would keep hidden good—who had never thought about his own hair or clothes or anybody else's hair or clothes until he saw that monkey nigger, [. . .] how it was the nigger told him, even before he had had time to say what he came for, never to come to that front door again but to go around to the back. (189)

Quentin's images and rhetoric are significant in that they evoke a specific imperially driven mythology, the late Victorian advertising campaign for Monkey Brand soap. In *Imperial Leather,* Anne McClintock explains that in the second half of the nineteenth century soap emerged as an important fetishized "cheap and portable domestic commodity" whose advertising articulated its ability to "mediate the Victorian poetics of racial hygiene and imperial progress" (209). The Monkey Brand advertising campaign, which hit its stride in the 1880s and would thus have been in full swing by the time of Quentin's birth, typically pictured "the fetish soap-monkey[, which] sits cross-legged on a doorstep, the threshold boundary between private domesticity and public commerce [. . .]. Dressed like an organ grinder's minion in a gentleman's ragged suit, white shirt and tie, but with improbably human hands and feet[, . . .] the soap-monkey is a hybrid: not entirely ape, not entirely human; part street beggar, part gentleman; part artist, part advertiser. The creature inhabits the ambivalent border of jungle and city, private and public, domestic and the commercial, and offers as its handiwork a fetish that is both art and commodity" (215). The "monkey nigger" whom Sutpen encounters stands on the threshold of a "smooth white brass-decorated door" wearing "broadcloth and linen and silk stockings" (189) in a striking replication of the Monkey Brand icon.

This context of threshold and hybridity informs both Sutpen's and Bon's hybridity. For Sutpen, it is the African American at the door who gives him his original imperial cue. Although it is clearly the white aristocrat Tidewater plantation owner who stands as Sutpen's model, it is through the hybrid threshold monkey figure that the model is articulated, and Sutpen never becomes anything more than a hybrid threshold figure himself: indeed, Wash Jones cuts him down with a scythe as he walks out of the cabin in which he has just denounced Milly's offspring.[6] Significantly, in Quentin and Shreve's imagination(s) Bon brings himself to the very threshold of his father's recognition only to be turned away by his father (now in the place of the "monkey nigger"), just as his father himself had been turned away.[7] Furthermore, Mr. Compson places Bon and Henry on both a literal and metaphorical threshold when the latter murders the former, as Henry "discharged [the ultimatum 'Do you renounce?'] before the gate to which the two of them must have ridden side by side almost" (105) and then inside the gate, Henry saying *"Dont you pass the shadow of this post, this branch, Charles;* and *I am going to pass it, Henry"* (106). Finally, Wash Jones, the poor white, sits "his saddleless mule before Miss Rosa's gate" as he tells her "Henry has done shot that durn French feller. Kilt him dead as beef" (106).[8]

The white male southern narrators' relentless focus on Bon and Sutpen highlights a nostalgic fetishizing of the white southern patriarchal romance. To Mr. Compson and, to a lesser extent, even Quentin (especially when the latter operates within a specifically southern patriarchal mythopoeic mode), the true Others are outside the narrative process altogether as subjects. The idea that Clytie's life might be tinged with tragedy never seems compelling to Mr. Compson, and Rosa, Wash, and Judith are largely afterthoughts, as he focuses almost exclusively on the actions of Henry, Bon, and Sutpen. Quentin's position is more complex, partly because he must negotiate his narrativizing between placement in Cambridge and in Jefferson; yet in the end, however much Rosa has insinuated herself into the text, or Clytie, Ellen, and Judith into his consciousness (and however much, as Irwin argues in *Doubling and Incest,* the thematic element of incest is the result of his own desires for his sister Caddy), Quentin follows in his father's footsteps in weaving a male-centered tale of fratricide and failed dynasty. The white male patriarchy as exemplified by Mr. Compson and as partially adopted by Quentin tends to look within itself to explain history, pursuing the elitist view of history, othering those of its own number and largely ignoring or silencing the true Others, the nonwhite nonwhites.[9]

Such a society of elites forms the core of the characters in *Mosquitoes,* Faulkner's first book-length work set in New Orleans. The novel opens with Talliafero admiring Gordon's marble statue of a torso that seems neither male nor female or both male and female—yet another of Faulkner's variants on the marble faun, only androgyny replaces racial ambiguity in this image. Still, the whiteness of the image is significant, especially in the context of generation of counterfeit Others and false nonwhites as Faulkner traces the exploits, or nonexploits, of a group of artists and would-be artists during an excursion on Lake Pontchartrain. In this novel, as well as in the other novels in which New Orleans plays a central role as a setting—*Pylon* and *If I Forget Thee, Jerusalem*—the city itself acts as a frame, as a clamp, that pins down the novel's potentially expansive and liberating action, holding that action within the vice-grip of mythic-imperial poetics. There are, in fact, two basic settings in the novel: New Orleans itself (ostensibly representing the center) and Lake Pontchartrain and its surrounding area (ostensibly the periphery). The periphery is negotiated by the yacht *Nausikaa,* which, with its Homeric overtones, is a sort of heterotopic vehicle that simultaneously bears away the *habitus* of the center as experienced by the New Orleans set while also negotiating the values of the periphery, at least as understood by the passengers, who would "go native" according to the ways they read (however incorrectly) the "peripheral" signs or breathe the "peripheral" air.

Faulkner constructs the frame in *Mosquitoes* according to an important model that features a group of elites escaping a diseased metropole to retreat to a healthy periphery while adopting a game of storytelling to "pass the time." The obvious example is Boccaccio's *Decameron,* as Robert Cantwell notes. In fact, Dawson Fairchild discourses on the problem of substituting "words for things and deeds, like the withered cuckold husband that took the Decameron to bed with him every night" (210). A chief variation on this model is Chaucer's *Canterbury Tales,* of course, but another and more immediate example that mediates the influence of both Boccaccio and Chaucer is Faulkner's own great-grandfather's bestselling novel, *The White Rose of Memphis.* In this work, the Old Colonel tells a story about the journey of the steamboat *The White Rose of Memphis* from Memphis down the Mississippi River to New Orleans, which will include, as part of its maiden voyage, a "grand masque ball" to serve as a diversion from Memphis's afflictions of "bad government and yellow fever epidemics" (2–3). This masque ball creates an immediate structure of fictional layers in the very performance of the passengers, for they masquerade as such figures as Mary Queen of Scots, Ivanhoe, Napoleon, and Ingomar, the barbarian chief, and Mary Queen of Scots declares that the time should be passed by telling stories.[10] Donald Philip Duclos suggests that Faulkner "intended to imitate Chaucer's *Canterbury Tales,* probably devoting one or two installments to each story" (163), and as in *The Canterbury Tales,* the various characters prefer stories that correspond in some way with the roles they perform, so that Ivanhoe says, "Give me something like the *Talisman,* or the *Heart of Midlothian,*" and Mary Queen of Scots prefers "love stories [. . .] like *Henrietta Temple, Alonzo and Melissa, Foul Play,* or *Little Dorrit,*" while the Queen of Sheba calls for "a patriotic story, such as the *Scottish Chiefs* or *Thaddaeus of Warsaw,*" saying that she admires "those noble-hearted heroes who are always willing to die for their country, but manage somehow not to do it," and George III says, "I prefer *Gulliver* or *Crusoe* [. . .]. I do not think I could command sufficient patience to listen to such a love story as *Henrietta Temple*" (21–22).

Ingomar, the barbarian chief, is designated as the first raconteur, and he presents his story, the only one actually told. His tale employs a multilayered narrative approach that includes frames within his frame, creating a texture of nested narratives similar to that in *The Canterbury Tales* identified by Katherine S. Gittes. It is primarily the story of three orphans, Edward Demar, Lottie Wallingford, and Harry Wallingford, who journey to Memphis and encounter a fourth child, Viola Bramlett, whom Harry saves from being run over by a train. As they grow older, Edward and Lottie fall in love, and Harry and Viola fall in love, and the story tells of the obstacles the lovers must overcome to remain together. Just as Chaucer draws on established forms such as the fabliaux, Ingomar draws on historical romance, love stories, and other forms of narrative. At the end of the tale, Ingomar reveals that he is in fact the hero of his own story, and it is further made known that Harry, Lottie, Viola, and one Benjamin Bowles, a scoundrel bent on destroying the others' relationships, are all aboard the boat as masquers. The frame thus features the denouement of Ingomar's story, in which the lovers come together at last.

The theme of healing and the motif of healing water pervade *The White Rose of Memphis*. Duclos notes the centrality of medicine in the novel and the plethora of hysterical fits, illnesses, fainting, and so on that plague the characters. Healing also operates thematically on the level of society in the interaction between and performance of the other passengers on the boat. Like Chaucer's *Canterbury Tales, The White Rose of Memphis* includes a list of passengers that ranges from lawyers to detectives to criminals, much like the passengers aboard the steamboat *Fidèle* in Herman Melville's *The Confidence Man,* which explicitly states its re-creation of the Canterbury pilgrimage's societal situation. In *The White Rose of Memphis,* the characters in Ingomar's story and the passengers on the boat establish their own unique society as they negotiate their differences. The most conspicuous bit of social healing is that of sectional reconciliation, exemplified in an exchange between a northern General Camphollower and a southern Colonel Confed:

> "For my part," said General Camphollower, "I think that our Government dealt too leniently with the rebels after the war."
>
> "I believe," replied Colonel Confed, "that the views you express were those held by men who never smelt burnt powder, or heard the whistle of a hostile bullet; but all brave soldiers who fought in the Union army, from General Grant down to the humblest private, were opposed to any harsh measures."

"I perceive," replied General Camphollower, "that you are not being much reconstructed."

"Gentlemen," said Captain Quitman, "pardon me for interrupting your conversation, but I would beg to suggest the propriety of eschewing politics while on this excursion. Let the past bury the past—let us cultivate a feeling of friendship between the North and South. Both parties committed errors—let both parties get back to the right track. Let us try to profit by our sad experience—let us teach forgiveness and patriotism and look forward to the time when the cruel war shall be forgotten. We have a great and glorious nation, of which we are very proud, and we will make it greater by our love and support. It was a family quarrel, and the family has settled it, and woe be to the outsider who shall dare to interfere!"

"Hurrah! hurrah for Uncle Sam!" was unanimously shouted by all the passengers.

"Uncle Sam shall live forever, and those unpatriotic politicians who have crippled him shall be driven into obscurity. Let peace and good will, brotherly love and good faith, exist between the North and South, and let Satan take those who wave the bloody shirt."

"Good! good! hear! hear!" was shouted long and loud by all the guests, while the two politicians shook hands across the table, and bumped their glasses together.

"Ladies and gentlemen," said Captain Quitman as his tall, handsome form rose high above the crowd, "fill your glasses and hear my toast." Some little confusion then ensued while each guest was having his glass filled, and then the captain's voice rung out as he spoke: "Here is to the Union as it was in the days of its purity." General Camphollower responded in an eloquent speech, and took his seat amid thundering applause. Then, reaching his hand across the table toward Colonel Confed, he explained: "Here is my hand, Colonel—let us shake across the table, and consider it the bloody chasm." (24–25)

I quote at length here because of the finely mannered and chivalric tone of the passage, which highlights what is all too obvious about the characters in the novel: that they are all of the white elite, are all *able* to take this pleasure cruise. Whatever their difficulties, they are all well versed in the writing of Sir Walter Scott, and even when they are down-and-out they matriculate within the upper levels of their society. Where such frame-narrative writers as Joel Chandler Harris, Mary Noailles Murfree, and Thomas Nelson Page presented truly othered regional poor white or African American narrators (those authors' own blinders notwithstanding), Colonel Falkner offers aristocrats masquerading as aristocratic models telling stories of themselves as Others. What the reader does not get from Falkner are narratives that detail the plight of blacks or poor whites unable to escape the city and therefore susceptible to yellow fever.

The implied historical threat of yellow fever, as well as the themes of healing and social intermingling, which is nevertheless limited to and contained by the white elite, also informs *Mosquitoes*. Faulkner could not have chosen a more appropriate insect in the history of New Orleans to use as a central trope in the novel, for it was the mosquito that had carried the yellow fever responsible for multiple epidemics in the city's history. Characterized by vomiting of blood, a black tongue, and jaundiced eyes, "Yellow Jack" devastated New Orleans because citizens kept cisterns, where the *Aedes aegypti* mosquito bred. Faulkner calls the mosquitoes themselves "a biblical plague seen through the wrong end of a binocular" (8). Doubtless thinking of John Donne's "The Flea," Faulkner seems to have realized the implication of racial as well as sexual mixing in the mosquito's occupation: it brings a disease that makes one yellow, the color of mulattos, quadroons, octoroons, the color of hybridity. Dawson Fairchild even insinuates the subtext of the disease when, faced with having to eat another of the grapefruits Mrs. Maurier offers as a meal, he complains that "my skin is getting rough and dry, with a kind of yellowish cast. If it keeps on, first thing I know I won't any more dare undress in public than Al Jack—" (276). The irony of this subtext of yellow fever, which was carried by mosquitoes spawned in standing water, is that it demonstrates that the medium of water can divide and conquer as well as facilitate democratic intermingling, that it can cause sickness rather than bring healing.

In fact, the two primary spaces in the novel—Lake Pontchartrain and New Orleans—emerge as complicated, contradictory figurations. Both settings ostensibly signify amalgamation, whether in the literal fluidity of the lake or in the social fluidity of the city. And yet, if anything, the elite main characters in the novel are even more isolated from the nonelite on the lake than they are in the French Quarter, where at least they must to some extent interact with poor immigrants and other such individuals. Mosquitoes, in the meantime, infiltrate both settings, and the novel's third-person narrator even evokes metropole-margin rhetoric when he notes that "as if at a signal, [the mosquitoes on the shores of Lake Pontchartrain] were all about them, unseen, with a dreadful bucolic intentness; unlike their urban cousins, making no sound" (83). Earlier, the mosquitoes come "cityward lustful as country boys, as passionately integral as a college football squad" (8). Apparently, the only place that is safe from these insects is the very center of the lake, but such a positioning in the heart of "fluidity" is also precisely the point of most isolation from the democratic mass for the members aboard the yacht: with the exception of Patricia, Mrs. Maurier's guests hardly associate with members of the *Nausikaa*'s crew as they while away the time on their cruise.

Fairchild's mention of Al Jack, or Al Jackson, highlights this problematic negotiation of a vexed center-periphery configuration by this counterfeit Other. The Al Jackson stories were a series of frame narratives that Faulkner and Sherwood Anderson developed explicitly in the vein of the Southwestern humorists' frame narratives, as Faulkner notes in a letter to his mother: "Al Jackson, grandson of Old Hickory[, . . . is] kind of like Sut Lovingood" (*Thinking of Home* 171). In *Mosquitoes*, Fairchild emerges as the sole owner and proprietor of the Al Jackson stories, and he transforms himself into the poor white (the pun, sadly, *is* intended) narrator of the Southwestern humorist frame narrative. With this narrative structure and context comes the same dynamic of center-periphery negotiation found in the local-color frame. Again, the irony lies in the fact that Fairchild is one of the elite; and Faulkner complicates even this complication by making Fairchild, if not as poor a white as Thomas Sutpen, at least a person of somewhat underprivileged origins, as demonstrated in his story about having to work to earn one year at college, where he had to work even to stay and did not even have time to join a fraternity (and was even swindled out of his attempt to join one by a rascal posing as a student—not an altogether uncommon creature) (116–20).

This artistic elite transforming itself into the body of an Other conforms to modernist artistic techniques. In *The Dialect of Modernism,* Michael North explains that T. S. Eliot, Ezra Pound, and other modernists used elements of African American dialect representation to forge a subversive dialect of their own. The passengers on the *Nausikaa* might also be thought of as establishing a plantation structure in which the "artists" are the slaves (Anderson and the other creoles—with a small *c,* signifying racially mixed) and Mrs. Maurier (the Northerner who married a plantation owner) is the "Ole Missus." The masquerade on this vessel then becomes a sort of minstrel show, with the "slaves" of the French "quarter" in New Orleans having their own sort of carnival-voyage with the head lady of the plantation, so that the yacht, which, again, carries the center's culture into the periphery, must carry a culture part of which is informed by a past that included "walls which had housed slaves long ago, slaves long dead and dust with the age that had produced them and which they had served with a kind and gracious dignity—shades of servants and masters now in a more gracious region, lending dignity to eternity. After all, only a few chosen can accept service with dignity: it is man's impulse to do for himself" (11).

The Al Jackson stories and the politics of their Southwestern humorist/local-color frames exemplify the interstices of hybridity, narrative, and imperial space. The victim of Fairchild's outlandish Al Jackson tales is the British sap Major Ayers, whose foremost goal in coming to the United States is to bottle a laxative in such a culturally enticing manner that Americans will buy it and use the bottle as a decoration. Fairchild immediately recognizes the imperial implications of this scheme and suggests that the "tweaky phial [. . .] all Americans will buy" should picture "[t]he American flag and a couple of doves holding dollar marks in their bills" (64). Major Ayers, like the passengers on *The White Rose of Memphis,* is a type: the British imperialist. Fairchild teases him mercilessly, saying things like "I guess you've shot lots of grapefruit in China and India, haven't you Major" (275) and reminding the Major of Britain's defeat at New Orleans even as he acknowledges the Major's own economic-imperial designs, observing, "Now here's a clean case of poetic justice for you. A hundred odd years ago Major Ayers' grandpa wants to come to New Orleans, but our grandfathers stop him down yonder in those Chalmette swamps and lick hell out of him. And now Major Ayers comes into the city itself and conquers it with a laxative so mild that, as he says, you don't even notice it" (66). Fairchild proceeds to explain to Major Ayers that Al Jackson grew rich in the business of fish ranching in the Gulf of Mexico, an enterprise that grew out of his brother Claude's having developed into an amphibious creature in his efforts to herd sheep that had developed gills and lived underwater. Jackson's business ventures were originally located in a swamp habitat, one Faulkner develops in terms of mythic layering. For example, he describes one swampy bayou at dusk thus: "The world was becoming dimensionless, the tall bearded cypresses drew nearer one to another across the wallowing river with the soulless implacability of pagan gods" (83). Faulkner echoes this description of the swamp when Patricia gazes through binoculars at the swamp and sees "pendants of rusty green moss [which were like] beards of contemplative goats ruminating among the trees and above a yellow strip of beach" (121). Traces of this layer emerge from beneath other layers in the form of "[h]uge cypress roots thrust up like weathered bones out of a green scum and a quaking neither earth nor water, and always those bearded eternal trees like gods regarding without alarm this puny desecration of a silence of air and earth and water ancient when hoary old Time himself was a pink and dreadful miracle in his mother's arms" (174). This landscape is that of New Orleans before there was a city, although not before there was a mythic New Orleans in John Law's mind or on French maps; this miasmic foundation is indomitable and asserts itself ubiquitously in the context of New Orleans.

The characters in the novel work to mediate, absorb, and comprehend the complexities of hybridity not only as dictated by their setting but within themselves. Just as Major Ayers is a "type" in the novel, so other characters are framed in such myth-informed typographies: Fairchild is the Writer, Mark Frost the Poet, Gordon the Artist, Mrs. Maurier the Patron, Patricia the niece, Jenny the soft-enveloping-thighs, Julius the Semitic man, and so on. With the possible exception of the young people (Patricia, Jenny, Pete, Josh), the characters strive to live according to their types but find them limiting in the face of the complexities of performance. The problems of the fictional "character" actually become the topic of conversation when Eva says, "I was thinking of how book people, when you find them in real life, have such a perverse and disconcerting way of liking and disliking the wrong things." Then she points out that Dorothy should like the music of Grieg, yet, as Dorothy herself notes, she actually prefers Chopin, proving that consistency (purity) is finally only an aspect of fiction, while reality must be inconsistent (hybridity) (182). Indeed, however ensconced the characters may be in their stereotypes (which is not much), they are infiltrated with unnamed and unnamable foreign elements when they are stung by the roving vessels and dispensers of hybridity, the mosquitoes.

And yet the frame that would keep these characters from changing is finally inescapable; this frame is the city of New Orleans, to which each of the passengers must return. Despite Fairchild's evoking the mythic-imperial moment of the Battle of New Orleans, Lake Pontchartrain and its purlieus represent an older, manifestly pagan and Homeric space. In fact, the suggestion that the Gulf of Mexico can be transformed into a ranch suggests that even such an aquatic space of openness and fluidity can be brought under imperial subjection, framed, fenced in. But the constrictions inherent in this peripheral space are nothing to the oppressive frame of multiple mythic-imperial layers present in the metropolitan space of the city. Layering is a key feature of Faulkner's description of the city, for he builds the environment as a sort of collage, with the "Pontalba and cathedral [. . .] cut from black paper and pasted flat on a green sky" (14) and Jackson Square itself "undimensional" and "feathered" with "stenciled palms" (13–14). Again, the frame itself is heterogeneous and ambiguous, its multiple aspects hazed over by its cultural and racial multifacetedness. Faulkner stresses the element of smoke at twilight, noting that the city "brooded in a faintly tarnished languor like an aging yet still beautiful courtesan in a smokefilled room" (10); in "a darkling corridor [. . .] are two people indistinguishably kissing" (13), and in the city are to be found "small indiscriminate shops" (15).

Despite its aura of free-flowing heterogeneity, however, in the end New Orleans is the place to which people return after a trip, a space of fluidity where they must resume their constrained everyday business. The novel's epilogue stresses that the decadent and romantic freedom the city exemplifies does not change the fact that it is a constructed space whose imperial nature imprisons lives in certain modes and settings. Away from the city, Talliafero might be able to "seduce" Jenny into dancing with him, but back in New Orleans whatever success he has had and whatever boldness he has developed are seen for the sham they are as a younger man steals her from him. Talliafero's very name is problematic; his real name is Tarver, from a family in Alabama, and so he is not the New Orleans Italian his false name and setting suggest he may be. Indeed, although he seems able to exploit the potentialities for mythic self-creation by changing his name, he cannot transform himself permanently into a dangerous seducer. In fact, as his selling women's clothing and the opening scene with Gordon and the milk bottle suggest, no amount of self-fictionalizing can obliterate what seems a homoerotic tendency on his part that renders him impotent in his efforts to fashion himself in the image of Rudolph Valentino.

Like Talliafero, Pete returns to his humdrum life in the city, where he works with his brother at his family's dance hall. Pete seems the most typical colonial subject on the yacht; his Italian features are mistaken by

Major Ayers for those of "one of your natives [. . .] red Indians" (65). Appropriately enough, this "subaltern" is the most bereft of speech on a yacht where the main activity is "[t]alk, talk, talk: the utter and heartbreaking stupidity of words" (186). Pete's family's business has transformed from a small restaurant to a dance hall that bears the iconography of American empire in the form of an "electric sign with the family name on it," which had "marked a climacteric" (295–96), for like other layers of New Orleans's successive imperial moments, this sign signified "the phoenix-like rise of the family fortunes from the dun ashes of respectability and a small restaurant catering to Italian working people, to the final and ultimate Americanization of the family" (296). With his return to the city, it becomes evident that even his relationship with Jenny, which had seemed more or less established and permanent (as he was forever urging her to "give papa a kiss"), was in fact only a thin, almost fictional thing when a woman who is apparently his real girlfriend shows up at the restaurant and chastises him for his recent absence. Interestingly, while Pete is a "colonized subject" on the yacht, he is part of a coloni*zing* force in the city, although in fact he is enclosed by his brother's and (apparent) girlfriend's own colonizing of his body.

In the context of Italian immigration, it should be noted that Faulkner describes a modern imperial moment in a strikingly Gramscian passage in which the Semitic man says to Fairchild, "Do you know who is the happiest man in the world today? Mussolini, of course. And do you know who are next? The poor devils he will get killed with his Caesar illusion. Don't pity them however: were it not Mussolini and his illusion it would be some one else and his cause. I believe it is some grand cosmic scheme for fertilizing the earth. And it could be so much worse [. . .]. Who knows? They might all migrate to America and fall into the hands of Henry Ford" (131). In light of Pete's family, it might be asserted that the family has already arrived. More importantly, the Semitic man's comments evoke the same signifying strategy as that found in the marble faun, in which a new empire resurrects the icons of a past empire, only in this case the new empire's layer would spread across the same space that the former one occupied and thus identify itself as an exact replica or even extension of that earlier imperial moment. Transferring the Caesar illusion to New Orleans would transform the city into New Rome and exemplify the configuration of mythic place and imperial space.

The one character who seems most comfortable with hybridity and most resistant to the frames that would enclose her is Patricia. Gordon notes that she mirrors the androgynous marble torso he has sculpted. She is a marble-faun figure, conforming to the elements in Fairchild's discourse on "Hermaphroditus [. . .]. Kind of like men nowadays are not masculine and lusty enough to tamper with something that borders so close to the unnatural. A kind of sterile race: women too masculine to conceive, men too feminine to beget . . ." (252). Tanned and natural, Patricia seems a creature of the woods, like Emmy in *Soldiers' Pay;* yet, though drawn to the forest, she does not belong there, as evidenced in her failed elopement with David. It is not surprising that Gordon, with his "silver faun's face" (152), would be attracted to such a nymph. In the end, even the city cannot hold her, as she plans to go to Yale with her brother. No marble bonds constrain her; her existence is not fraught with the traces of empire in materiality. She is, rather, immediate and rife with motion and completely unconcerned with narrative-generated iconography; she is never more delighted than when people act in ways that their types dictate they should not. In fact, for Patricia is reserved the one opportunity in the novel to leave behind the terrestrial matrix of mythic place and imperial space and experience something seemingly unrestrained. At one point while on the yacht, Gordon lifts her off the ground and swings her through the air. Faulkner describes her experiencing "that sensation of flying, of space and motion and his hard hands coming into it; and for an instant she stopped in mid-flight, hand to hand and arm braced to arm, high above the deck while water dripped from her turned to gold as it fell. Sunset was in his eyes: a glory he could not see; and her taut simple body, almost breastless and with the fleeting hips of a boy, was an ecstasy in golden marble, and in her face the passionate ecstasy of a child" (82). Where the pagan gods of a former mythic layer protrude through the watery swamp, and where even open waters might be colonized by fictional fish ranchers, the medium of air would seem to be entirely free of constraints. Yet, ironically, it is in this moment of flight that Patricia's body achieves the rigidity of marble that she resists on solid ground.

Faulkner would take up the dynamics of the space of air in *Pylon.* As in *Mosquitoes,* in this novel New Orleans operates as a frame surrounding a peripheral space of ostensible openness. In fact, the two spatial components are the same as those found in the earlier novel, but recast in a mythic revision: New Orleans and Lake Pontchartrain here are "New Valois" and "Lake Rambaud." Faulkner's explanation for the name changes is interesting; he wrote to Hal Smith that "'New Valois' is a thinly disguised (that is, someone will read the story and believe it to be) New Orleans. [. . .] But the incidents in Pylon are all fiction and Feinman is fiction so far as I know [. . .]. Someone may or may not see a chance for a suit. You might decide whether there would be grounds for a suit, whether a suit would help sell the book, or whether to alter the location, etc., so there would be no grounds" (*Selected Letters* 86–87). Whatever concerns Faulkner may have had about the novel being too close to reality for comfort, there was something clearly important about grounding the events in the story in the framing historical space of New Orleans. It is noteworthy that in a novel so concerned with the proclivities of rootlessness, Faulkner found it necessary to draw on the historical signifying of the Crescent City—that he should be so concerned with "grounds" and the implications of space of hybridity, myth, and imperialism implicit in them.

It is appropriate that Faulkner overlays New Orleans with a new mythic place, for the novel focuses on the creation of the mythic-imperial layer. Where Dawson Fairchild engages in romantic mythopoeism to promulgate the narrative of Al Jackson's transforming an aquatic space into an imperialized space, the reporter struggles with his own prescribed mythmaking role in regard to those who would imperialize the air. A central issue in the novel is whether the reporter will use the materials of imperially driven mythic place to valorize the ordering and defining of the skies just as Faulkner uses the mythically and imperially layered New Orleans to create New Valois, a space where the name draws attention to itself for its very masking function, which more thoroughly accentuates the true signifier it masks rather than developing itself as a full-functioning space. Hybridity and the atmosphere of the carnivalesque are clearly the primary signifiers of New Orleans in the novel, as the events of the plot occur concurrently with Mardi Gras, with its purple and gold bunting and clouds of confetti contributing to a *mise en scène* of gaudy ambiguity. Ultimately, New Valois emerges as Faulkner's posited birthplace of a future in which region becomes redefined altogether, a new mythic place foreshadowing a mythic cosmos utterly bereft of regions as formerly understood, effecting a bricolage in which the old regionalism is reconfigured into a tenuous relationship with any terrestrial space whatsoever.

It is important to remember the centrality of flying in Faulkner's life and writing, whether in the world of his material existence or in the created world of his imagination. Flying airplanes is directly related to one of

Faulkner's foremost role-playing tropes, whether he was playing the Royal Air Force cadet or the limping war hero. The RAF represented a type of modern military glory that approached that of the cavalry in the wars of his forefathers. John Faulkner explains his brother's fascination with building and flying planes, a fascination that began in childhood and continued throughout his life, even after his youngest brother was killed in a crash and even after Malcolm Cowley's prying into his war experience led him to back away from his professed flying glory. The airplane was one of the tools of modern empire defending and empire building and figured strongly in Faulkner's layered mythology of his own body and person.[11] Ward L. Miner offers a reading of flying in Faulkner's writing, suggesting that the "period 1920–1940, or the period between the wars, adds events more violent. This violence is accentuated by the standards of materialism within our modern, mechanized society. Frequently Faulkner uses the airplane to symbolize this destructive, depersonalizing force" (83). Miner goes on to assert that from

> the love of the land is derived what is so intense in Faulkner, the necessity for roots, or loyalty to one's region. The strength acquired by those having roots is frequently contrasted by Faulkner to the weakness of those without roots. In *Pylon* he uses this idea as one to characterize the fliers whom the reporter meets at the air races. [. . .] An individual acquires strength from his roots in a particular region. But this is true only when the region is a non-urban one and thereby provides that intimate association with the earth so necessary for a true sense of loyalty. (146)

Miner's reading of the Faulknerian airplane as a destructive and negative presence might be contrasted with André Bleikasten's slightly more subtle reading of flight. Examining *The Sound and the Fury,* Bleikasten compares the scene of the trout and the medium of water to the gull and the medium of air. "Conjoining stability and suppleness, gravity and grace," Bleikasten writes, "the trout stands for a mode of being in which self-possession does not preclude adjustment to a changing environment. The fish achieves balance in the vortex, immobility in motion, eternity in time." He notes that "[t]he obvious parallel to the fish suspended in the water is the bird posed in the air [. . .]. As the aerial counterpart of the trout, the *gull* is another model of delicate poise and dynamic immobility. Yet its meaning for Quentin is more ambiguous. The gull seems to hover above the flux of time" (*Ink of Melancholy* 101).

Taken together, Miner's and Bleikasten's somewhat oppositional readings approach an explanation of the powerful function of flight in the machinery of Faulkner's imagination. This machinery might best be articulated by drawing on the very helpful material regarding flight, aerodynamics, and aviation terms that Robert Harrison offers in *Aviation Lore in Faulkner*. In his opening summary of aerodynamics, Harrison concretely identifies what Bleikasten impressionistically refers to as a "vortex." Harrison explains that flight requires the negotiation of four forces: thrust, drag, lift, and weight. These forces might be understood as constituting a sort of axis, as thrust (or forward motion) opposes drag (rearward wind created by thrust) and lift (which pushes upward) opposes weight (the gravity that pulls downward). The airplane pilot must maneuver within what is essentially a "vortex" of these forces by manipulating various moveable parts of a plane (ailerons, elevators, and rudder) to adjust the vehicle's "angle of attack" or the angle in relation to the surface of the earth the plane takes into the air. Each manipulation of one force creates a new force of wind that also requires attention; in fact, each of these forces becomes actuated by the propeller and wings, which initiate thrust and thereby create drag and lead to the introduction of lift and therefore weight into the moment of flight. In essence, these forces are all relative, inextricably interconnected and therefore requiring the flyer's constant attention.

Although Harrison offers explanations for the aviation jargon in Faulkner's stories and novels, the important implication the material offers is that flight as an arresting of motion on an axis of wind bears great resemblance to Faulkner's description of writing as an arresting of motion. It does not seem unreasonable to assume that these elements of aerodynamics, which Faulkner learned at such an early age as a cadet in Canada (the rudiments of which he probably already knew even then), entered into and informed the very machinery of the craft that would become his life's work. It seems almost superfluous to mention that Faulkner's first published story, "Landing in Luck" (1919), was a tale about a cadet's first landing experience and that a large number of works that followed in his career were about or included elements of flight. For the dynamics of flight are the dynamics of Faulkner's art.

In *Pylon*, the problems of motion and art in flying and their implications of imperial definition of space occupy the focus of action and meaning. The very rotunda of the Feinman Airport sports a mural that "presented the furious, still, and legendary tale of what man has come to call his conquering of the infinite and impervious air" (800).[12] The reality of the venture of flight is that it cannot achieve the escape from "roots" that Ward assigns to it, nor does it hover above the flux of time; actually, flying carries with it the same imperial impulses that have defined the history of humankind. John Faulkner makes a significant comment about his brother's understanding of imperialism and the phenomenon of flight, writing that in a speech in Denver, "Bill said that if man ever did finally succeed in destroying himself and there were as many as two of him left, they'd be found making a do-it-yourself rocket to leave the world they had ruined. But already they'd be arguing about which direction to take to find some new world to conquer" (224).

The flyers in *Pylon* are thought by certain characters and media in the novel to represent a new hybrid race destined to colonize the air. Just as the mosquitoes of *Mosquitoes* are the vehicles of amalgamation, the airplanes in *Pylon* are "those little ships that look like mosquitoes" (803); they are "motionless wasps" (794), "[w]aspwaisted, wasplight, still, trim, vicious, small and immobile" on the airport runways (787). The beings that fly them or are associated with them are hybrid, "granted that they have kinfolks or are descended from human beings [. . .]. Because they aint human [. . .]; they couldn't turn those pylons like they do if they had human blood [. . .]; crash one and it aint even blood when you haul him out: it's cylinder oil the same as in a crankcase" (804). Even Jiggs, who is neither pilot, parachutist, nor any other type of aerial performer but still maintains connections to planes as a mechanic, is a pagan hybrid figure, "the vicious halfmetamorphosis between thug and horse" centaur (960); like the marble faun, who cannot fit into his present mythic moment, Jiggs cannot fit into the boots he would wear over his tennis shoes.

The future face of these new colonists is Jack, the offspring of Laverne and either Roger Shumann or Jack Holmes, the parachutist. The photographer for the paper that the reporter and Hagood work for thinks about the kid and his conception: "'That's it,' he thought quietly, with that faint quiet grimace almost like smiling; 'they aint human. It aint adultery; you cant anymore imagine two of them making love than you can two of them aeroplanes back in the corner of the hangar, coupled.' With one hand he supported the boy on his shoulder, feeling through the harsh khaki the young brief living flesh. 'Yair; cut him and it's cylinder oil; dissect him and it aint bones: it's little rockerarms and connecting rods—'" (933–34). These inhabitants of the air will have the unique quality of being free from the problem of regions, from the boundaries of nations, because they have "[n]o ties; no place where you were born and have to go back to it now and then" (805); Jack as a child has seen more of the world than the reporter has and can never be as impressed with the fact of his mobility as the reporter can. Indeed, these air-people are "creatures imbued with motion though not with life and incomprehensible to the puny crawling pain-webbed globe" (793). The airport—the mediating space between earth and air—is itself "a mammoth terminal for some species of machine of a yet unvisioned tomorrow, to which air earth and water will be as one" (786).[13]

Faulkner uses New Orleans as the model for the site of his exploration of this new hybrid race because of the city's liminal nature, its history of renewal, and its suggestions of openness. Complicated though it may be, Faulkner seems to want to embrace the city's cosmopolitan centeredness and imagine that just as French, German, African, and Irish immigrants colonized New Orleans and mixed to form a new race of New Orleanians, so the air-people might be understood by those on land, and from this site of amalgamation and rebirth might spring a new phoenix with mightier wings than any before it. It seems particularly appropriate that the only African American who appears in the novel is the reporter's maid, who is hybrid, a "thin youngish lightcolored negress" (865).[14] In fact, despite its brutality and its tragic elements, the novel maintains a largely celebratory and even hopeful tone, as the new race of air-people seems a good thing that might move humanity forward, a new race of fauns released from their marble bonds into the ultimate medium of fluidity and infinity.

There is, however, a dangerous, neoimperialist trick that haunts the rhetoric in Faulkner's depiction of these flyers as a new race. Just as an uneasy sense of hidden cruelty and oppression lurks in Bill Spratling's recanting of the BB-gun experiences, so the optimism about these new colonists tends to obfuscate the reality that their invasion of the air, however benign, represents an act of imperialization as determined by ideologies presented in media representations of the flyers' activities. Ostensibly, the aviators escape the earth and represent a new, infinite horizon of freedom, free from the implements of power and control entrenched on earth. The reporter suggests that the air-people "dont need money; it aint money they are after anymore than it's glory [. . .] except only now and then when they come in contact with the human race like in a hotel to sleep or eat now and then or maybe to buy a pair of pants or a skirt to keep the police off of them" (805–6). Like Tarzan, the flyers are part of a wilderness, though (also like Tarzan), they are not entirely part of that wilderness. Like Tarzan and like the celebratory aspect of Orientalism, the air represents a romanticized space (another important connection to New Orleans). Although the flyers in *Pylon* are not military, the implication of the sky as the next frontier resounds throughout the text.[15]

This idea of the flyers as imperialists is particularly strengthened and defined in media treatments of the airshow. The novel opens with the mechanic Jiggs staring at a pair of boots in a shop window arranged to evoke a specifically U.S.-informed imperial ideology:

> [s]lantshimmered by the intervening plate [the boots] sat upon their wooden pedestal in unblemished and inviolate implication of horse and spur, of the posed countrylife photographs in the magazine advertisements, beside the easelwise card-board placard with which the town had bloomed overnight as it had with the purple-and-gold tissue bunting and the trodden confetti and broken serpentine—the same lettering, the same photographs of the trim vicious fragile aeroplanes and the pilots leaning upon them in gargantuan irrelation as if the aeroplanes were a species of esoteric and fatal animals not trained or tamed but just for the instant inert, above the neat brief legend of name and accomplishment or perhaps just hope. (779)

The shop window presents a bricolage composed of two elements. The first is a "natural" one that recreates images derived from media: the boots evoke cowboy iconography as promoted in Western shows, books, stories, films, and advertising that among other things encodes a U.S. imperial myth of westward expansion, a peculiarly American white man's burden that calls for the eradication of Native Americans and the acquisition of land; at the same time, the arrangement of the boots mimics advertisements of a glossy genteel country living, advertisements that, whether referring to ranch life or to aristocratic riding (such as at the Virginia hunt clubs with which Faulkner would later be involved), describe a distinctly white and empowered experience.[16] The second element in the window is one of pure medium: the placard announcing the airshow and containing images of the airplane pilots and their planes, the two (pilot and plane) posed together as if they are horse and rider, as the planes seem in the pictures like "a species of esoteric and fatal animals not trained or tamed but just for the instant inert." With their own "busted broncos," the pilots thus emerge in this scene as the cowboys in a new imperial project, riding their own animals into the new frontier of the sky and therefore the new imperial heroes in a new space.

Depicted as "blooming," the components of this image achieve a peculiar and powerful reversal in which the representation actually precedes the natural event and thereby works to infuse the natural event with a narrative bathed in imperial impulse that amounts to no less than mythic layering. Jean Baudrillard describes this order reversal in what he sees as an "age of simulation," whose space "is no longer that of the real, nor of truth [. . . and which] begins with a liquidation of all referentials" (167). Whereas "representation tries to absorb simulation by interpreting it as false representation, simulation envelops the whole edifice of representation itself as simulacrum" (170). Therefore, simulation "is no longer that of a territory, a referential being or a substance. It is the generation by models of a real without origin or reality: a hyperreal" (166). The representation thus precedes the real, and Baudrillard makes his point in a way that practically addresses the creation of New Orleans itself, as he recounts a story in which a map creates natural space, observing that in simulation "territory no longer precedes the map, nor survives it. Henceforth, it is the map that precedes the territory—*precession of simulacra*—it is the map that engenders the territory" (166). This sort of "hyperreality" is promoted in media, whether in advertising or film, because, as Mary Cross points out, advertising "has become our culture's primary visual reference" (xii).[17]

Other media combine with the shop window to carry out a primary mythmaking campaign. In addition to its mural, which contextualizes the flyers both spatially and temporally as the new colonialists in the same manner that "pulp magazines [offer] war stories in the air" (963), the Feinman Airport further enshrines flying as an economic as well as a cultural and military imperial act: "High overhead the dome of azure glass repeated the mosaiced twin Fsymbols of the runways to the brass twin Fs let into the tile floor and which, bright-polished, gleaming, seemed to reflect and find soundless and fading echo in turn monogrammed into the bronzed grilling above the ticket-and-information windows and inletted friezelike into baseboard and cornice of the synthetic stone" (800). The hieroglyphic *F* can be read as standing for both *Feinman* and *flying*, as it collapses them and emblazons their greatness in the sky, on the earth, and in the place that really counts and combines the two—the ticket booth. The rotunda itself functions as an advertisement, and Faulkner stresses its status as simulation, with its painted sky and tiled earth; even its constructed space—the baseboard and cornice—is made of "synthetic stone." This advertising shrine thus conditions consumers as they pass through it to witness the natural event it advertises, hyping the show and its constituents and infusing them with and installing them within the ideology of capitalism in which Feinman and at least a few of the flyers "gain" economically as they demonstrate to the audience humankind's "gain" of control over the sky. (The barnstormers' gravity- and death-defying acts may be read as updated versions of cowboys' horse stunts in Wild West shows.)[18]

Further promoting this mythmaking activity is the amplified voice at Feinman Airport, because there "was an amplifyer in the rotunda too [. . . that] filled rotunda and restaurant even above the sound of feet as the crowd moiled and milled and trickled through the gates onto the field, with the announcer's voice harsh masculine and disembodied [. . .] reverberant and sonorous within the domed shell of glass and steel in a running commentary to which apparently none listened, as if the voice were merely some unavoidable and inextricable phenomenon of nature like the sound of wind or erosion" (791–92).[19] Continuing the shop window's mythic-imperial function, the amplified voice attempts to capture a colloquial "natural" image of the settled West, describing Roger's making his way toward first place in the race by saying that if "we were all back on the farm now I would say somebody has put a cocklebur under Roger's—well, you know where: maybe it was Mrs Shumann did it [. . .] maybe she told Roger if he dont come in on the money he needn't come in at all" (796). Speaking in a colloquial style and evoking "the farm," the voice tells a story to the "folks."[20] Later, when narrating Roger's fatal flight, the voice describes Roger's and Ord's planes as two "horses from the same stable, folks, and two pilots both of whom are so good that it is a pleasure to give the citizens of New Valois and Franciana the chance to see them pitted against each other" (934). In fact, the "farm" seems to be a "ranch" set in the new frontier that is the sky, and the amplified voice implicitly works to spread this imperial ideology to this new space.

Contrasted with these primary mythmaking forces is the editor, Hagood, who may be seen as a consummatory mythmaking force, as he seeks to curtail and control the narratives of the flyers. The editor and his newspaper represent control and codification. The newspaper stands in for authority and truthfulness, at least as presented under the leadership of Hagood, who is not interested in the subversive potentiality of journalism. He chastises the reporter, explaining that the "people who own this paper or who direct its policies or anyway who pay the salaries, fortunately or unfortunately I shant attempt to say, have no Lewises or Hemingways or even Tchekovs on the staff: one very good reason being that they do not want them, since what they want is not fiction, not even Nobel Prize fiction, but news. [. . .] I expect you to come in here tomorrow night with an accurate account of everything that occurs out there tomorrow that creates any reaction excitement or irritation on any human retina [. . .]" (808). Hagood here is the censor, and he keeps a pragmatic eye on the material conditions of the paper, promoting its role as reinforcer of "accuracy," of a report that is more than simply information and less than the subtle and questioning medium of fiction. The editor keeps a wary eye on forces that might romanticize the flyers and their deeds, seeking instead to give a more objective, unglorified account of the things that happen.

Between these media forces stands the reporter. In fact, the reporter is caught within two three-part coercive structures: he is positioned first as a romantic mythmaker between primary and consummatory forces and second in a psychological interrelationship in which the amplified voice represents the id, the editor the superego, and the reporter himself, the mediative ego. These two structures coalesce around a central element, which is the titular and foremost symbolical element of the novel—the phallic pylon, the pen jutting into the sky and delineating points in the air races. And the reporter spends his days struggling with the pylon and how to negotiate his position. He first performs a mediative function by writing a romantic version of the story, thus wielding the pylon as a romantic mythmaker ejaculating the seeds of romantic myth of the air, which will herald the imperialization of that spacious frontier. After Shumann's death, the reporter writes an account of his experiences that casts the flyers' experiences in mythic anthropomorphic terms of cosmic proportions:

> On Thursday Roger Shumann flew a race against four competitors, and won. On Saturday he flew against but one competitor. But that competitor was Death and Shumann lost. And so today a lone aeroplane flew out over the lake on the wings of dawn and circled the spot where Roger Shumann got the Last Checkered Flag, and vanished back into the dawn from whence it came.
>
> Thus two friends told him farewell. Two friends, yet two competitors too, whom he had met in fair contest and conquered in the lonely sky from which he fell, dropping a simple wreath to mark his Last Pylon. (991)

Full of symbolic elements, this story presents a mythology-informed story. The wings here might be the rays of sunrise, the soaring glory of

Apollo's chariot come to commemorate his son Phaethon, who falls like a star to his death from the heavens. In the meantime, Shumann's "Last Pylon" is just that—his final erection, his final narrative inscription. Undoubtedly, the reporter remembers the story of Laverne's first parachute jump, when she crawled into the cockpit with Roger "clawing blindly and furiously not at the belt across his thighs but at the fly of his trousers," where soon "he was outnumbered, he now bore in his own lap, between himself and her wild and frenzied body, the perennially undefeated, the victorious" (909).[21] Possibly, another use of his "pylon" produced the child Jack (e-Jack-ulation?). Again, the reporter sees the child as a sort of Creole—an Old World person born in the New World, in this case, the Sky—as he "was born on an unrolled parachute in a hangar in California; he got dropped already running like a colt or a calf from the fuselage of an airplane [. . .]. Talk about your immaculate conception" (806–7). Perhaps this child is the next hybrid Christ figure, for whose cause crusades later will be led and new tracts of sky will be claimed in a gorging of imperial hegemony. Whatever the case, Shumann here is the heroic pioneer, the airplane-busting cowboy, the Christopher Columbus and father figure of the sky.

Thus the first version of the story promulgates a romantic narrative, but that story is not the one the reporter submits to Hagood; instead, he gives the editor a story already metamorphosed from romantic to consummatory myth. This version of the story, which lies "on Hagood's desk [. . .] weighted neatly down by an empty whiskey bottle," reads:

> At midnight last night the search for the body of Roger Shumann, racing pilot who plunged into the lake Saturday p.m. was finally abandoned by a threeplace biplane of about eighty horsepower which managed to fly out over the water and return without falling to pieces and dropping a wreath of flowers into the water approximately three quarters of a mile away from where Shumann's body is generally supposed to be since they were precision pilots and so did not miss the entire lake. Mrs Shumann departed with her husband and children for Ohio, where it is understood that their six year old son will spend an indefinite time with some of his grandparents and where any and all finders of Roger Shumann are kindly requested to forward any and all of same. (991–92)

This version is accompanied by a note that reads: *"I guess this is what you want you bastard and now I am going down to Amboise st. and get drunk a while and if you dont know where Amboise st. is ask your son to tell you and if you dont know what drunk is come down there and look at me and when you come bring some jack because I am on a credit"* (992).

In writing this second version of the story, the reporter changes from a romantic to a consummatory mythmaker as he enacts the role of the mediative ego, and this latter role casts him as a Spivakian speaker trapped between two powerful voices and attempting to negotiate the language of the two. Indeed, like the monkeys in the advertising of Monkey Brand soap, the reporter lies across the threshold to his own apartment house, "his nondescript hair broken down about his brow and his eyes closed and peaceful and his shirt and awry tie stiff and sour with vomit" (856) when the flyers leave him after spending the night in his apartment (having had no money to stay anywhere else). And like Ichabod Crane (the traveling gazette who resembles a scarecrow), the reporter resembles "a scarecrow in a winter field" (793), and implicit in the similarity is the notion of the explorer, the "white man who knows the red man," the native informant. There are two problems with this position for him, however: first, as Spivak also points out, the moment the subaltern adopts the language of the oppressor, the person is no longer a subaltern and thus cannot speak as a subaltern; second, the reporter was never a "native" in the first place, for he is not one of the flyers, nor does he ever grasp their motives and desires. He may attempt to write in two "languages," but both are those of the empowered. Neither succeeds in promoting narrative revolution; rather, they confirm an order that will maintain unswaying power. Indeed, Hugh M. Ruppersburg, along with other critics, would cite the "impotence of language" (67), arguing that the reporter "yearns for explanations beyond the ken of journalism, beyond even the capacity of language to express or the human mind to comprehend" (66). But it is a mistake to read language as impotent when the very central image of the novel—the pylon—is one of overwhelming potency. If anything, the problem in the novel is not the absence and/or failure of communication but rather the superfluity of communication, which is everywhere evident not simply in written language but in its host of media forces.[22]

The reporter's changed evaluation is precipitated by a signal reinscription of region, a return to the terrestrial, a radical and (to the reporter) unanticipated displacement, namely, Laverne's consigning Jack to earth by taking him to his grandparents. The reporter finally realizes that the flyers do not share his grand vision of a future race of nonregionalists/nonimperialists. Laverne does not merely put the child in someone else's hands; she removes (according to the reporter's thinking) the hope of a nonimperialist future and obliterates the hope of the freedom of flight. The reporter attempts to fund Laverne and her child's future by planting money in the toy airplane he sends to Jack by Jiggs, but, ironically, this very action cinches the child's grounding in the inscribed space of the land instead of air when Doctor Shumann finds the money and interprets it as a sign that his son Roger had saved it for Jack, "proving" that Jack was his own child. The Trojan Horse imagery evoked by the money concealed in the plane renders it a vivid symbol of the material underpinnings of a vehicle that the reporter has romanticized; the image stands as a brilliant manifestation of the imperial practicality within the shell of the sacred.

That Laverne installs Jack in Ohio is significant because it reinforces the very model of regionalism that the reporter and, in a larger sense, the novel itself would want to escape. Composed contiguously with *Absalom, Absalom! Pylon* seems an effort to move away from the weighty material of Faulkner's South, an effort to envision something new and different. New Valois is indeed something new, a new phase in Faulkner's construction of a mythic cosmos that builds on the New Orleans model but also attempts to blaze new and original trails into his imaginative world. Faulkner struggles to expunge the themes of the South—even when Colonel Feinman acknowledges himself as a "country lawyer to Washington" (928), he avoids evoking the South per se—as he attempts to reimagine space in radically different ways. The space of Ohio, however, marks a return to the model of regionalism and to the most famous literary influence in Faulkner's career and on modernism generally, Sherwood Anderson. Just as Jack finally must remain on earth to carry on the terrestrial history of empire and oppression, so Faulkner cannot escape Anderson and the plan of regional writing, however powerfully universal it may have eventually been considered to be.

This displacement is actually a component that accompanies Faulkner's imagination of New Orleans, appearing in *Mosquitoes* in the form of Dawson Fairchild, whom Faulkner modeled on Anderson. To Faulkner, Anderson represented autochthony; in his essay "Sherwood Anderson" he observes that "[m]en grow from the soil, like corn and trees: I prefer to think of Mr. Anderson as a lusty corn field in his native Ohio" (132–33), indeed a "field of corn with a story to tell and a tongue to tell it with" (139). Early in the novel, while still in New Orleans, Julius calls Fairchild "Corn belt [. . .] Indiana talking. You people up there are born with the booster complex, aren't you?" (52), to which Fairchild replies, "Oh, well, we Nordics are at a disadvantage [. . .]. We've got to fix our idea on a terrestrial place. Though we know it's second rate, that's the best we can do" (52). Compared with the excitement and at least ostensible fluidity of New Orleans, Fairchild's imagined home community is characterized by stagnancy, workaday boredom, rural plainness. Juxtaposed against New Orleans and its difference, heightened by Fairchild's own descriptions of it, the Midwest represents the sort of regionalism/regionalizing that Faulkner would escape.[23]

Where the Midwest tags along with New Orleans in *Pylon* and *Mosquitoes,* Faulkner imagines a very elaborate juxtaposition of other spaces in relation to New Orleans in *Absalom, Absalom!* In this novel, in which southern autochthony is a prime element, Faulkner draws graduated concentric configurations of center and periphery. To Mr. Compson, New Orleans is an Oriental and exotic space, but in Cambridge, Massachusetts, Quentin and Shreve collapse the entire space of the South into an Oriental space. Shreve picks up the thread of Mr. Compson's views of an Oriental Charles Bon, asserting that the latter is "the esoteric, the sybarite, the steel blade in the silken tessellated sheath" (256). But whereas for Mr. Compson New Orleans represents an Orientalized space within the South of which Bon is the representative, for Shreve the entire South becomes conflated into a single miasmic Orient, the simultaneously centered yet peripheral forest primeval of which Quentin as well as Bon is a representative.

Faulkner draws the contrast between Shreve and Quentin and their respective places in quite clear terms. Whereas "Shreve [is] the Canadian, the child of blizzards and of cold in a bathrobe with an overcoat above it, the collar turned up about his ears; Quentin [is] the Southerner, the morose and delicate offspring of rain and steamy heat in the thin suitable clothing which he had brought from Mississippi" (276). Mississippi, which is to Shreve simply the South, emerges as global South, a faraway and exotic fantasyland full of wild and romantic people and adventures that is an extension of the space of New Orleans.[24] As Quentin lies in bed shivering, Shreve says:

[I]f I was going to have to spend nine months in this [northern] climate, I would sure hate to have come from the South. Maybe I wouldn't come from the South anyway, even if I could stay there. Wait. Listen. I'm not trying to be funny, smart. I just want to understand it if I can and I don't know how to say it better. Because it's something my people haven't got. Or if we have got it, it all happened long ago across the water and so now there aint anything to look at every day to remind us of it. We don't live among defeated grandfathers and freed slaves [. . .] and bullets in the dining room table and such, to be always reminding us to never forget. What is it? something you live and breathe in like air? (289)

Mississippi, which metonymically serves as the global South for Shreve, is a romanticized/Orientalized place, and Quentin is its immediate Oriental representative. Where scholars would suggest that the United States is the South writ large, here Faulkner seeks to make the South New Orleans writ large.

The presence of other spaces in Faulkner's imagination of the space of New Orleans is exploited most in *If I Forget Thee, Jerusalem*, the final novel anchored by the place of the Crescent City. Displacement constitutes a central focus in the novel, whether it be the displacement of elements (primarily water), feelings, individuals, or power. The importance of displacement emerges in the title's imperial implications, a quote from a Hebrew lament over being removed from the homeland. Early in "The Wild Palms," Charlotte Rittenmeyer explains that she is a sculptor (one who places, displaces, and replaces clay, brass, or stone); when she meets Harry Wilbourne, she draws "his finger-tips along the base of her other palm" as she tells him about her art, describing her sculpted work as "something you can touch, pick up, something with weight in your hand that you can look at the behind side of, that displaces air and displaces water and when you drop it, it's your foot that breaks and not the shape. Not poking at a piece of cloth with a knife or a brush like you were trying to put together a jig saw puzzle with a rotten switch through the bars of a cage" (35–36). Charlotte's statement might be read as the thesis of the entire novel. For in this book Faulkner explores the theme of severing, whether it be the cut that leads to Charlotte's death or the dynamiting of the levee that breaks apart the tall convict's newly forged home life. Charlotte and the woman whom the tall convict saves represent the noncarceral; they are the figures who would disrupt the puzzles that Harry and the tall convict struggle to keep together from behind their penitentiary bars. Most important, the main characters in the novel seek, through their own attempts to alter their places, ways to negotiate the forms their societies would use to imperialize their bodies, lives, and speech.

Both of the male protagonists in the novel early in life ingest nationalistic myths that lead to their respective initial incarcerations. Harry Wilbourne adopts the Benjamin Franklin plan of self-denial, industriousness, and temperance during medical school, "stopping tobacco for a year" to be frugal with the "two thousand dollars to be stretched over four years" his father left him (28); even so, there "was nothing left over for squiring girls" (28). He works to fit the dynamic emotions, desires, and experiences of living into this overarching mythology, thinking to himself once he has arrived in New Orleans, "*I have repudiated money and hence love. Not abjured it, repudiated. I do not need it; by next year or two years or five years I will know to be true what I now believe to be true: I will not even need to want it*" (30). In "Old Man," the tall convict lands himself in prison because of a failed train robbery because he believes the myths of "the Diamond Dicks and Jesse Jameses and such—whom he believed had led him into his present predicament through their own ignorance and gullibility regarding the medium in which they dealt and took money for, in accepting information on which they placed the stamp of verisimilitude and authenticity [. . .]" (20).

Furthermore, both characters are victims of myths of heroism forged by nationalistic propaganda; both try to escape the influence of those myths by striving for patterns of behavior that are the opposites of those myths and in so doing become hybrid figures. Harry tailors his behavior to conform with a plan of sobriety and law-abiding honesty, but in his relationship with Charlotte he leads a life of transgression. The tall convict falls prey to a literal interpretation of the paradoxical myth of heroism through transgression but moves from a life of outlawry to a pattern of heightened order, becoming a proletariat worker/husband (if alligator grappling can be labeled as working). In terms of their behavior, the two characters essentially cross paths in a movement that informs the very structure of the novel; indeed, much has been made of the contrapuntal nature of the novel's structure, but the movement of the two male protagonists of "Old Man" and "The Wild Palms" is also strikingly chiasmic. Harry moves initially from Oklahoma to New Orleans, crossing Louisiana to the eastern shore of the Mississippi River. The tall convict, identified as a "hill-man," comes from some region east and probably north of the Delta and moves westward through Parchman into Louisiana, presumably across the river during his time with the Cajun and then back onto the river and down to New Orleans. These men trade one form of captivity for another, crossing over into other lifestyles and finding in the end only more incarceration because neither transgression nor conformity can free them.

Harry and the tall convict attempt to speak out of their respective spaces of marginalization, but both face formidable barriers. Harry's virgin naiveté resulting from his industrious life of abstinence and sobriety renders him incompetent in the idiom of everyday affairs, whether it be in the ways he speaks to Charlotte's husband, Rat, or in his ridiculous attempt to get a whore to help him perform Charlotte's abortion. When he and Charlotte go to the Utah mine, he is unable to speak to the Poles, walled off from them because of their differing languages. Likewise, the tall convict approaches the world from the naive perspective of the reader of pulp fiction written by people "he did not even know were not actual men but merely the designations of shades who had written about shades" (22). And halfway through his journey down the Mississippi he encounters a steamboat full of French-speaking Louisianans and barely avoids a catastrophe when he cannot understand the Cajun who tells him that the levee will be dynamited and his new-found home flooded.

In fact, the great horror of the condition of both characters lies in the fact that the sounds they would make cannot be heard. Faulkner explores this problem slightly in *Pylon* when he implies that the paper for which the reporter works is a minor publication and that whatever may or may not be said in it runs the even greater risk of never being read anyway. But the theme of the inaudible and its juxtaposition against the all too audible is strong in *If I Forget Thee, Jerusalem*. In "The Wild Palms," the sound of "the palm fronds clashing with their wild dry bitter" noise (8) contrasts in its loudness with Harry's almost inaudible "palm clashing and murmuring dry and wild and faint" (272) in his jail cell after Charlotte's death. Here, Harry has grasped the phallic instrument that would "speak" his memory of Charlotte, but the sound cannot signify, having no listener save himself. The tall convict, on the other hand, finally finds his voice back at Parchman as he tells the other convicts about his adventure. But while on that adventure, he never manages to explain to those he meets that "the last thing I want to do is run away" (140). Indeed, his trying to explain that he is not an *escaped* but rather a *lost* (and law-abiding) convict is no more than the "wasting of precious breath, speaking to no one now anymore than the scream of the dying rabbit is addressed to any mortal ear but rather an indictment of all breath and its folly and suffering," for in the end, as he would put it, "All in the world I want is just to surrender" (146).

However, while myths serve as the catalysts for the incarceration of these characters, mythologies opened up by the disruptive presence of women also provide their opportunities for freedom. Once Harry and Charlotte are in Chicago, Charlotte's making money through sculpting plays an integral role in their relationship's being free of confining conventions. Significantly, she sculpts "historical figures about Chicago, this part of the West. You know—Mrs. O-Leary with Nero's face and the cow with the ukelele, Kit Carson with legs like Nijinsky and no face, just two eyes and a shelf of forehead to shade them with" (74). Harry eventually falls prey to the same pulp hero worship that haunts the tall convict, as he begins writing stories for magazines, buying his meals as he works toward the role of a working husband, "like a little boy with a new Daniel Boone suit hoarding crackers in the improvised forest of a broom closet" (104). The move westward to Utah roughly re-creates the imperial moment of the search for the gold in El Dorado that established New Orleans; although Harry and Charlotte do not go to the Utah mine seeking riches, they do hope to forge a new and different life for themselves, if not for any offspring, and to achieve the freedom inherent in the signifier of New Orleans. New Orleans itself cannot hold for them the freedom it normally signifies because Charlotte's family is there, and so she and Harry attempt to transmigrate, to shift their *habitus* into a new landscape, making a move westward (always the direction of imperial expansion in the vernacular of U.S. continental history).

The tall convict too finds freedom as well as confinement in the mechanisms of myth. In addition to the Arthurian overtones of his quest down the river, he wields "a light club the size and weight and shape of a Thuringian mace" (214) to engage in the business of wrestling and killing an alligator, a performance of mythical proportions (resembling Boon Hoggenback and Old Ben in "The Bear") in which he is likened to Hercules (219). The tall convict's grasping the "mace" is a seizing of the power of speech in the same manner as Harry's grasping the literal phallus, but as in Harry's case, problems arise in the capabilities of the audience. The Cajun takes on the role of primary mythmaker, telling his friends about the epic battle between the convict and the alligator, but he does so in French. In a sharp twist of irony, the very language that establishes the mythic texture that gives the convict notoriety among the Cajuns and the status of pseudohusband to the woman is the very language that is never accessible to him; again, his inability to understand the Cajun's explanation that the levee will be dynamited prevents him from going with the Cajun to find a new home and finally leads to his return to Parchman.

Cynthia Dobbs argues that the feminine force in the novel is uncontrollable, as symbolized in the flowing of the Mississippi River, but it is important to remember that however little control the men in the novel seem to have over the female force, the novel's women protagonists, as it were, must also negotiate forms of incarceration. However successful Charlotte may have been initially in selling her sculptures, the very mythic "historical" figures of Chicago that served her enterprise fail her. Charlotte understands the importance of trying to exist in the interstice between center and periphery. She seeks to escape her family life in New Orleans, which is characterized by a centeredness, being sanctioned by society; at the same time, she realizes, more than Harry, the importance of remaining on the periphery in relation to the national mythology of the bourgeois-sanctioned family if they are to maintain freedom rather than simply move into another form of centered behavior. Yet the very fabric of myth fails her when she seeks to copulate while still avoiding having the child, who, like Jack in *Pylon,* would signify some future generation to colonize the space of the earth, for she finds false the myth she was told when she "was young then, that when people loved, hard, really loved each other, they didn't have children, the seed got burned up in the love, the passion" (172).

The young woman in "Old Man" is at the mercy of an overarching male-defined incarceration despite the uncontrollable and disruptive power of her femininity. Trapped and pregnant in the flood early on, she has the child that would, if raised by herself and the convict, become something new for them, a new type of person in a new place, sprung from the half-free, half-imprisoned roots of its "parentage." And yet, even the place of the Louisiana swamp, with its implications of fluidity and amalgamation, with its "goats' beards of moss" (140), harbors the constrictions of the cultural center. Even though the convict and the Cajun speak "in their two patois, the one bastard English, the other bastard French" (218), the convict is tempted to conform to something akin to societal norm in his relationship with the woman. For her part, her relationship with the convict quickly becomes "that rapport of the wedded conferred upon her by the two weeks during which they had jointly suffered all the crises emotional social economic and even moral which do not always occur even in the ordinary fifty married years" (213). Just as importantly, however, they are bound by being the offspring of a similar heritage, "stemmed at some point from the same dim hill-bred Abraham" (213); that is, these people are Snopeses, bound to overrun the country. Yet they too resist the colonizing impulse; they do not marry—do not even have intercourse—as she returns home, presumably, and he returns to the societal margin, the prison.

What emerges as a common and constant problem throughout the novel is the problem of material, for, as the tall convict puts it, "Money aint got but one language" (212); and wherever speech may succeed or fail for the characters, the material always remains in control. Here again, paper continues to register its importance. Rittenmeyer's check for three hundred dollars for Charlotte's return tantalizes Harry but always remains unspent and therefore always a constriction. The tall convict revels in the pleasure of working to make money, becoming more and more enmeshed in the superstructure of currency only to have his hope of getting money dashed, precipitating his return to a form of incarceration that is at least dependable and constant. He is himself inscribed in paper: the poor whites on the raft who turn him away call his prison uniform "billboards" (139), and he later wraps those garments "in a six-months-old New Orleans paper" (212). Even though he removes his "wrapping," he still drifts back to the centeredness of currency, the very paradoxical centeredness, recorded on the pages of pulp fiction, that first sentenced him to a life of imprisonment. No matter how thoroughly these characters entrench themselves in the periphery—Harry and Charlotte in the mining camp in Utah, the tall convict and the woman in the swamp in Louisiana—they cannot escape the power of the center. Hence, in the end they are vanquished, returned to the periphery as sanctioned by and ensconced in the narrative power of the cultural center, the women silenced (Charlotte dead, the young woman back home) and the men speaking, but powerless and largely unheard.

To some extent, *If I Forget Thee, Jerusalem* marks a summation of Faulkner's earlier treatments of New Orleans. "The Wild Palms," like *Mosquitoes,* features the ordeal of the elite, the self- and ultimately societal Othering of the privileged resulting from the tweaking of narratives. Just as Charles Bon may be othered to the extent of being transformed in narrative into an Oriental body, so Harry becomes transformed from model working citizen of New Orleans into outcast murderer, something not altogether pure or legitimate but rather hybrid, *"that bungling bastard Wilbourne"* (271). From the beginning of "Old Man," the tall convict is not entirely white, being instead something of an Indian bandit such as might be found in the stories of Jesse James, having "a sunburned face and Indian-black hair and pale, china-colored outraged eyes" (20). He is hybrid also, for when he encounters the boatful of Louisianans, he distinguishes himself from them by noting that they "were not white people," and when asked, "You mean niggers?" he replies, "No. Not Americans" (201). And like the flyers in *Pylon,* he would occupy an untamed wilderness characterized in this case not by air but by water; swimming in the swamp water and fighting the alligators, he might be Al Jackson, the man who grew gills and would have opened a fish ranch in the Gulf.

Faulkner uses New Orleans as an anchor in much the same way as in the other novels. Again it is the space of amalgamation and hope, but also a space with a history of imperialism and oppression, a simultaneous playground always framed, for the

> city was there [. . . but the tall convict] had not seen it yet and would not—the low constant glare; Bienville had stood there too, it had been the figment of an emasculate also calling himself Napoleon but no more, Andrew Jackson had found it one step from Pennsylvania Avenue. But the convict found it considerably further than one step back to the ship canal and the skill, the coca cola sign dim now, the draw bridge arching spidery against the jonquil sky at dawn: nor did he tell, anymore than about the sixty-foot levee, how he got the skiff back into the water. (231)

The passage drips with imperialism, not just that of Bienville, Napoleon, and Jackson, but also, perhaps even more significantly, that of the Coca Cola sign, the signification of American (and conspicuously southern) cultural hegemony in all of its paradox marching to homogenize the U.S. landscape and culture by marshaling the forces of media. For in this novel, the Creoles are absent, vanished in the face of the American march toward domination. The frame of empire finally has closed upon its subjects, however loudly their rabbit screams may pierce the indomitably oppressive air.

CHAPTER THREE

Sold into Egypt
The Raiding of Mythic Place

Roth Edmonds sold my Benjamin. Sold him in Egypt. Pharaoh got him—
—*Go Down, Moses*

Few places so thoroughly and flexibly represent imperialism in Western history as Egypt. As an ancient empire, Egypt has been seen by Western civilization as the starting point of greatness, its power handed down through subsequent empires. The desire to recuperate, seize, and appropriate Egyptian glory helped generate the entire discipline of Orientalism, beginning with Napoleon Bonaparte's invasion of Egypt, which resulted, as Edward Said notes, from "the memories and glories that were attached to Alexander's Orient generally and to Egypt in particular" (80) and led to Napoleon's establishing the Institut d'Égypte, which produced the volume *Description de l'Égypte*. From this beginning, what would become known as Egyptology grew into a scholarly discipline that inundated European culture. The discipline produced Sir John Gardner Wilkinson's gargantuan study *Manners and Customs of the Ancient Egyptians*, as well as other studies of Egyptian history, mummification, and art, all of which culminated in the "Egyptomania" of Britain's evocation of Egypt in art, architecture, and literature for the purpose of aligning its own empire with the precedent of ancient Egypt.

As has been recently shown in Scott Trafton's *Egypt Land*, ancient Egypt as elaborated in biblical as well as Orientalist narrative also formed a flexible and conflicted metaphor in the founding and development of the United States. Noting that "[t]hroughout American history the iconography of empire—that of its wielders as well as its resisters—was lavishly drawn from that of ancient Egypt" (2), Trafton explains that "much of nineteenth-century American racial and national identity can be said to partake of a schematic split structured by the conflictual visions of ancient Egypt [. . . which] is indicative [. . .] of an overall and widespread instability in American racial and national identity that, through American visions of ancient Egypt, was often stylized as a split" (4). As Trafton goes on to explain, the splitting and doubleness of Egypt in U.S. figuration was complex, as various American groups attempted to fix themselves within overlapping paradigms of center and periphery in the various moments and movements of U.S. development and expansion. These attempts appeared in arguments regarding whether the ancient Egyptians were white or black and consequently in arguments regarding who were the centered and who were the marginalized within the rhetoric of Egypt as a narrative economy.

A glance at some central elements of U.S. appropriations of Egypt as a mythic place and imperial space will be useful in understanding Faulkner's use of an Egypt-informed mythic layer. On one hand, much of the iconography of the founding of the United States depicted (conspicuously white) Americans as the Israelites escaping the Egypt of religious oppression that was Britain. Accompanying this vision was a paradoxical embracing of Egypt in which white Americans, many of whose leaders were Freemasons, came to see their new country as another in the long line of civilizations descended from Egypt.[1] Thus, as Trafton notes, Benjamin Franklin's "early proposal for the Great Seal of the United States, featuring Moses leading the chosen people *out* of Egypt, would eventually be replaced in its reverse by the iconography *of* Egypt, crowned by an all-seeing eye" (20). From the founding of the nation and throughout the nineteenth century, the United States was caught up in its own Egyptomania, from the popularity of Egyptian architecture to the public unwrapping of mummies. In essence, white America moved from seeing itself as the oppressed to adopting the trappings of the oppressor; for example, such an Egypt-influenced structure as the Washington Monument celebrated George Washington as both Moses-like liberator from European domination and champion of the new American imperial impulse.

As the nineteenth century progressed, bringing with it conflict over slavery and intensified arguments over the origin and nature of race, African Americans appropriated the nation's Egyptian-informed rhetoric to subvert the narrative of the oppressor. On one hand, proslavery Orientalists worked to produce evidence that the ancient Egyptians had black slaves, showing that race-based slavery was therefore a natural part of the "new Egypt," as it were. At the same time, a number of scholars, including African American Orientalists, argued that the Egyptians themselves were black, an assertion that situated the black race as the origin of civilization. In still another appropriation of ancient Egypt large numbers of African Americans saw themselves as Israelites enslaved in the land of the Egyptians, a perspective that found particular expression in the slave spirituals.[2] In these various appropriations and treatments, ancient Egypt emerged as a flexible entity that could be used to articulate multiple viewpoints and political designs.

The influence of this Egyptomania on literature was broad. Multitudes of British writers, from Keats and Coleridge to Haggard and Doyle, employed images of and themes about the "Orient," and Egypt in particular, in their writing. Nineteenth-century American literary treatments of Egypt have been documented most thoroughly and impressively in Trafton's work and in John T. Irwin's *American Hieroglyphics,* which shows the importance of the trope of the hieroglyph in the works of Melville, Emerson, Thoreau, and others, particularly Poe. These works are helpful in understanding Faulkner's use of Egypt to construct his mythic-imperial space; however, some additional attention must first be given to the historical connections between Faulkner's South (specifically the Mississippi Delta region) and Egypt in terms of myth and empire. Attention must be paid, that is, to the history that Trafton and Irwin for the most part do not discuss—the history of cotton and empire in Egypt and the ways these enterprises interrelated with the U.S. South not only in the nineteenth century but even into the twentieth century, when Faulkner was writing.

Much like the rest of the nation, the South was constructed on the powerful narrative significance of ancient Egypt as expounded by the Bible and the Orientalists. This construction was particularly conspicuous in that region along what Abraham Lincoln would refer to as the "American Nile." Here lay the perfect topographical features for recreating ancient Egypt: a major river, the Mississippi, with its own delta. Accordingly, cities with Egyptian names, such as Cairo and Memphis, appeared along its banks.[3] Not only does the development of the region mark a point in the westward movement of the growing empire of the United States but as people began to realize that cotton would grow well in the Delta's rich soil, the Delta's leaders also positioned it within the machinations of the global market.[4] This presence in the global market drove the national conflicts regarding the nature of westward expansion, as southern planters sought to spread slave-worked cotton plantation culture, a project carried out in direct contradiction to northern visions of the nation's future. By the time the southern states seceded, the U.S. South was the leading supplier of high-quality cotton to Great Britain, a prime factor in that country's tendency to recognize the Confederate States of America as a legitimate nation.[5]

During the Civil War, however, the South was surpassed in its cotton production and exportation by a new competitor, Egypt. In fact, cotton had been a player in ancient Egypt; its presence, growth, and uses are mentioned by Herodotus and later described by Pliny.[6] A high-quality long staple cotton had continued to grow in Egypt but had been overlooked by would-be economic imperialists until the early nineteenth century, when Louis Alexis Jumel, a French textile engineer, discovered it growing in a garden and began cultivating it.[7] Jumel had come to Egypt with other Europeans at the behest of the Egyptian leader Muhammad Ali, who sought to bring the country out of an economic abyss through various attempts at industrialization and increased agricultural production. Soon this cotton was grown along the Nile, and cotton exportation steadily increased, though Egypt remained a minor supplier of cotton to Britain until 1860. When the Civil War started in America in 1860, and the North's blockade severely constricted the South's exportation, the British turned to other sources of cotton, first to its original and second-ranked supplier, India, but then to Egypt for its higher-quality cotton, and soon Egypt's exportation and its economy were booming. Though Egypt never eclipsed India in the amount of cotton exported, it effectively replaced the U.S. South as the primary supplier of high-quality cotton.

Now the old Egyptian empire itself might be renewed, but this economic glory quickly faded. The same crop that had helped fuel the rise of the southern states and formed the impetus for its dreams of imperial expansion had also played a significant role in reviving Egypt. And just as it brought what white aristocratic southerners saw as northern imperialism during and after the Civil War, it brought the fury and might of the British Empire onto Egypt. For obvious economic reasons (made especially urgent by the rise of cotton mills in the United States, especially in the South) and also in reaction to a rising sentiment of "Egypt for Egyptians," Britain moved to tighten its grasp on Egypt; by July 1882 it had significantly increased its control over Egypt and its cotton production. In the second decade of the twentieth century, George Bigwood wrote of his concern that U.S. mills were consuming the bulk of their nation's cotton, which in the past had been exported to England. He said that the aim of the British Cotton Growing Association was "to encourage in [cotton growth] the natives and settlers in the different Colonies and Protectorates" (72).

The theme of empire in histories of Egypt and the U.S. South and in relations between them is therefore significant. Part of the glory of ancient Egypt was its cotton, and the U.S. South, particularly the Mississippi Delta, had modeled itself on the ancient Egyptian model. The South's own imperial impulses were severely restricted during the Civil War, giving rise to a renewal of Egyptian cotton culture, which in turn led to Egypt's experiencing another wave of imperial oppression. Indeed, as Edward Mead Earle writes,

> [O]ne cannot study the history of Egypt without being profoundly impressed by the importance of the American Civil War in the making of modern Egypt; without realizing that the production of Egyptian cotton, stimulated by the blockade of Southern ports, contributed materially to the development of important British interests in Egypt; without feeling that the resulting increase in cotton exports from the Nile Valley to Lancashire was a factor in the eventual British occupation of Egypt [. . . . Where] the discovery of America and of the sea routes to the east in the fifteenth century resulted in an economic decline of the Mediterranean region, from which Egypt in common with her neighbors suffered severely[, . . .] four years of civil war in America in the nineteenth century offered Egypt an opportunity which she eagerly seized to make herself once more an integral part of the complicated economic organism of the world. (520–21)

Perhaps the greatest and most significant development in this relationship of imperial contiguity and reciprocation between the United States and Egypt emerged as the twentieth century progressed, for from the beginning of the century U.S. cotton became increasingly hybrid, mixing American and Egyptian species.[8] The optimum type of cotton was Extra-Long Staple, the foremost variety of which was cultivated in the Sea Islands, off the coast of Georgia, Florida, and South Carolina. The cotton Jumel discovered in Egypt was of slightly lesser quality, not being quite as long. These varieties were crossed in 1825 in Egypt. From a later strain of this American-Egyptian cotton, which was named Mitafifi, a new variety was developed in 1908 and began to be grown in the southwestern United States. This new variety of cotton was named Yuma, and subsequent strains were given names that were variations on the name Pima. This American-Egyptian cotton was the premier variety grown in the United States throughout the twentieth century and has been the most important of cotton crops since the 1950s.

Cotton thus emerges as an emblem of hybridity and empire. The very expansion of cotton into the Southwest that southern planters envisioned came to pass (although under ostensibly different circumstances), and the hybrid strains of cotton produced were given Native American names—an ideal way to establish a sort of renewed nativity, a resuscitation of the cigar-store Indian motif. Moreover, the strain itself combined the best of the "first" great empire of Western civilization and a new great economic empire modeled on Egypt itself. Cotton's uses in empire building were many: Thomas Edison's choice light-bulb filament was made of cotton; the Wright brothers stretched cotton across the wings of the first plane to fly successfully; cotton was used in the manufacture of automobile tires; and cotton materials were employed in the making of smokeless gunpowder during World War I.[9] Stephen Yafa stresses cotton's imperial importance, writing that for

> a scrawny, gangling plant that produces hairs about as insubstantial as milkweed, cotton has exerted a mighty hold on human events since it was first domesticated about 5,500 years ago in Asia, Africa, and South America. Cotton rode on the back of Alexander the Great all the way from India to Europe, robed ancient Egyptian priests, generated the conflicts that led to the American Civil War, inspired [Marx and Engels's] *Communist Manifesto*, fooled Columbus into thinking he had reached Asia, and made at least one bug, the boll weevil, world famous. It also created the Industrial Revolution in England and in the United States, motivated single American women to leave home for the first time in history, and played a pivotal role in Mahatma Gandhi's fight for India's independence from British colonial rule. [One finds in cotton's history] the empires cotton built and destroyed, the fortunes it created, and the revolutions it stirred up along the way as it journeyed west from India to continental Europe, then to Great Britain, and from there to the United States. (1)

And here was the United States prospering from the southern model, with the peculiar institution apparently abrogated and yet also curiously present, for the name Pima "was given in honor of the Pima Indians who were helping to raise the ELS [Extra-Long Staple] cotton on the USDA experimental farm in Sacaton, Arizona" ("History of Pima Cotton").

As the twentieth century progressed and the United States emerged as a world power, its cotton industry would take steps to eclipse its Egyptian counterpart altogether in yet another chapter in this rivalry. Toward the end of World War II the 1943–44 international edition of the *Cotton Trade Journal,* published by the New Orleans Cotton Exchange, was celebrating the United States' success in war in an article entitled "Cotton in Victory," while another article announced the importance of "Rayon . . . Today and Tomorrow" (rayon was another cotton product used in making tires and parachutes). The issue also features an article entitled "Egyptian Cotton States Its Case" in which Anis Azer, commercial counselor of the Royal Egyptian Legation, pleads with the United States, which has taken a predominant role in world affairs, to lift a tariff imposed by the Hawley-Smoot Tariff Act. According to Azer, the "intention of the legislation was apparently to protect the United States Pima cotton-grower who could not compete with the Egyptian grower on account of the lower labor cost" (50). This reduction in price differential had increased domestic sales of U.S. cotton but correspondingly reduced its foreign sales, since European manufacturers had taken advantage of the situation to buy Egyptian cotton. Still, these European manufacturers were not as large and so did not purchase as much as American manufacturers had, hurting Egyptian cotton sales as well. What seems obvious is that the United States had secured its position of power in global affairs; it could impose tariffs simply because it could, regardless of long-term practical values or balance in the global economy. The United States had been becoming and now was the new ancient Egypt.

The presence of Egypt as a trope of imperialism and hybridity in Faulkner's cosmos was therefore vivid and very much alive rather than a mere holdover from the nineteenth-century Egyptomania. This presence is perhaps best exemplified by the 1934 Memphis Cotton Carnival, which made Egypt its theme.[10] Memphis, Tennessee, had long capitalized on being named after the Egyptian city, and the nineteenth-century Memphis Mardi Gras was reincarnated as the Cotton Carnival in 1931, when, adopting an "Old South" theme, the city celebrated the closely connected crop that had contributed to its own greatness and the ancient empire that had served as its model. And Memphis was merely the northern gateway to the Delta, the region that in 1932 was "known to the trade throughout the world as the home of 'Delta Staples,' [as] the site of an area which produces approximately three-fourths of American's better fibered cotton" ("Kingdom of the Negro, the Mule, and Cotton" 49), and the Stoneville, Mississippi, research facility was considered the "nerve center of the World's cotton trade" (Black 94). The gateway at the opposite end of this cultural region was New Orleans, and the two cities share several similarities, both having been developed from the exploration of La Salle and Bienville, both participating in traditions of carnival, and both being afflicted by yellow fever carried by the mosquito *Aedes aegypti,* whose name takes on particular significance in light of the importance of Egypt in American figuration.

In fact, the historical reciprocities between Memphis and New Orleans are worth recounting in considering the raw material of Faulkner's cosmos. Both cities signify layers of imperial history. As John E. Harkins notes, ancient Memphis was situated "at the junction of the newly united kingdoms of Upper and Lower Egypt" and then was conquered in turn by Alexander, the Romans, and the Arabs, who took "much of its remaining stone [downriver] to be used in building Fostat, destined to become the Arab capital of Cairo" (17). So, too, Harkins describes Memphis, Tennessee, as being situated between the Deep South and the North, close to Missouri and Kentucky in a sort of liminal border region. And in language uncannily reminiscent of Grace King's, Harkins notes that after successive yellow-fever epidemics, "like the phoenix of Egyptian legend, Memphis renewed itself from the figurative ashes of its devastation" (91).

Furthermore, Faulkner uses Egypt as part of his treatment of New Orleans. Highlighting the city as an Oriental space, the narrator of "Mirrors of Chartres Street" asserts that "[e]ven those who carved those strange flat-handed creatures on the Temple of Rameses must have dreamed New Orleans by moonlight" (16). In *Mosquitoes* Faulkner describes Patricia as getting "her seemingly boneless body into an undimensional angular flatness pure as an Egyptian carving" (20), thus situating her in the nexus of the century-long debate over the race of the ancient Egyptians in a manner that further highlights her androgyny. And it is worth noting again the implicit connection Faulkner draws between the Egyptian plagues and New Orleans when he describes mosquitoes as "a biblical plague" (8). Moreover, André Bleikasten has shown the centrality of signs of Egypt in *Pylon,* pointing out that Shumann's name might be derived from the Egyptian god of the air, Shou, and arguing that the reporter "is the pencil pusher for the country of shadows. One could almost take him for a clownish avatar of Thoth, the Egyptian god of writing and death."[11] In fact, had he not perished in Lake Rimbaud, Shumann might have been the Moses of the flyers; certainly the pylon that so dominates the narrative evokes the obelisk constructed to commemorate the U.S. liberator George Washington.[12]

Egypt lurks about the text of *If I Forget Thee, Jerusalem.* Trafton explains that one of the central motifs of Egyptomania in nineteenth-century American literature was that of the puncture in the earth, showing the globe to be hollow and to contain a lost race of Egyptians. This motif appears in "The Wild Palms" when Harry and Charlotte go to the mining camp in Utah, a state that has a conspicuous Egypt-informed imperial past, for, as Irwin points out, Joseph Smith (whose Mormon followers would colonize Utah) claimed that *The Pearl of Great Price* had been translated from an Egyptian papyrus and hypocephalus. In Utah, the puncture is present in the form of the mine, which is also the site of would-be Polish colonists. The miners emerge from this puncture in the earth in which they live with "faces of a poorly made-up and starving black-face minstrel troop" (168)—Egyptians in the most complete sense, being both white and black—at which point Harry and Charlotte realize that they have had babies recently and are in need of a doctor.

To communicate with these people, Charlotte strikes upon a most natural method, in light of the Egyptian-informed significance of the moment: she begins drawing hieroglyphics, the language the "lost race" of "Egyptians" best understand. After drawing a picture representing the miners, Charlotte begins to draw another picture, in which

> Wilbourne saw his face emerge from beneath the flying chalk; anyone would have recognized him: they did at once. The sound [of the chalk] ceased, they looked at Wilbourne then at one another in bewilderment. Then they looked at Charlotte again as she ripped the paper from the wall and began to attach a fresh sheet; this time one of them stepped forward and helped her, Wilbourne too watching the flying crayon again. This time it was himself, indubitably himself and indubitably a doctor, anyone would have know it—the horn glasses, the hospital tunic every charity patient, every hunky gutted by flying rock or steel

or premature dynamite and coming to in company emergency stations, has seen [. . .]. (169–70)

The two "groups" in this scene are, in fact, doubled in two different configurations of center-periphery: Harry and Charlotte are the moderns, who discover the Egyptians and attempt to communicate with them; the Polish people are the Israelites, who work in the mines (building the pyramids?), the non-"white" slaves who must be led out of bondage by some Moses. Their Moses is Harry, who is both like and unlike them, the hybrid liberator who cannot himself speak and so has his Aaron (Charlotte) to handle the duty of communication.[13] Like Moses, Harry himself cannot leave the wilderness with these "Israelites" and ultimately cannot cross over into the Promised Land of a life with Charlotte, for instead of "speaking" (making the precise cut in Charlotte's anatomy that "lets the air in" to cause abortion), he has "smitten" (cut in the wrong way, causing Charlotte's death) and finds himself in prison looking out the window at what might have been his.

The Sound and the Fury is inundated with the poetics of Egypt and the dynamics of race and power that they encode. The Compson family occupies a central position in the colonization and creation of Yoknapatawpha County; the Compson Appendix traces the family all the way back to Quentin MacLachan, whose neighbor in Kentucky was "Boon or Boone" (705).[14] The Compsons are present from the moment of Ikkemotubbe, which is the time of Andrew Jackson. And the generations proceed to Maury, "rechristened Benjamin by his brother Quentin (Benjamin, our lastborn, sold into Egypt)" (718). From the lastborn to the firstborn of this final generation of Compsons, an Egypt-informed mythic layer informs the novel's text, spawning questions of racial identity and tortured difficulties in speaking from unstable paradigms of center and periphery.

A layer of Egyptian-Hebraic narrative is evoked in both the beginning and the end of *The Sound and the Fury*, channeled through the hybridity of Benjy. This hybridity emerges in the racialization present in the multiple explanations for his renaming. He is originally named for his uncle Maury Bascomb, but his mother changes his name to Benjamin. The novel does not explain exactly why his name is changed; instead, it strangely begs what is apparently not a non sequitur to Mrs. Compson or to Caddy, who explains to Dilsey that his *"name's Benjy now."* In answer to Dilsey's question why his name was changed, she replies, *"Benjamin came out of the bible. [. . .] It's a better name for him than Maury was. How come it is, Dilsey said. Mothers says it is, Caddy said"* (58). As has already been mentioned, the Compson Appendix, written later, states that it was Quentin and not his mother who renamed him Benjamin, because he was "our lastborn, sold into Egypt," but this explanation does not help at all, since not only has the name of the renamer changed but in the biblical account it was Joseph and not Benjamin who was sold into Egypt. In the novel, the thought passes through Quentin's mind, "Benjamin the child of mine old age held hostage into Egypt" (170), which is a more accurate rendering of the narrative evoked but raises the question, what sort of Egypt is he held hostage in, that of his own mind? Or that of the African American space in which he is placed? Yet another explanation is supplied by Versh, who tells Benjy:

> *Your name Benjamin now. You know how come your name Benjamin now. They making a bluegum out of you. Mammy say in old time your granpaw changed nigger's name, and he turn preacher, and when they look at him, he bluegum, too. Didn't use to be bluegum, neither. And when family woman look him in the eye in the full of the moon, chile born bluegum. And one evening, when they was about a dozen them bluegum chillen running around the place, he never come home. Possum hunters found him in the woods, et clean. And you know who et him. Them bluegum chillen did.* (69)

The lack of clarity regarding the reason for Benjy's renaming signals the flexibility of myth and the ways different groups can wield it as a heterogeneous medium. Whatever confusion there may be, however, it is clear that he is cast as an Israelite, and in a way that registers the conflicted discussions of Egyptian and Israelite identity present in nineteenth-century American Egyptomania. On one hand, Benjy's being made into one of the sons of Jacob simultaneously casts the rest of the family as part of that of Jacob, progenitors from the line of Abraham of a great nation. But it is also important to note that when he is "sold" into Egypt, he becomes a different kind of Israelite, for he has crossed over into another racial figuration of that kind of personage: now he is one of the race of the enslaved, the figurative African American Israelites in the American Egypt. The Compsons themselves become reconfigured as the enslaving Egyptians, and Benjy emerges as hybrid, placed within African American space, with its own myth-informed explanation for his name change, and yet still somehow a Compson (despite his name being taken from the Bascomb side of the family, which carries implications of being a lesser and perhaps even "darker" name).

Like Donald Mahon in *Soldiers' Pay,* Benjy is also enslaved inside his own mind and cannot speak in any intelligible way. He tells his tale with the help of an omniscient narrator who can somewhat mediate (or at least record) his thoughts. And to some extent Luster knows Benjy's tale, for he realizes the effect of the signifier *caddy,* which does very much signify something and with a great deal of fury. What is interesting is that the word that so sparks Benjy's emotions should carry different meanings not in its sound but in its spelling. The hieroglyphics for this phoneme *(caddy* and *caddie),* which is so remarkably fixed for Benjy, fail in their textual signifying for him, and he cannot read the context that differentiates between the sound's two meanings. In a strange role reversal, the bawdy and linguistically talented Luster might himself become the Egyptian, for however much he may be Benjy's servant, Benjy is certainly the unempowered figure in their relationship. Indeed, as much as Benjy participates in both whiteness and blackness, his mental limitations seem to place him within his own space, which is neither of the racial constructs between which he stands at the same time that it is both. The isolation of his hybridity is well demonstrated by Frony's telling Dilsey on Easter Sunday, "I wish you wouldn't keep on bringin him to church, mammy [. . .]. Folks talking" (290). To which Dilsey responds, "And I knows whut kind of folks [. . .]. Trash white folks. Dat's who it is. Thinks he aint good enough fer white church, but nigger church aint good enough fer him. [. . .] Tell um de good Lawd dont keer whether he bright er not. Dont nobody but white trash keer dat" (290).

The events of this Easter Sunday play with the signifiers of the Egypt-informed mythic layer, with its implications of hybridity and its constitutions of mythic-imperial space. "Nigger Hollow" marks a peripheral space in relation to the town of Jefferson or to the Compson estate, but as Dilsey and her companions make their way to that location for Easter services, the dynamic of center and periphery shifts. This area is situated on a lower geographical plane than the "white" land around it: the narrator notes that there the "street became a dirt road. On either hand the land dropped more sharply" (290). As the group enters this place, "negroes spoke to them as they passed" (291). When the setting has shifted entirely to this thoroughly African American space, the racial markers *negro* and *nigger* disappear and "normal" generic pronouns take their places. In the church building "[m]ost of the *women* were gathered on one side of the room. [. . .] the congregation turned its head as one as six small *children*—four *girls* with tight pigtails bound with small scraps of cloth like butterflies, and two *boys* with close napped heads—entered and marched up the aisle [. . .] followed by two *men* in single file" (292–93, emphasis mine). Here, the people involved are described merely as people; the passage might just as easily describe a *white* Easter service.[15] One can imagine the narrator having to note the presence of a "white" person as a marker of difference—as a representative of a space that is in fact peripheral to this raced center.

Introduced into this scene is Revered Shegog, himself a hybrid figure whose accustomed space is that of the threshold. "He had a wizened black face like a small, aged monkey," the narrator notes, an "insignificant looking man sitting dwarfed and countrified by the [regular] minister's imposing bulk" (293). Dressed "in a shabby alpaca coat," Shegog seems to signify the periphery to the extent that Frony wonders, "En dey brung dat all de way fum Saint Looey" (293). Yet, his cosmopolitan near-whiteness displays itself immediately as he begins to speak, his voice and diction "like a white man['s]. His voice was level and cold" (293). At length, the "white" part of his sermon closes as "with a sort of swooping glide he came to rest again beside the reading desk [. . .] his monkey body reft of all motion as a mummy" (294). The dressed-up threshold monkey is now a mummy to be unwrapped—the white Egyptian wrapping will now be removed to reveal the true black Israelite underneath. The congregation "did not mark just when his intonation, his pronunciation, became negroid" (295), but now the preacher is one of them, one of the oppressed black Israelites, transformed amazingly from Egyptian to child of Israel, launching immediately into the double figuration of oppression present in the narrative of ancient Egypt: "When de long, cold— Oh, I tells you, breddren, when de long, cold. . . . I sees de light en I sees de word, po sinner! Dey passed away in Egypt, de swingin chariots; de generations passed away. Wus a rich man: whar he now, O breddren? Wus a po man: whar he now, O sistuhn? Oh I tell you, ef you aint got de milk en de dew of de old salvation when de long, cold years rolls away!" (295). Where Benjy is the white hybrid outsider in the congregation, Shegog is the black hybrid outsider, both being figures of explicit hybridity and both being present within a mythic framework. Shegog ties Egyptian and Roman layers of narrative together in the central motif of the Crucifixion, stressing that the recollection and the blood of the Lamb offer joy and freedom in the afterlife, a theme tailored to his hardworking audience, bereft of the power of the center, which Shegog on some level does possess. He wields the power of myth. He may have spoken of Egypt in his white as well as his black voice, for all the audience knows. Ostensibly, Benjy signifies nothing in the sounds he makes; rather, he is a sort of canvas (although not a tabula rasa) upon which to paint narrative, as the explanations for his renaming above show. What is significant in both characters is that their complex hybrid identities are registered by means of an Egypt-informed mythic layer, both moving back and forth across what would seem an impermeable membrane between center and periphery.

Benjy, Shegog, and African American space and poetics of resistance and deferred freedom in salvation represent the most obvious evocations of Egypt in the novel, but the importance of this mythic layer by no means ends with them. In his pursuit of the "golden fleece" that is cotton, Jason is not merely the leader of the Argonauts but also a white southerner invested in the global market for cotton, with its intricate connections to Egypt. W. E. B. Du Bois makes the connection between the myth of Jason's quest for the Golden Fleece and the South's pursuit of cotton production: "This is the Black Belt of Georgia," he writes. "Dougherty County is the west end of the Black Belt, and men once called it the Egypt of the Confederacy" (100). He notes that the Black Belt of the New South is part of the quest for this "golden fleece" and that "the Negro is still supreme in a Cotton Kingdom larger than that on which the Confederacy built its hopes" (112). Du Bois's observations easily transfer to the Mississippi River Delta, the American Nile, and Faulkner's Jason not only operates within his own Greek-informed mythic significance but also maintains a simultaneity with the mythic place of Egypt.

Jason's monologue contains a number of overtures on the topic of cotton production and trade, articulating his fury in ways that encode shifts in conceptions of margin and metropole and express either his empowerment or lack thereof accordingly. Early in his section, he chides Job for working so slowly, telling him, "You'd better be glad you're not a boll-weevil waiting on those cultivators [. . .]. You'd work yourself to death before they'd be ready to prevent you" (189). Jason also enjoys a degree of empowered centeredness when he goes to the telegraph office to check on the cotton market, for he takes leave to speak to the telegraph clerk as roughly as he pleases. As his employer intimates, Jason possesses the power of being a Compson, descendant of one of the first white colonizers. At the same time, Jason is painfully aware of his peripheral position in relation to the true location of power in the cotton business. As he tells the drummer who appears in the hardware store where he works, "Cotton is a speculator's crop. They fill the farmer full of hot air and get him to raise a big crop for them to whipsaw on the market, to trim the suckers with" (191). "They," as has been noted earlier, are the "dam eastern jews" (191) at the New York Cotton Exchange, "that New York crowd" (227), and Jason wonders "how a city no bigger than New York can hold enough people to take the money away from us country suckers" (234). In fact, section 3 of the 1910 charter for the New York Cotton Exchange stated that the "purposes of said corporation shall be to provide, regulate and maintain a suitable building [. . .] for a Cotton Exchange [. . .], to adjust controversies between its members, [. . . and] to establish just and equitable principles in the trade" (New York Cotton Exchange 2), but speaking from the periphery, Jason realizes the oppression also encoded in its overriding hegemony to "promote the cotton trade of the city of New York" (2).

Although he never says so, foreign influences on the market are implicit in Jason's championing of whiteness and Americanness. In his frustration with the telegraph office, Jason exclaims to himself, "I'll be damned if it hasn't come to a pretty pass when any dam foreigner that cant make a living in the country where God put him, can come to this one and take money right out of an American's pockets" (192). His invective is couched in a larger complaint about Jews, but also implied in his rhetoric is the presence of Indian and Egyptian cotton, the threats of the global market. That he is a Compson means nothing to anyone in New York City or anywhere else in the global market, where he is just one in a million peripheral southerners who themselves compete against other peripheral cotton suppliers. Jason thus emerges as a partly empowered and partly unempowered figure, a modern Egyptian trying to ply his way in the global market who is aware of his importance, his centeredness in that market, as well as his peripheral status in relation to it.

As a "modern Egyptian," Jason harbors his own hoard, a treasure saved over the course of years in his scamming of Caddy; his gold is raided in the punctured-earth fashion that Trafton describes. Quentin robs her oppressor, Jason, by breaking his window and literally exhuming the money he has saved from beneath his floor. She thus transfers the treasure of the Compson empire (not something left over from the past, but treasure gained profanely) and takes it elsewhere to establish her own life, presumably—her own narrative. Jason chases her to Mottson and there encounters the man with the hatchet, who attempts to kill him, at which point Jason realizes that he is no longer in the center of his power, is no longer the Pharaoh on his own throne: "for the first time [he] saw clear and unshadowed the disaster toward which he rushed" (310). This entire scene transpires under the gaze of a hieroglyph, the sign with the picture of a "human eye with an electric pupil" in the space between "Keep your" and "on Mottson" (311); this eye would be the all-seeing eye of Egypt atop the pyramid on the seal of the United States, and perhaps Benjy, whose most remarkable feature is his blue eyes, finally is neither a bluegum nor Benjamin son of Jacob but Benjamin Franklin himself, with his all-seeing eye atop the pyramid gazing upon Jason from the dollar bill to which he is a slave. For Jason has attempted to evade the Franklin ethic, has violated the distinct American mythic plan of frugality, and now his evil has brought him to his inevitable end: he the profane robber and oppressor has himself been robbed of his glory.

Such a situation roughly corresponds to the plot of the film *Land of the Pharaohs*. Although Faulkner was only one of the script's three writers, it is worth pausing to mention it at this point, for while it was written and produced toward the end of Faulkner's career and was not wholly his creation, the film nevertheless manifests recognizable Faulknerian elements. The story is presented from the perspective of Hamar, Lord High Priest of Egypt, who acts as a scribe, "preparing a chronicle of the reign of Khu-fu, ruler of Egypt." At the beginning, Hamar explains that "word has come that again [Khu-fu] has been victorious in the war against our enemies, and now Egypt has taken its place as the greatest of all nations in the world. Today, Pharaoh and his army return." The scene then shifts to a fabulous procession, and when Khu-fu appears on the screen, Hamar's voice is heard saying, "This was Pharaoh. Direct descendant of our deity Amon, God of the Sun, who rules the Heavens as Pharaoh rules the earth. Again he brought treasure—gold and precious jewels taken from our enemies. For to Pharaoh, riches were power, and power was to be desired. And also again he brought many captives, for is it not by slaves that one becomes even richer? And then has more power."

Pharaoh is, of course, Thomas Sutpen as much as he is Jason Compson, for once he arrives home, he tells Hamar that he wants to keep his treasure forever, and he tells his wife that he is ready to have a child and set to work establishing a dynasty. Khu-fu's greatest hope is to build "a tomb that no man can violate," and to design this tomb he enlists one of the slaves from the nation he has just conquered. In true Faulkner fashion, this personage is an architect. Pharaoh promises the architect, whose name is Vashtar, that he will set his people free if Vashtar will design this tomb so that it can never be penetrated.[16] The people of Egypt work for Pharaoh, at first voluntarily and then by force, to complete the pyramid in which the tomb will be housed. These workers behave very much like African American slaves, as many of them are very dark-skinned and they spend a great deal of time singing in amazingly harmonious and echoic voices that sound uncannily like the Fisk Jubilee Singers.

As time progresses, it is Pharaoh himself who violates his dream of impenetrability by permitting into his life a patently penetrable person: Nellifer, Princess of Cypress. After marrying Khu-fu, she rids herself of her chief rival for his fortune (the true queen, Pharaoh's first wife) by having her bitten by a cobra, much as Cleopatra was. By various other schemes, she manages to get Khu-fu killed and thus positions herself to acquire his wealth when he is buried. But Vashtar has ingeniously designed the pyramid in such a way that when the tomb is sealed, the entire labyrinth leading to it is sealed as well, so that when Nellifer accompanies Hamar into the tomb as part of the burial procession, she is herself sealed in and unable to take Khu-fu's wealth. Caddy's daughter Quentin is more successful than Nellifer in her burglary, but the Faulknerian poetics of imperialism and the U.S. South are marked in *Land of the Pharaohs,* and reading *The Sound and the Fury* back across the film exposes the flexibility of the Egyptian narrative.[17]

Quentin Compson—the man—also moves within the dynamics of a racially charged, Egypt-informed mythic matrix. What Toni Morrison calls an Africanist presence is strong in Quentin's section, as his shadow marks his progression through the final day of his life, counting down the hours of that day as it shifts in relation to his own body. The instability of Quentin's whiteness and of his concept of whiteness is noteworthy, and he often recognizes his shadow in connection to an encounter or a thought that exposes racial instability. For example, early in his section, Quentin finds himself seated by an African American man on a streetcar (an obviously charged site of segregation in the South if not in Massachusetts). This violation of what Quentin thinks of as normal racial division leads him to begin to think about the situation as a means to cope with the presence of the black man. Quentin explains, "I used to think that a Southerner had to be always conscious of niggers. [. . .] When I first came East I kept thinking You've got to remember to think of them as colored people not niggers." He goes on to comment that "I realised that a nigger is not a person so much as a form of behavior; a sort of obverse reflection [read "shadow"] of the white people he lives among" (86). His thoughts lead him from this moment of displacement and disorder to a memory of replacement and reorder as he remembers seeing an African American man from his train window while stopped in Virginia on his way home for Christmas. He had beaten the man to the punch with the tradition of calling out "Christmas gift" and found that he "really had missed Roskus and Dilsey" (86–87). At home, in place in the South, this folk-culture act, actually participated in by both whites and blacks, allows him to speak, and to do so in a way he cannot in Cambridge, where the interracial interactions proceed according to different strategies. The strategies of his *habitus* do not travel well to the North, where the black man is no longer safely placed outside on a "gaunt rabbit of a mule" (87) but is rather inside the vehicle, sitting beside Quentin, even so bold as to touch Quentin's knee and speak to him in standard English, "Pardon me" (89). When Quentin exits the car, one of the first things he notes is his shadow in the river, and then he evokes that "consolidating" southern folk culture, noting that "[n]iggers say a drowned man's shadow was watching for him in the water all the time" (90).

Then there is Deacon, the con who meets all the southern students in an "Uncle Tom's cabin, patches and all" but who soon "was calling you Quentin or whatever, and when you saw him next he'd be wearing a cast-off Brooks suit" (97). Again, Deacon marks a presence of instability, obviously playing the role of the African southerner, but even then having a white boy carry students' luggage at the train station. Significantly, "once he had heard you speak, he could name your state" (97), but Deacon himself understands language as performance, being able to weave back and forth between dialect and standard speech. Still, Quentin can participate in this game of signifying, and whatever threat Deacon poses, Quentin can feel some kinship, for he believes that Deacon is really one of the folks, able to perform "that self he had long since taught himself to wear in the world's eye, pompous, spurious, not quite gross" (100). It is interesting that Quentin uses the word *world,* as it expresses quite literally his sense of his southerner's peripheral status in "the world": if Deacon and himself could just be inside the safe bubble of the South, then they could avoid having to perform for "the world" and live according to what Quentin sees as the natural order. Note the following exchange when Quentin gives Deacon an envelope. Deacon asks:

> "Something for me, you say?"
> "Yes. A present I'm making you."
> He was looking at me now, the envelope white in his black hand, in the sun. His eyes were soft and irisless and brown, and suddenly I saw Roskus watching me from behind all his whitefolks' claptrap of uniforms and politics and Harvard manner, diffident, secret, inarticulate and sad. "You aint playing a joke on the old nigger, is you?"
> "You know I'm not. Did any Southerner ever play joke on you?"
> "You're right. They're fine folks. But you cant live with them."
> "Did you ever try?" I said. But Roskus was gone. (99)

This confluence of displacement and race becomes particularly potent when it emerges that Quentin's own racial status is unstable. When he encounters the three boys going fishing and then swimming in the countryside—in the periphery, a space that could be mistaken for the South given its anti-Italian brand of racism and rural ways—they think "[h]e talks like they do in minstrel shows [. . .] like a colored man" (120). This observation seems to contrast with Quentin's cosmopolitan sheen, which is evident when he is at home and Herbert Head notes that "you dont look like these other hicks" (108). Indeed, in the Massachusetts countryside (the space that apparently most resembles his own home space), Quentin's "little sister" is an Italian, whose "two patent-leather pigtails" might be those of an African American (125). And despite Gerald's and Shreve's attempts to explain that Quentin comes of a good family and background, the country judge does not extend any of the privileges of empowerment that Quentin would have enjoyed at home (the privileges that Jason, in fact, takes advantage of). In the court scene, the configuration of center and periphery is slippery; Quentin is peripheral enough to the entire space of Massachusetts to be as nonwhite as the Italians, and yet he lives in the central location of Harvard (itself peripheral to Boston), and he cannot speak to the country judge (representative of the center of power in this peripheral space) any more than he can speak the tongue of the Italians (the peripheral figures in that space). The only noise he can make is that of his laughter, a Titus Andronicus–type expression of a complex intersection of powerful competing forces of control.

All of these elements of racial instability and problems of empowerment key into Egyptian place when Quentin chooses to drown himself, to cross over figuratively to a realm free from sexuality, race, and life in general; he is crossing over from Egypt to a land of freedom. Faulkner uses this trope of crossing in numerous instances. For example, in *Light in August* Joanna Burden's grandfather evokes the scene of Israelites crossing to articulate the perspective of the abolitionist, as he "got off on Lincoln and slavery and dared any man there to deny that Lincoln and the Negro and Moses and the children of Israel were the same, and that the Red Sea was just the blood that had been spilled in order that the black race might cross into the Promised Land" (251). His assertion becomes an incarnation in "Raid," the third section of *The Unvanquished,* when freed slaves follow Northern soldiers in their march through the area, chanting, "going to Jordan [. . .] Going to cross Jordan" (91). At length, they reach a river, and the bridge over it collapses in a manner that George W. Van Devender argues replicates the Red Sea's swallowing the Egyptians: the Jordan becomes instead the Red Sea, so that "[v]arious concepts have become confused in these people's minds: the Israelite Exodus with its crossing of the Red Sea, its conclusion, after forty years of wandering, with the crossing of the Jordan [. . .]" (146). In this event, which Van Devender calls a "black exodus," the slaves' escape to freedom goes sour, as "Canaan has turned out to be not heaven, not even a promised land on this earth, but a place of suffering and disillusionment, [. . .] their deliverers [. . .] Yankee soldiers who have made no real provisions with them, who find them at best a burden or a hindrance to the work of fighting of a war" (148). Just as the black characters' confusion of details both permits and undercuts their perspective, so exploiting the typical paradigm of white South as empowered Egypt and blacks as chosen people realigns those parallels to empower the Southern whites. For the "Red Sea" has swallowed the Northern "Egyptians," and as Van Devender notes, Granny Millard becomes Moses leading the chosen people (148), although it must be acknowledged that she merely appears on the scene in search of her silver, stolen by one of her former slaves.

At the heart of this hybrid motif of Jordan/Red Sea crossing is a dual configuration of center and periphery. One crosses the Jordan River into the Promised Land, which flows with milk and honey and lies bathed in the sunshine of freedom—a center one travels to from the periphery of the wilderness and the rootless activity of wandering. The crossing of the Red Sea, on the other hand, is an "exodus," a leaving of a center of oppression for the periphery of the wilderness. Exodus is perilous, fraught with the snapping of the oppressor's teeth at the fleeing heels of the oppressed; crossing the Jordan, on the other hand, is an imperial act invigorated by the assurance of prophesy and driven by a grand hegemony. And so in "Raid" is established a complex set of motives that not only identify white aristocratic slaveholding Southerners as the centered oppressors but also highlight a certain imperial hegemony in the freeing of the slaves, who not only are fleeing the center but hope to establish a new center. This element emerges clearly in "Skirmish at Sartoris," another section of *The Unvanquished,* in which John Sartoris and his band of men (plus Drusilla, a sexually liminal character) prevent the establishing of the black Cassius Q. Benbow (note the imperial implications of his Roman name) as marshal of Jefferson.

A scene of crossing also occurs in *As I Lay Dying,* but in a different context of race and class. On the way to Jefferson, the Bundrens must cross a swollen river with a sarcophagus of their own, one that Vardaman has already punctured. This crossing over is, again, both an exodus out of the country and an entry into the city, for the Bundrens are not merely taking Addie to her chosen burial ground; several of them also seek the amenities of town life. Anse, Cash, Dewey Dell, and Vardaman all want to align themselves with the centered culture of the town by obtaining teeth and a new town wife, a graphophone, an abortion, and bananas, respectively. Meanwhile, Jewel remains an Other, scuffling with a "town fellow" when they enter Jefferson (230); at the same time, Darl refuses to conform to this new value system and is removed to Jackson under the charge of insanity (however tenuous Cash suspects that "diagnosis" may be). Like the Texas pony he earns, Jewel may be harnessed, silenced, marginalized, and set to brood in some dusty corner of civilization, but his spirit remains that of the periphery, while those members of the family now settling in Jefferson gladly embrace the values of the center.[18]

Quentin's experience with the river in Massachusetts registers the same dynamics, for he simultaneously flees the problematics of sexuality and race in his life and strives to establish a new center of consolidation with "little sister Death." In one sense, Quentin occupies the position of the empowered Egyptians in his crossing of the Red Sea as the waters close upon him, but his drowning also clearly signifies a crossing over from the land of physicality, life, and time to a Platonic land of nonphysicality, death, and timelessness. He would use the traces of an Egypt-informed mythic layer to make his way into a marble faun's imagined world of eternal freedom, although this unchanging realm would also be devoid of the taint of sexuality so obviously present in the pagan mythic layer. Faulkner makes this theme of fleeing oppressed/invading colonizer explicit in the Compson Appendix, beginning with Quentin MacLachan and moving through Charles Stuart and the Jasons, who would establish the Compson presence in Yoknapatawpha County, "the solid square mile of land which some day would be almost in the center of the town of Jefferson" (707). Of course, Quentin is not black, and as has been noted, his difficulties as a manufactured counterfeit Other pale in comparison with the material oppression of the African American slaves in *The Unvanquished*.

At the center of *The Sound and the Fury* stands Caddy, and like Eula Varner, she is the queen, Cleopatra herself. Arguments about Cleopatra's racial and ethnic identity pervaded the nineteenth century, as Trafton shows; her body as sexualized icon occupied the center of the gaze of Orientalist discussion. So the racializing of the sexuality of Caddy occupies the obsessions of the Compson brothers. Quentin asks his sister, "*Why wont you bring him to the house, Caddy? Why must you do like nigger women do in the pasture the ditches the dark woods hot hidden furious in the dark woods*" (92). Jason's comment about Caddy's daughter also articulates his attitude toward Caddy: "When people act like niggers, no matter who they are the only thing to do is treat them like a nigger" (181). And from his liminal space of mixed blackness and whiteness, Benjy actually witnesses Caddy's sexual escapades in the pasture, his pasture. Although Caddy is the very center of the novel, in terms of its obsessions and its gaze, throughout the novel she lurks about the periphery, is almost wholly absent; when she is present, she is up in the trees or standing in a dark alley or waiting along the side of the road. When Quentin puts the point of a knife against her throat, he might just as well be putting the fangs of a snake against the breast of Cleopatra, and Caddy may be left for dead alongside the mummified bones of Nancy, the relic of Quentin's obsessions with her chastity (151–53).

With Caddy physically marginalized, her daughter becomes a center of attention, primarily for Jason, who enforces his dominance over her, hoarding the riches that are hers but that he considers rightfully his. On April 6, 1928, Quentin appears at the breakfast table dressed in a kimono, an Orientalized figure, a neo-Caddy-Cleopatra. When she defies her uncle's command that she put up her coffee cup and get dressed for school, he grabs her and attempts to drag her off and whip her; as he does so, her "kimono [comes] unfastened, flapping about her, dam near naked" (184). This scene evokes the nineteenth-century obsession with the undressing of Cleopatra; an iconography of the Egyptian queen developed that represented her as half-barbaric and half-civilized, half-Greek and half-Egyptian, half-dressed and half-undressed, one breast concealed and the other exposed. The Compson house itself, full as it is with the ghosts of the family's imperial past, is Quentin's own confining space, where she, daughter and copy of Caddy-Cleopatra, is, like nineteenth-century marble statues of Cleopatra, a body to be controlled yet one that is ultimately uncontrollable. Jason, the quintessential white southerner, tied in critical ways to the global market and having stolen the glories of ancient Egypt (whether in his involvement with the cotton market or in his stealing of Caddy/Quentin's treasures), is dispossessed in the end, the proud, white, aristocratic, imperial-tomb-raiding, Egypt-replicating southerner usurped by the resurrected Egypt.

Faulkner approached the story of the Compsons by means of repeated layers of myth generating, confirming, and questioning, and this same approach of primary, romantic, and consummatory mythmaking characterizes his treatment of another Cleopatra-like figure, whose throne stands for some time in Memphis, Temple Drake. Like Caddy, Temple is, in *Sanctuary,* the focus of a consistent and mostly male gaze, and as nineteenth-century artists and scholars would seek to undress Cleopatra, so the men in the novel would undress Temple. Lying in bed, "her hands crossed on her breast and her legs straight and close and decorous, like an effigy on an ancient tomb" (71), Temple is a mummy to be violated, and the criminal Popeye is more than happy to oblige. He then installs her in Reba's Memphis brothel, which presents itself as an Oriental, feminized, exoticized space, replete with "lithographs of spurious Greek scenes" (212) and women in robes like Temple's "spurious Chinese robe splotched with gold dragons and jade and scarlet flowers" (230). There Temple moves like Cleopatra from one lover to another, at least one of whom evokes Rome, for Gavin Stevens reveals in *Requiem for a Nun* that Popeye is part Italian (Red's name also perhaps signifies an Italian presence, as it echoes Major Ayers's misreading of the Italian Pete's features as Native American in *Mosquitoes*).

Reading Egypt into a novel that makes no explicit reference to it may be the worst sort of symbol mongering, but the presence of cotton, the Delta, and Memphis in Faulkner's mapping of center and periphery in *Sanctuary* suggest the mythic-material presence and relationship of both the ancient and the modern civilization of Egypt. The novel opens with Horace Benbow's exodus from the Delta: on his way from Kinston to Jefferson, he stops at a spring to drink. The motif of the spring, again, suggests Moses and the rock; moreover, Horace must cross the water that "flow[s] away [from the spring] upon a bottom of whorled and waved sand" (3) to enter what he thinks of as the Promised Land, his hometown of Jefferson. His experience in the Delta has been one of the "forced" labor of unloading shrimp for his wife, and he flees the entrapment of his relationship with Belle as well as that of his sexual attraction to/involvement with little Belle. The Delta space of Kinston thus renders Horace a servant to female control, and a similar situation arises when he goes to Reba's whorehouse in Memphis. Of course, Horace's subjugation to female control is not limited to Delta spaces; he is equally under the thumb of Aunt Jenny and Narcissa when he goes to Jefferson.

But reading Delta spaces in the novel as sites of unadulterated female empowerment oversimplifies the situation. For Reba's "Oriental" space is nonetheless constantly threatened by civil law: no matter how many policemen may patronize her business, she must be vigilant to prevent interference from the male-inscribed city law. The whorehouse, for whatever Oriental exoticism it evokes, is a peripheral space within the city and in its aberration does not necessarily contribute to an Egypt-informed portrait of Memphis. Furthermore, whatever power Temple might struggle to grasp, no matter how successfully she manipulates the men around her, she remains always the center of a controlling male gaze, always under the murderous control of Popeye; even her condemnation of Lee Goodwin must be articulated within a male courtroom. In the end, however much the novel attempts to marginalize Horace, he nevertheless emerges as yet another white male figure fetishized as an Other, when he is actually one of the Jefferson elite.

Requiem for a Nun, Faulkner's retelling/revisioning of not only Temple's story but also that of Jefferson and Yoknapatawpha County makes the encroachment of one layer of imperialization upon another explicit. It is in this hybrid work, both drama and novel, that Gavin Stevens famously pronounces, "The past is never dead. It's not even past" (535). It is also in this work that Faulkner offers the metaphor of the transparent layer with its signifying trace, noting regarding the glass with Cecilia Farmer's name etched on it that

> the faint frail illegible meaningless even inference-less scratching on the ancient poor-quality glass you stare at, has moved, under your eyes, even while you stared at it, coalesced, seeming actually to have entered into another sense than vision: a scent, a whisper, filling that hot cramped strange room already fierce with the sound and reek of frying pork-fat: the two of them in conjunction—the old milky obsolete glass, and the scratches on it: that tender ownerless obsolete girl's name and the old dead date in April almost a century ago—speaking, murmuring, back from, out of, across from, a time as old as lavender, older than album or stereopticon, as old as daguerreotype itself. (643–44)

Faulkner's discussion of successive imperial moments in the prose parts of the text includes an overture on cotton and its economic importance; he refers to the plant as "a commodity in the land now which until now had dealt first in Indians: then in acres and sections and boundaries:—an economy: Cotton: a king: omnipotent and omnipresent" (625). And although the text makes no specific reference to Egypt, Faulkner alludes to the plagues sent by Jehovah upon Egypt when he describes the arrival of carpetbaggers in the South as "a migration of locusts" (633).

At the center of the book, though no less at the mercy of white male aristocratic hegemony than in *Sanctuary,* stand Temple and Nancy Manigo, the two together making a Cleopatra-esque whole. Doubled as they are, they form the hybrid center, the two "whores." While Temple continues to be the center of the male gaze, she describes Nancy as the "nurse: guide: mentor, catalyst, glue, whatever you want to call it, holding the whole lot of them together—not just a magnetic center for the heir apparent and the other little princes or princesses in their orderly succession, to circle around" (579). Both women are incarcerated within the dictates of their *habitus,* their tragedies misunderstood by the men who largely control their destinies. And both women struggle to speak from their tortured center/margin positions, Nancy speaking in court when she should not and Temple trying to speak over Gavin's ceaseless controlling drone.

Faulkner's most extended meditation on the mythic place/layer of Egypt centers on the Beauchamp family in *Go Down, Moses* and *Intruder in the Dust.* The Egyptian context of the first novel is evident in its title, taken from the spiritual of the same name. The novel's primary focus is the oppression of African Americans, but it is important not to overlook the hybridity of the McCaslin-Beauchamp-Edmonds clan. The dynamics of oppression and empowerment within the trope of an Egypt-informed mythic layer are predictably complex and contradictory. Note the following exchange between a student and Faulkner at the University of Virginia:

> Q. I'd like to probe your question, your statement, that no nation can exist with second-class citizens. I'm not aware of any civilization either ancient or modern that has not in some form had second-class citizenry. For example, the Hellenic civilization probably reached its flower because the leisure of one class was made possible by the labors of one who were not only second-class citizens, but worse—I'm not defending second-class citizenship, but it seems that some civilizations exist not only in spite of it but in fact because of second-class citizenship. So I would like to know if there is historical precedent for your statement.
>
> A. This: I don't know any of those civilizations that have not had a second-class citizenship, but I don't know of any of them in which that second-class citizenship was an arbitrary condition compelled on the second-class citizen by the others. He found his own second-class level. He was not compelled to it by the color of his skin. If that second-class citizen could rise from his second-class citizenship he was allowed to, there was nothing to stop him. In our economy it's pretty hard for the Negro to get very far. That's the only difference.
>
> Q. In Egypt many thousands and tens of thousand and hundreds of thousands of workers were held in slavery, and they could not get out....
>
> A. True, but some of them broke out. You know Moses led a big gang out himself. (*Faulkner in the University* 219)

Faulkner's comments are striking because they blame a race for disunity while empowering it as capable of and thus responsible for the future of achieving that unity. The conversation leading to this sequence involves Faulkner's arguing that "[t]his nation cannot endure containing a minority as large as ten percent held second class in citizenship by accident of physical appearance" (209). Actually, Faulkner immediately contradicts himself, asserting that such relegation of class status may not occur by accident but rather because "perhaps the Negro is not yet capable of more than second-class citizenship" (210). Thus, white people in the South must make the black person "cease forever more thinking like a Negro and acting like a Negro" (211). Yet, in the lengthy exchange quoted, he asserts that second-class citizenship is an option the second-class citizenry chooses.

While Faulkner delivers his comment about Moses off the cuff, equating Moses and Israelites to slaves endows the latter with a will and dignity that masks what is in fact a double-edged problematic that ultimately serves white desire for control. The first aspect of this problematic is that African Americans may rise in status if they choose and that if they do not, it is their fault. Whites will not impede that rise—only the "economy" will do that—if for no other reason than that "we are a nation established on the fact that we are only ninety percent unified in power. With only ninety percent of unanimity, we would face (and hope to survive in it) an inimical world unified against us even if only in inimicality. We cannot be even ninety percent unified against that inimical world which outnumbers us, because too much of even that ninety percent of power is spent and consumed by the physical problem of the ten percent of irresponsibles" (210). The second problem in Faulkner's rhetoric, which ostensibly champions the slave's cause only to strengthen whites, is his maneuver of equalizing southern and northern whites. Faulkner, like certain other white southern writers, saw the North as spreading its imperial control over the South, and one way he saw to help loosen the North's grip and resuscitate the white South's cultural and political power was to write stories of reconciliation that elevated southern whites to the same level as northerners.[19] This equating was accomplished by setting the white southerner on an equal footing with white northerners against the black "second class," thus taking focus away from and eliding the difference in status between the northern and southern whites, and thereby equating the two and empowering southern whites. Southern whites then, rhetorically at least, rise beyond *their* second-class citizenship on the national scene. And then, ideally, with southern whites' help, African Americans should do so as well, in the interest of national unity, yet they *cannot* do so because they are incapable of rising to a higher level.

Egypt therefore suggested to Faulkner shifts in power and potentiality for freedom from oppression in a manner that *focuses* on the condition of southern blacks while actually *serving* the cause of southern whites. Accordingly, Faulkner's fictional treatment of Egypt in *Go Down, Moses* generally centers on African Americans and their drawing parallels between the Mississippi Delta and the biblical Egypt. Ostensibly, such a discussion of Egypt posits the South as the empowered Egypt, with white southerners representing Egyptians and African Americans representing Israelites. But Faulkner problematizes this dynamic in ways that undercut the black characters' situations and perspective and privilege the white characters' positions by subverting the North's superiority and control over white southerners, thus addressing the configuration of the Delta as a colonized region resembling modern British-controlled Egypt.

These maneuvers appear in the story "Go Down, Moses" when Mollie Beauchamp announces to Gavin Stevens, "whose serious vocation was a twenty-two-year-old unfinished translation of the Old Testament back into classic Greek," that "Roth Edmonds sold my Benjamin. Sold him in Egypt. Pharaoh got him—" (353). As in the renaming of Benjy in *The Sound and the Fury,* the allusion does not exactly explain because Joseph was the one sold into slavery in Egypt. Furthermore, the analogy initially seems inaccurate to Stevens, who remembers Samuel's turbulent, crime-filled youth: "at nineteen he had quit the country and come to town and spent a year in and out of jail for gambling and fighting" before running away from the area altogether (354–55). Later, though, Stevens reflects that Mollie's analogy does accurately describe the situation when he recalls that "it was Edmonds who had actually sent the boy to Jefferson in the first place" (355). To Mollie, then, Jefferson is Egypt in relation to the Edmonds plantation, but this rendering of Jefferson as the space of Egyptian bondage and the plantation as the place of Israelite freedom is a reversal of Faulkner's depiction of space in the earlier parts of the novel.

In "Was," Tommy's Terrel crosses a Jordan/Red Sea body of water on his way to romance Tennie, but the most he hopes for is to pass from one owner to another, remaining in slavery no matter what. In "The Bear," Fonsiba leaves the McCaslin plantation to live on a farm in Arkansas, which her husband calls "the new Canaan" (267), against which the Mississippi plantation is juxtaposed as an Egypt to be escaped. And in "Delta Autumn," Ike encounters a descendant of the offspring of Tommy's Terrel and Tennie and urges her to leave the oppressive Delta/Egypt for the North, where she can marry "a man in your own race" (346).

Ike's conception of the Delta should not be oversimplified, though. When Tennie's Jim's granddaughter leaves him, Ike reflects on

> This Delta. *This land which man has deswamped and denuded and derivered in two generations so that white men can own plantations and*

> *commute every night to Memphis and black men own plantations and ride in jim crow cars to Chicago to live in millionaires' mansions on Lakeshore Drive, where white men rent farms and live like niggers and niggers crop on shares and live like animals, where cotton is planted and grows man-tall in the very cracks of the sidewalks, and usury and mortgage and bankruptcy and measureless wealth, Chinese and African and Aryan and Jew, all breed and spawn together until no man has time to say which one is which nor cares [. . .].* (347)

Indeed, the Delta is such a space of amalgamation that even delineating differences between races is practically impossible. Gavin Stevens becomes conscious of this fact when Miss Worsham visits him, explains that she and Mollie "grew up as sisters would," and gives him twenty-five dollars to "take care of the immediate expenses" of having Samuel's body returned to Yoknapatawpha County (356–59).

By the end of "Go Down, Moses," Faulkner would have all of Yoknapatawpha part of one race. Mollie and her brother Hamp continue to see Jefferson as Egypt, chanting

> "Sold my Benjamin," she said. "Sold him in Egypt."
> "Sold him in Egypt," Worsham said.
> "Roth Edmonds sold my Benjamin."
> "Sold him to Pharaoh."
> "Sold him to Pharaoh and now he dead." (362)

But Gavin Stevens solicits money for the return and burial of Samuel's body from people in town, and when "the train [bearing Samuel's body] came in Stevens and the editor began to notice the number of people, Negroes and whites both" (363). The "people" here become one, Israelites receiving their own from the faraway Egypt of the North, where Samuel has literally been imprisoned and executed. The very context of the spiritual for which the story and the novel are named thus emerges as problematic: Go down in Egypt and let my people go—but what people? African Americans on the plantations? Native Americans in the Delta? The white people equally enslaved to their slaves and imprisoned by the curse of their oppressive heritage? Faulkner's answer, tortured as it is, seems to be yes, all of the above.

In the center of this heritage of amalgamation and mutual enslavement stands Lucas Beauchamp, the hybrid Other who, unlike most of

Faulkner's marble-faun figures, is a true Other who simultaneously refuses and seizes both the power and freedom of his white ancestry and the disempowerment and oppression of his black ancestry. Lucas in his stubbornness resembles another hybrid figure in the Faulknerian cosmos, one that Faulkner explicitly links with "the Negro": the mule. The link between the mule and "the Negro" appears most famously in *Flags in the Dust*:

> Some Cincinnatus of the cotton fields should contemplate the lowly destiny, some Homer should sing the saga, of the mule and of his place in the South. He it was, more than any one creature or thing, who, steadfast to the land when all else faltered before the hopeless juggernaut of circumstance, impervious to conditions that broke men's hearts because of his venomous and patient preoccupation with the immediate present, won the prone South from beneath the iron heel of Reconstruction and taught it pride again through humility and courage through adversity overcome; who accomplished the well-nigh impossible despite hopeless odds, by sheer and vindictive patience. Father and mother he does not resemble, sons and daughters he will never have; vindictive and patient (it is a known fact that he will labor ten years willingly and patiently for you, for the privilege of kicking you once); solitary but without pride, self-sufficient but without vanity; his voice is his own derision. Outcast and pariah, he has neither friend, wife, mistress nor sweetheart; celibate, he is unscarred, possesses neither pillar nor desert cave, he is not assaulted by temptations nor flagellated by dreams nor assuaged by visions; faith, hope and charity are not his. Misanthropic, he labors six days without reward for one creature whom he hates, bound with chains to another whom he despises, and spends the seventh day kicking or being kicked by his fellows. Misunderstood even by that creature (the nigger who drives him) whose impulses and mental processes most closely resemble his, he performs alien actions among alien surroundings; he finds bread not only for a race, but for an entire form of behavior; meek his inheritance is cooked away from him along with his soul in a glue factory. Ugly, untiring and perverse, he can be moved neither by reason, flattery, nor promise of reward; he performs his humble monotonous duties without complaint, and his meed is blows. Alive, he is haled through the world, an object of general execration; unwept and unsung, he bleaches his awkward, accusing bones among rusting cans and broken crockery and worn-out automo-

bile tires on lonely hillsides, while his flesh soars unawares against the blue in the craws of buzzards. (313–15)[20]

I quote this passage at length to show that here, in the germ of Faulkner's apocrypha, lies the blueprint for the architecture of Faulkner's African Americans. Here are Nancy's bones bleaching in the sun in "That Evening Sun" and *The Sound and the Fury*. Here is Quentin's observation that being a "Negro" is a form of behavior. And here, too, is the image of the hybrid, which, ironically, Faulkner clearly applies to "Negro," the stubborn figure who exhibits the same "passive recalcitrance" of the Faulknerian soil that Ike McCaslin dwells on obsessively. Here, in short, is Lucas Beauchamp.

While Lucas wields multiple imperial positions in different situations, his primary role is that of tomb raider. With his Grecian name, Lucas emerges as a sort of black marble faun prepared to operate in the capacity of Greco-Roman to use the treasures of Egypt to construct his own glory. "The Fire and the Hearth" primarily follows Lucas's efforts to find and exhume the riches of the McCaslins in a sequence that very much resembles Ratliff's search for treasure in *The Hamlet*. Attempting to hide his moonshine still by burying it in an "Indian mound," Lucas discovers a shard of broken pottery and a coin. This discovery illustrates the simultaneity of successive imperial epochs—Native American, European American, and African American—showing the presence of those opaque traces of past civilizations in the earth. The progression began with the "nameless though recorded predecessors who built the mounds to escape the spring floods and left their meager artifacts," as Faulkner states it in *Requiem for a Nun,* and moved through the successive "obsolete and the dispossessed, dispossessed by those who were dispossessed in turn because they too were obsolete" (541). The new dispossessors are the African Americans, as Fonsiba's husband says to Ike in "The Bear": "You're wrong. The curse you whites brought into this land has been lifted. It has been voided and discharged. We are seeing a new era, an era dedicated, as our founders intended it, to freedom, liberty and equality for all" (267).

Lucas manipulates Chick Mallison as his helper in another tomb-raiding/punctured-earth scenario in *Intruder in the Dust* (the title itself suggests the intrusion of burial chambers). In fact, Faulkner had depicted a scene in which a sepulcher is punctured and a mummy is found in "A Rose for Emily." When the townsmen break down the door to Emily Grierson's bedroom with a violence that "seemed to fill this room with pervading dust," they find that a "thin, acrid pall as of the tomb seemed to lie everywhere upon this room decked and furnished as for a bridal," or perhaps for a journey into the afterlife with accompanying treasures, as they find it "upon the dressing table, upon the delicate array of crystal and the man's toilet things backed with tarnished silver" (120–30). The body of Homer Barron itself bears a "profound and fleshless grin," and "[w]hat was left of him [was] rotted beneath what was left of [his] nightshirt" (130). Homer, named after the Greek poet, represents a seeping through of a Grecian-informed mythic layer of Old South poetics now obsolete and dispossessed in a new epoch.

In *Intruder in the Dust* a body must be taken out of the ground in order to prove Lucas's innocence. Charged with and arrested for the murder of Vinson Gowrie, Lucas urges Charles Mallison to exhume the body to inspect the gunshot wounds, which would prove that Lucas's gun had not been used. But when Chick, Aleck Sander (Alex-ander?), and Miss Habersham arrive at the Caledonia cemetery, they find the tomb already raided and Jake Montgomery's body in the coffin instead. Just as Miss Worsham helped Mollie retrieve her son's body in "Go Down, Moses," here, incarnated as Miss Habersham, she helps Lucas. Significantly, representatives of marginalized groups manage to "speak," to empower themselves, by means of the Egyptian trope of the punctured earth/mummy unwrapping, as women, African Americans, and (in the context of the novel) children defy the overarching cultural myth that demands, in its "few simple clichés," that it see "the nigger acting like a nigger and the white folks acting like white folks and no real hard feelings on either side" (320).

The premise of *Intruder in the Dust* resembles that of *Pylon,* but the outcome is more hopeful. In the earlier novel, the child Jack Shumann cannot carry the banner of a new race sprung from the amalgamation of the earth to colonize the sky because he finds himself grounded. In the later novel, Charles Mallison might be the white man who can carry southern society a step farther even than Ike McCaslin by joining forces on more equal terms with women and African Americans. Clearly, Gavin Stevens, with his tiresome and endless defense of the South's "privilege of setting [Sambo] free ourselves" (400–401), cannot conceive of race relations in terms that are not defensive of the aristocratic white South's racist attitudes and past. Stevens is constantly aware of place, whether it be Beat Four or Freedman Town, but it is Charles who in the very first episode related in the novel has both fallen into and then crossed the Red Sea/ Jordan River into the Promised Land domain in which Lucas dwells and which he rules. It is Charles, fished out of the icy creek on the Edmonds plantation as Moses was drawn from Egyptian waters, who might be the leader of a new dawn for Yoknapatawpha race relations.

It is important not to read Faulkner's seemingly hopeful vision of the future of southern race relations too exuberantly or too naively, but it is also important to note that within a set of signifying tropes on the mythic place and imperial space of Egypt, Faulkner would have his marginalized groups—women, Native Americans, poor whites, and especially African Americans—speak. Reverend Shegog, Mollie Beauchamp, and Lucas (who has the last word in *Intruder in the Dust*) all speak in ways that resist containment at the same time that they negotiate the containment of white supremacy they cannot escape. On the other hand, Jason Compson, a white male character who embraces, enforces, and promotes his supremacy within a context of economic competition with Egypt, finds himself under the thumb of Egyptian mythic place, held under a gaze that supersedes even his own empowered white gaze as his niece evades his grasp. However problematic the empowerment of marginalized groups may be, the poetic of Egypt offers a subversive economy of speech and signifying that results from the richness of the matrix of myth and empire, place and space.

CHAPTER FOUR

Fabulous Immeasurable Camelots and Carcassonnes
The Quest of Imperialism

For there is death in the sound of it, and a glamorous fatality, like silver pennons downrushing at sunset, or a dying fall of horns along the road to Roncevaux.

—*Flags in the Dust*

The influence of the Arthurian legend is strong and ubiquitous in Faulkner's writing. Scholars have not failed to comment on this fact, although they tend to address more generally chivalric elements in the work rather than to explicate Faulkner's specific uses of Arthurian material.[1] Also, scholars have typically seen the chivalric-Arthurian vision as being located in the narratives of the aristocratic white South, a means by which that group might articulate its nostalgia for a lost civilization and its greatness. Recent scholarly attention to the hegemony of the white aristocratic narrative suggests reading this nostalgia as a trick of the aristocrat who marginalizes him or herself, the tortured narrative of the counterfeit Other. While this often "invisible" aspect of the chivalric-Arthurian white aristocratic southern narrative appears in the Faulknerian cosmos, it should be noted that Faulkner's use of the legend does not inform southern contexts only, but rather what Faulkner would probably posit as a "universal," transcendent dynamic of human interactions and mythmaking that includes not only aristocratic white southerners but even such unempowered figures as poor whites.

The Arthurian legend utilizes a rhetoric that provides a usable antetype for the aristocratic southern narrative that informs so much of the context of Faulkner's writing, for its rhetoric articulates victory and defeat simultaneously. Britain, and specifically Camelot, are sites of contestation, liminal sites where one empire falls to another as a new civilization supersedes the one before it, building mythic-imperial layers that render a bricolage that registers a binding thread of translation of empire. The narrative thus is characterized by successive victories, the converse of which are successive defeats; in this half-full, half-empty sort of manner, England developed as a nation-state with a mythology of simultaneous victory and loss, with a hero who even in defeat prophesied a second coming and the promise of more victory. Camelot was both beautiful and corrupt, chivalric and dishonorable, victorious and doomed. Furthermore, like New Orleans, the legend offered Faulkner a place-model of mythic-imperial development and a vivid example of the assembly of bricolage and its resulting palimpsest.

The legend of King Arthur, Camelot, and the deeds of the Knights of the Round Table originated in historical and pseudohistorical documents of the early Middle Ages.[2] The king's historical moment is the late fifth and early sixth centuries, when the Angles, Saxons, and Jutes invaded his home island, Britain. Arthur was said to have led forces against the invaders, which is ironic in light of the fact that many people who would later glorify him were of Saxon stock. As Arthurian myths developed, the hero-warrior-king now known as Arthur became transformed from a Roman into a Briton and ultimately into an Englander, a movement that highlights the translation of empire in the mythic place of Camelot. The first mention of the figure later to be identified as Arthur appears in 540, when the monk Gildas, in *De exidio et conquestu britanniae,* discusses an Ambrosius Aurelianus, of royal Roman descent, who defeated the Saxons in an unnamed battle.[3] In 731 Bede repeated Gildas's account in his *Historia ecclesiastica gentis anglorum.* The name Arthur first appeared about 800, in Nennius's *Historia brittonum;* apparently, Nennius changed the name Ambrosius to Arthur. The *Annales Cambriae* records the information on the "Year [516] The Battle of Badon, in which Arthur carried the Cross of our Lord Jesus Christ on his shoulders for three days and three nights, and the Britons were victorious" (Brengle 7); the list also introduces the name Medraut, which anticipates Mordred. And in his *Gesta Regum Anglorum* (1125) William of Malmesbury offers the ambivalent simultaneity of signifiers peculiar to such a bricolage when he suggests that the Britons "would have [. . .] immediately perished [at the hands of invading Saxons] had not Ambrosius—alone of the Romans surviving, who reigned as king after Vortigern—overpowered the presumptuous barbarians with the distinguished service of the warlike Arthur" (Brengle 8).

From these pseudohistorical accounts and verbal legends, various writers/historians pieced together full narratives of Arthur's life and the lives of those connected with him. Geoffrey of Monmouth in 1130 composed a narrative of Arthur's entire life and death in *The History of the Kings of Britain,* positioning Arthur as the last and greatest of Britain's kings, whose defeat by his nephew, Mordred, marks the end of that civilization. It is in Geoffrey's romantic mythmaking account that the wizard Merlin first appears. And Sir Gawain is the chief among Arthur's knights, as he continues to be in the English tradition of the legend's development, while Lancelot, the Round Table, and the French form of chivalry do not appear at all. After Geoffrey, French and English writers further developed the legend by adding new characters, events, and themes to his story. In France, Wace and Layamon translated Geoffrey's work in 1155 and 1174, respectively, adding numerous embellishments, such as the Round Table. In the mid-twelfth century, in a series of stories Chrétien de Troyes added the story of Tristan and Iseult—which accentuated and developed chivalry in the legend—and introduced and positioned Lancelot du Lak as the foremost knight of the Round Table. In England, the late-fourteenth-century *Sir Gawain and the Green Knight* focused on Gawain's ongoing preservation of his honor. And the anonymous *Alliterative Morte Arthure* combined the British and French legends into one account, presenting the story of King Arthur's life and death while also chronicling many of the exploits of his knights and their ladies. Of these grand tellings of the Arthurian legend, the grandest and most influential on future generations was Sir Thomas Malory's *Le Morte Darthur.* This work, first printed in 1485, gathered practically all of the known stories pertaining to Arthur and his companions into twenty-one books to form what is at times an awkward but engaging text of primary, romantic, and at times even consummatory mythmaking.

The basic Arthurian story resulting from these texts begins with Arthur's unusual birth and ends with his questionable death. Uther Pendragon and Igraine, the wife of Gorlois, Duke of Cornwall, beget him when Merlin tricks her by magically transforming Uther into Gorlois's likeness. As it happens, Uther's men kill Gorlois before Arthur's conception. Arthur becomes king at age fifteen, when Uther dies. With Merlin's help, he quells Saxon and Roman enemies and establishes his kingdom's center in Camelot, where he installs the system of honor that comes to be known as chivalry. While there, he marries Guinevere and sets up the Knights of the Round Table. Lancelot du Lak comes from France to join this group of warriors, and he becomes one of Arthur's greatest knights. Lancelot immediately falls in love with Guinevere, and Guinevere with him. At length, Mordred, Arthur's nephew, creates an alliance with Arthur's enemies and attacks Arthur, who is killed and taken to Avalon to be buried, though actually he disappears and no one knows whether he is dead or alive or whether he might some day return to lead the Britons again.

By this point in the legend's development, the theme of loss had changed from a fall due to external forces to a collapse from conflicts within. In the historical accounts, all of Arthur's victories, though glorious, do not stay the oncoming defeat at the hands of the Saxons. His reign is the one bright spot in a story of destruction. Beginning with Geoffrey (though he too considered his work to be historical), that loss comes not only at the hands of invading Saxons but also from conflict and treachery within Arthur's own realm. Geoffrey presents Mordred as Arthur's nephew, who forms alliances with Scots and Picts and others who hate Arthur. They defeat and kill Arthur. All of his fighting takes place during the Britons' final demise. In his text, Malory further tightened the interrelations among the characters by making Arthur kin to many Camelot inhabitants and by infusing his character with a democratic quality and position resulting from Merlin's having raised him in a nonroyal setting. The story of Arthur and his knights becomes a family saga by Malory's positioning the wife of King Lot of Orkney, who is Sir Gawain's mother, as Arthur's sister. Before Arthur realizes their relationship, he begets Mordred by her. Because of these realigned kinships, the fall of Arthur's kingdom comes not only from within the nation and family but from a father-son dynamic.

Malory was the last significant writer to attempt a complete treatment of the Arthurian legend until Tennyson did so in *Idylls of the King*. Between Malory and Tennyson (the latter of whom drew heavily on the former), most writers used the legend as a backdrop to inform their own narratives. For example, Edmund Spenser made an Arthurian world the setting of *The Faerie Queene,* and the Red Cross knight is certainly a questing hero in the tradition of Ivain and Galahad. Additionally, Pre-Raphaelite writers and artists revisited Arthurian characters and themes in a nineteenth-century Arthurian revival that would lead to Tennyson's work. By this time Arthur was no longer a champion of the Britons but of England, and the themes of loss that had so thoroughly characterized the works from Geoffrey to Malory were less important than the theme of Arthur's return, specifically the return of the greatness of Camelot in the form of the greatness of the British Empire. Camelot as a mythic place now symbolized the British imperial impulse.

Another nineteenth-century writer who used the Arthurian legend as a backdrop against which to work out narratives of resistance was Sir Walter Scott. Writing before the Pre-Raphaelites and Tennyson and articulating the political situation of Scotland rather than that of England, Scott accentuated the perspective of the loser, the oppressed, the threatened Camelot. Writing from a peripheral space not unlike the U.S. South, Scott found in the chivalric world of a romantic past the possibilities for heroes in Scottish history. Scott is important because it is his work that serves as the most visible basis for the chivalric elements in the white aristocratic literature of the U.S. South. William Taylor explains the cultural shifts that fueled aristocratic championing of the feudal-chivalric elements in Scott's romances from the United States' beginnings and into the nineteenth century and that appear in the writing of George Tucker *(The Valley of the Shenandoah)*, James Kirk Paulding *(Westward Ho!)*, William Alexander Caruthers *(The Kentuckian in New York, The Cavaliers of Virginia,* and *The Knights of the Horseshoe)*, and Beverly Tucker *(The Partisan Leader and George Balcombe)*. As Taylor notes, throughout the nineteenth century, aristocratic white southerners went so far as to stage jousting tournaments and medieval masquerades (the party aboard *The White Rose of Memphis* being an excellent example of such a performative spectacle). Indeed, by 1874 Mark Twain was lambasting Sir Walter Scott for driving "the [southern] people mad [. . .] with his medieval romances. Admiration of his fantastic heroes and their grotesque 'chivalry' doings and romantic juvenilities still survives here" (332–33).

In noting the presence of generally chivalric elements in nineteenth-century aristocratic southern writing, it is important not to overlook the specific influences of the Arthurian legend. Writing in the 1830s, William Gilmore Simms and John Pendleton Kennedy looked primarily to Scott's world to paint their portraits of chivalric aristocratic southern culture. These writers were building another Scotland, having their characters speak from a peripheral space, a more genteel and romantic sphere that was beginning to see itself as different from the northern states. Their developing South had not yet fallen but was rather an alternative space, a space apart. However, after the South's defeat in war, as Lucinda MacKethan has suggested, "the plantation literature that arose from the ashes of the past had as its primary quality a tone of nostalgia evoking, without questioning, an aura of Camelot" ("Plantation Fiction" 211). The world of Scott would inform the Ku Klux Klan–dominated world of Thomas Dixon, while in the writing of Thomas Nelson Page, the South's foremost writer of reconciliation, it is Tennyson's name that appears, articulating not only the nostalgia of loss but the promise of resurgence, the hegemony of the New South in its drive to attain cultural ascendancy.

This period saw the birth of the Lost Cause myth, a sort of bricolage that exemplified the translation of empire so manifest in the Arthurian legend. In addition to explaining the marked religiosity of the Lost Cause myth, which in fact served as a civil religion in the South, Charles Reagan Wilson observes that an

> important aspect of Southern mythmaking was the tendency of ministers to place their myth in the context of other legends and past history, suggesting that they were aware of their function as mythmakers. Clergymen alluded to the Arthurian tales, visualizing the Confederates "on a field of chivalry more glorious than any since the Round Table." Southerners identified with another lost cause, the failed Scottish rebellion immortalized in the novels of Sir Walter Scott. Another popular comparison was with the ancient Greek heroes. In a 1905 oration the Episcopal minister and Confederate veteran Randolph McKim claimed that the Southern heroes were not matched by Agamemnon, Achilles, Ulysses, Ajax, Militiades, "nor by Leonidas himself at Thermopylae." After considering the ancients, the Baptist preacher S. A. Goodwin, at the time of Jefferson Davis's funeral in 1889, insisted that "In all the galaxy of fame there is no brighter constellation than that of the 'Heroes of the Lost Cause.'" (*Baptized in Blood* 39)

While the aristocratic white South clung to the heroic-chivalric worlds of Scott and Tennyson, the Arthurian legend elsewhere entered into a strikingly consummatory phase of development, signaled by J. M. Dent's edition of Malory's *Le Morte Darthur*. Reacting to the prudery of Tennyson's *Idylls,* this new edition of Malory, published between 1893 and 1894, repackaged the text, which was risqué enough on its own, in the context of illustrations by Aubrey Beardsley. Beardsley's drawings resulted in what Edmund V. Gillon Jr. refers to as "a Malory such as the world has never seen, with fauns and satyrs peering from behind trees, and greater nudity and sexual frankness than one associates with the Middle Ages"

(Beardsley v). Actually, Beardsley's drawings simply accentuated sexuality that was already present in Malory's work, but Dent's edition presented *Le Morte Darthur* as a reaction not only to alleged medieval abstemiousness but also, more significantly, to Victorian repression of explicit sexuality in art and in the Arthurian legend. The Dent edition both launched the Beardsley look, which was soon imitated by other artists, and resurrected Malory's power of presenting the mythic truth of the Arthurian legend.

The Dent edition influenced a number of U.S. writers, the most influential of whom in turn was James Branch Cabell, who satirized the Arthurian legend. Cabell's numerous Arthurian works include *Jurgen,* the 1923 edition of which featured illustrations by Ray F. Coyle drawn in the Beardsley style. This novel, which particularly influenced Faulkner, relates the adventures of a pawnbroker named Jurgen who has a "high-spirited [wife] with no especial gift for silence . . . [whom] people by ordinary call Dame Lisa" (9). Walking home one evening, he encounters a Cistercian monk who, mad about tripping over a brick, stands cursing the devil. Jurgen chides him and defends the devil, an action that the devil, whom Jurgen meets later down the street, rewards by ridding him of his termagant wife. The devil then sends him on a quest through a realm filled with satyrs and nymphs. Most of his activities during this trek involve affairs with such famous beauties as the Lady of the Lake and Guinevere. Jurgen welcomes these adventures after being tormented so long by Dame Lisa's incessant scolding. But in the end, he finds these relationships unsatisfying. The novel concludes with Jurgen's being offered the most beautiful women of all time, including, ultimately, Helen of Troy. He rejects them all and returns to his wife and her scolding, for he realizes that "as a man gets on in life he changes in many ways. He handles a sword and lance less creditable, and does not carry as heavy staff as he once flourished" (351).

Jurgen and the Dent edition of *Le Morte Darthur* had a powerful influence on Faulkner's developing art, and this influence appears most explicitly in his one expressly Arthurian work, *Mayday*. A hand-lettered, illustrated, and bound novella, *Mayday* relates the quest of a knight named Galwyn of Arthgyl for his ideal woman, whom he envisions in a stream at the novella's beginning. She has a face "all young and red and white, and with long shining hair like a column of fair sunny water" (50). Traveling with embodiments of Hunger and Pain, Galwyn encounters three women who remind him of his ideal: Yseult, Elys, and Aelia. But when none of them can hold his attention, his companion Hunger beckons Galwyn to see his sister. Galwyn finds that the face he saw in the water was that of Hunger's sister, whose name is Death. Seeing her, Galwyn steps "forward into the water and Hunger and Pain went away from him, and as the water touched him it seemed to him that he knelt in a dark room waiting for day and that one like a quiet soft shining came to him, saying: 'Rise Sir Galwyn; be faithful, fortunate, and brave'" (87). Now drowned, Galwyn has escaped the pain and loss of life, and the beautiful maiden is his forever.

Mayday's plot and presentation derive most directly from *Jurgen* and also draw from numerous Arthurian texts, but the novella conforms to the precedent set by the Dent edition of *Le Morte Darthur*. Cleanth Brooks notes in his article "The Image of Helen Baird in Faulkner's Early Poetry and Fiction" that Faulkner's Arthurian prose style ultimately links back to *Le Morte Darthur*. The title evokes Malory's use of May as a motif of ironic contrast between beauty and tragedy. The impact of Dent's edition is most evident in Faulkner's illustrations, which Alan and Barbara Tepa Lupack suggest were "influenced by Aubrey Beardsley's designs for *Morte d'Arthur*" (173). A comparison of Faulkner's frontispiece and an illustration from the Dent edition shows striking similarities in terms not only of style but even of composition. Beardsley's image of Arthur's symbolic dream, with Pan and a pathway curving up toward Camelot and intersected by a crescent-shaped dragon, furnishes Faulkner's image of the entire dream that is Galwyn's life, with its swath of light situated between Hunger, a smooth, rounded figure, and Pain, with its jagged head. *Mayday* offers an example of a way Faulkner explores the multivalence of mythic language. The Arthurian legend serves as an excellent model for Faulkner's art because it contains both hegemonic and subversive aspects; the romantic Tennyson and the ironic Cabell both ply their trade within the rich and flexible economy of the Arthurian legend. At the same time, the legend offers a tremendous functioning example of the layering of mythic place, as it contains Greek, Roman, and British places as parts of the foundations of Camelot.[4]

Indeed, Faulkner thoroughly understood the imperial element of the Arthurian legend. This awareness, as well as the subversions of empire through the enabling structure of mythic place, may be noted in a New Orleans sketch that has been mentioned several times already, "Mirrors of Chartres Street." This sketch represents a slice of Faulknerian cosmos that manifests its mythic-imperial strata. In this New Orleans site, Egyptian, Greek, Roman, and now Arthurian layers may be identified. Again, this story features a tramp with "eyes wild and soft as a faun's," who claims for himself a room of his own in a New Orleans of which "those who carved those strange flat-handed creatures on the Temple of Rameses must have dreamed" (16). To these Greco-Roman and Egyptian elements, discussed above, might be added the narrator's description of the protagonist's "untrammelled spirit" as "the heaven-sent attribute for finding life good which enabled the Jews to give young Jesus of Nazareth with two stars in His eyes, sucking His mother's breast, and a fairy tale that has conquered the whole Western earth, which gave King Arthur to a dull world, and sent baron and knight and lads who had more than coronets to flap pennons in Syria, seeking a dream" (16). For Faulkner, then, the Arthurian legend is the great imperial narrative of Christianity, the dream of Camelot driving the Western quest for control of the East, and the white project of dominating the dark. Christ and Arthur, with their utopian visions, codes of honor, and promises of resurrection, are inextricable in Faulkner's cosmos. And Camelot just as much as Jerusalem is a place that signifies a Christian layer of narrative.

Camelot itself emerges as yet another liminal place in Faulkner. On one hand, it is a center of chivalry and virtue, a place to rally crusaders in their conquering of the periphery, the center of an empire. On the other hand, it is a place in a "dark" world threatened not only by outside forces but also by evil that has crept inside its pristine walls, falling partly at the hands of a marauding victimizer, partly because of inner turmoil, and partly (when viewed through the lens of Faulknerian rhetoric) because of flaws inherent in imperial projects to which the imperializer is blind. Camelot's hegemonic iconography of the cross in the crusade represents a crossroads; this same iconography parallels the geographical layout of Jefferson because, as Ruzicka shows, Faulkner transforms the actual road layout of the Oxford, Mississippi, square into that of a crossroads in the Jefferson, Mississippi, square (57). Indeed, the paths of imperializer and imperialized cross in the very mythic place that occupies a center of Faulkner's fictional efforts.

The liminality of Camelot is best demonstrated in Rosa Coldfield's pairing of that mythic city with another city of peculiar historic significance in terms of the Crusades: Carcassonne. Describing Thomas Sutpen's distracted behavior during his return after defeat in the Civil War, Rosa notes that he "sounded like the bombast of a madman who creates within his very coffin walls his fabulous immeasurable Camelots and Carcassonnes. Not absent from the place, the arbitrary square of earth which he had named Sutpen's Hundred [. . . who] would not even pause for breath before undertaking to restore his house and plantation as near as possible to what it had been" (129). Located in southern France, the city of Carcassonne was a unique one in Western history in that it was actually a target *of* crusaders in the late twelfth and early thirteenth centuries. The city was a center of a religion named Catharism, which saw itself as Christian but was anti-Catholic, a stance that brought on the fury of Pope Innocent III in the form of the Albigensian Crusade.[5] This conflict congealed around oppositions between northern "France" and southern "Provence," between the Catholic and the heretic, between competing centers of culture. What Faulkner apparently saw was another case similar to that of the U.S. South in which a type of imperial project normally reserved for the Other (those further South than the inhabitants of Provence, the Moors) was aimed at and carried out in a space in-between, not quite the East and yet not exactly the West. Eiko Owada observes that as "a response to 'an internal threat,' the Albigensian Crusade [. . .] was a massacre of Christians by Christians" (129), but the true horror of the story that would have registered with Faulkner was that the victims of the crusade were, in fact, counterfeit Others, Europeans who were not quite Europeans, "Christians" who were not Catholics, in short, proto–white aristocratic southerners.

Faulkner develops the ambivalence of Carcassonne as a mythic place in an early story entitled "Carcassonne." The story has a number of things in common with "Black Music," as it is set in Rincon and the protagonist sleeps under tarred roofing paper just as Midgleston does in a building owned, in this story, by the "Standard" rather than the "Universal" Oil Company. As Robert Hamblin has noted, Carcassonne emerges as a "symbol of imaginative invention [. . .] identified not with the real world, with actuality, but with a private, inner vision that opposes and negates" reality (148–49).[6] As a mythic place, the city overlays the port of Rincon. The narrator carries on a conversation between his self-in-his-mind and his self-in-his-bones, imagining that he is riding a Norman steed in a crusade rather than lying around as a tramp in a Caribbean port. Reading Camelot back across Carcassonne as a place helps explain the ambivalence of the Arthurian mythic place in Faulkner's art. Sutpen (in Rosa's mind) builds Camelots and Carcassonnes because both cities resist the outer world, resist the hegemonies of larger political systems. Both purport to be bright spots of resistance in the world around them. And both are composed of mythic-imperial layers. At the same time, both places are part of Western imperializing imagined communities, the one located in empire-building England, the other in France. Both are spaces of victimizers and victimized. And both have a markedly "southern" flavor, Camelot because of its appropriations in aristocratic white U.S. writing and Carcassonne as a literal "southern" European city characterized by resistance and liminality like that Faulkner recognized in the U.S. South. Furthermore, both locations exemplify mythic-imperial layering, as Hamblin further notes that Carcassonne survived "centuries of war and empire-building" (151) in a manner resembling the history of the construction of New Orleans.

Regarding the function of chivalric literature–Arthurian myth in southern contexts, it might first be noted that Faulkner's Mississippi abounds with aristocrats who must negotiate the chivalric values their *habitus* demands that they adopt. Unable to "get religion and that galloping cavalry and his dead grandfather shot from the galloping horse untangled from each other, even in the pulpit" (*Light in August* 62), Gail Hightower seems the quintessential priest of the Lost Cause civil religion described by Charles Reagan Wilson. Virginia Du Pre, with her "high-bridged Norman nose," thinks that Carolina Bayard's "face wore that expression of frank and high-hearted dulness which you visualize Richard First as wearing before he went crusading" (*Flags in the Dust* 33, 14). And riding his horse, Jupiter, Colonel John Sartoris, modeled on Colonel Falkner (the "Knight of the Black Plume," whose killing of Thomas Hindman was precipitated by his allegedly having black-balled the latter in an election for membership in the Knights of Temperance), seems the quintessential southern chivalric aristocrat; indeed, his library includes "a complete Walter Scott, a complete Fenimore Cooper, a paper-bound Dumas complete, too, save for the volume which [he] lost from his pocket at Manassas (retreating, he said)" (*The Unvanquished* 16).

Quentin Compson is a central aristocratic-chivalric figure. Described by Herbert Head as a "half-baked Galahad" (*The Sound and the Fury* 110), Quentin constantly fails as a chivalric knight. In fact, as scholars have noted, Quentin is a reworked version of Galwyn of Arthgyle, as the two share character traits and dialogue. In *Mayday* Galwyn looks into a stream, encounters the personification of Time, speaks with St. Francis of Assisi, and drowns, choosing death in an attempt to obtain eternal love.

In *The Sound and the Fury* Quentin ponders the passing of time, stands on a bridge looking into a stream, imagines talking with St. Francis of Assisi, and drowns to escape the fleeting chastity of his sister, Caddy. He fails to perform the cavalier role Mrs. Bland expects him to play; at the same time, though, he succeeds where Gawain in the Arthurian tales fails, for despite his claims to the contrary, he seems never to have soiled himself with physical consummation of love. Mrs. Bland draws a distinction between the aristocratic southern cavalier and "ignorant lowclass Yankees" (146), highlighting the distinctness of the South as Camelot, the bright spot of high-class virtue in a dark and low-class world that is mere periphery to the chivalric center. Much of Quentin's section in *The Sound and the Fury* focuses on the experience of southerners away from southern spaces, developing a theme of quixotic displacement here spatial, where Quixote's displacement is temporal. This displacement is central to the Arthurian quest, in which the values of Camelot are carried into the dark periphery. The Arthurian quest charts not merely the journey and ordeals of the hero but also the portability and endurance of the hero's *habitus*. Chivalry must be carried as a torch, an imperial project that calls to mind the Baptist preacher Faulkner describes in "Mississippi."

Whereas Mrs. Bland articulates a white aristocratic conviction that the white South beams the all-healing light, the movement of the quest in *The Reivers* suggests a different trajectory in which a journey into the heart of darkness of moral degradation provides vital education in more dynamic and, ideally, more productive social strategies and interaction. Lucius Priest encounters the same whorehouse Temple Drake stays at in *Sanctuary*, an "Oriental" space, the target of a crusade. When the dwarf Otis (a figure resembling the dwarfs in the tales of Chrétien de Troyes) speaks disparagingly of Everbe's activities as a prostitute, Lucius assumes the role of chivalric champion and attacks him. Although Boon accuses him of being eleven "years old [. . .] and already knife-cut in a whore house brawl," Everbe, dressed in a kimono, realizes that Lucius "fought because of me. I've had people—drunks—fighting over me, but you're the first one ever fought for me" (854).[7] From the beginning of his visit to Reba's whorehouse, Lucius continually "makes his manners" and thereby models and exemplifies the "culture" that Everbe has brought Otis to Memphis to learn about. And Lucius comes from a mythically established and promoted line of chivalric figures: before he and Boon steal his grandfather's car and depart for Memphis, he describes his social superiority to

Boon, noting that "secure behind that inviolable and inescapable rectitude concomitant with the name I bore, patterned on the knightly shapes of my male ancestors as bequeathed—nay, compelled—to me by my father's word-of-mouth, further bolstered and made vulnerable to shame by my mother's doting conviction, I had been merely testing Boon; not trying my own virtue but simply testing Boon's capacity to undermine it [. . .]" (765–66). When Lucius's trip is over and he has to learn how to live with his unvirtuous ways, his grandfather explains to him that he can live with his wrongs because a "gentleman always does. A gentleman can live through anything. He faces anything. A gentleman accepts the responsibility of his actions and bears the burden of their consequences, even when he did not himself instigate them but only acquiesced to them, didn't say No though he knew he should" (969).

In *The Reivers*, chivalry emerges as the behavioral medium that binds classes and races together in an enveloping patriarchal hegemony. The Priests represent the aristocratic figures, but nonaristocratic characters form connections with them based on chivalric principles.[8] For example, Lucius (in the role of grandfather speaking to his grandchildren) explains that John Powell's gun was a moral problem for both John and his father, "and both of them knew it and handled it as mutual gentleman must and should" (729), so that when Boon takes John's gun, "the whole edifice of *entendre-de-noblesse* collapsed into dust" (730): although John is not an aristocrat, he and Lucius's father can form an alliance in a gentleman's agreement, as it were. Boon Hogganbeck, the third party in this particular triangle, also operates within a chivalric code as he steals the gun in order to shoot Ludus because Ludus has insulted him and he, Boon, "aint even got any choice. Me, a white man, have got to stand here and let a damn mule-wrestling nigger either criticise my private tail, or state before five public witnesses that I aint got any sense" (735). Boon draws the line of gentlemanly behavior racially (with Ludus as the "black"-guard), but a gentleman's agreement may cross racial differences. Later, when Lucius's grandfather buys a car, he and Ned would meet "on some unspoken gentleman's ground regarding it: Ned never to speak in scorn or derogation of its ownership and presence, Grandfather never to order Ned to wash and polish it as he used to do the carriage" (754). Lucius also observes that both Ned and Lucius's grandfather are Masons, an Egyptian as well as Arthurian imperial brotherhood and another example of a way that men of different races may stand on a level plain.[9]

Boon actually signifies an Arthurian presence on multiple levels. He emerges as a courtly lover, and Boss's car is "his soul's lily maid, the virgin's love of his rough and innocent heart" (747). Lucius describes Boon's maneuverings with Boss to secure permission to drive the car as fencing techniques in which he strove "all out, win or lose; logistics came into it, and terrain; feint thrust and parry" (750). Boon not only treats the vehicle with supreme (almost Astrophil and Stella–like) reverence; he also adopts chivalrous manners to accompany his use of the car, so that when the car spooks a horse leading a wagon "when a woman had the lines, telling Boon to stop and himself getting out, [he did so] talking quietly and steadily to the spooked horse until he could get hold of the bit and lead the vehicle past and remove his hat to the ladies in the buggy and come back and get into the front seat" (756). Boon evokes Arthurian legend most vividly when he behaves in a rash way, his own "rash boon" being the catalyst that starts the quest in the very lusty month of May to Memphis, where he, Gawain-like, finds his way past lust to true love and finally marriage to Miss Corrie/Everbe. This quest involves his resisting attacking his own "Green Knight" foe, Butch, who makes advances to Everbe while Boon struggles with his jealousy,

> furious and seething, restraining himself who never before had restrained himself from anything. Not from fear; I tell you, he was not afraid of that gun and badge: he could and would have taken them both away from Butch and then, in a kind of glory, tossed the pistol on the ground halfway between them and then given Butch the first step toward it; and only half from the loyalty which would shield me—and my family (his family)—from the result of such a battle, no matter who won it. Because the other half was chivalry: to shield a woman, even a whore from one of the predators who debase police badges by using them as immunity to prey on her helpless kind. (867)

Indeed, Faulkner seems to want the reader to see Boon as a figure who embodies the layering of mythic-imperial place. A liminal figure emerging from a wilderness space, Boon lives in "a single rented room in what in my grandfather's time was the Commercial Hotel," which, Lucius explains, has passed through multiple layers, first "established in hopeful rivalry of the Holston House [. . .] then in my time [it became] the Snopes Hotel [. . .] then for a brief time in the mid-thirties leased by a brassy-haired gentlewoman who came briefly from nowhere and went briefly back [and] known to your father and the police as Little Chicago [... and now the hotel has become] Mrs Rouncewell's boarding house" (743–44).

The mishaps of Lucius, Boon, and Ned's trip to Memphis culminate in an event that in its democratic nature allows such nonaristocratic and (at least on some level) unempowered figures as Ned and Boon not only to exercise their notions of honor but also to lift themselves to the level of the empowered aristocrats. In order to save Bobo from his gambling debts, Ned arranges to have Mr. Van Tosch's horse Coppermine race at Parsham, the name of which Ned colonizes by pronouncing it "Possum." Ned takes his cohorts to the home of Uncle Parsham (Possum) Hood, who seems the black version of the planter, as he is "an old man very dark in a white shirt and galluses and a planter's hat, with perfectly white moustaches and an imperial" (860), which Butch later calls a "goat-whisker" (865). Like Lucas Beauchamp's, Uncle Parsham's name comes from the patriarch who started the hamlet in which he lives. While Lucius's sleeping in the same bed with Uncle Parsham signifies the former's acquiescence to the flattening of relations created by the medium of honor, Ned stands as a Rabelaisian force who most easily and fluidly moves among various social circles (this fluidity is one of the most powerful things Lucius discovers during the trip). He makes his presence in the car known by farting, and throughout the novel he laughs in a manner that evokes Bakhtin's comments on laughter as subversion. Most importantly, Ned thrives at the racetrack, a site of democratic effort in which black jockeys might defeat white jockeys and a homogeneous group of people may gather and gamble.[10] It is at the racetrack that Ned may be empowered enough even to tell a white law-enforcement officer what to do, for when the constable insists that he does not want Lucius to stay with Uncle Parsham while Ned and Boon are in jail, Ned tells him, "There's somewhere the Law stops and just people starts" (921).

In fact, "just people" seems to be what Faulkner wants to get at in the novel. Just as the two mules that pull cars out of the mire at Hell Creek are "color blind" (798), so Faulkner seems to want to write a novel that at least promotes color blindness even as it acknowledges that prejudices in regard to color are embraced by people. To be sure, there are differences between black and white people in the novel. Ned explains that there are things white people "cant know," and he tells Colonel Linscomb, "You're the wrong color. If you could just be a nigger one Saturday night, you wouldn't never want to be a white man again as long as you live" (960).

Although he does not rearrange power in any official way in the novel, Ned nevertheless asserts enormous control and manages to subvert the systems that would control him as a black person and the people who administer those systems. At the same time, while Reba's whorehouse corrupts Temple, somehow Lucius learns important life lessons in a negotiation of his small-town chivalric principles and the Memphis whorehouse's lack of principles. Lucius's experience is not unlike Bayard's in *The Unvanquished* when the latter refuses to kill his father's murderer; both young men learn alternative strategies of honor and thus revise their aristocratic experience and principles. In Lucius's case, this negotiation is charged with distinctions in class: his encounter with lower-class attitudes and values leads him to question and adjust the aristocratic white southern value system. Stated another way, "Camelot," figured in terms of class as well as place (Lucius's family in Jefferson), becomes the periphery to "Syria" (a lower-class place in Memphis).

The Reivers thus ostensibly represents a new direction for Faulkner, as different races and classes seem to dwell on a somewhat level field, but this egalitarianism is suspicious because it most effectively binds only *men* in a fraternal bond that is at best complicated, while leaving women largely unempowered and outside the discourse of Arthurian-informed chivalric strategies. That is not to say that the women in the novel have no power; for example, Reba's power is undeniable, but it is moderated by Mr. Binford, whom Reba cannot control but whom she also cannot live without. Likewise, Miss Corrie/Everbe takes her cue from Lucius's chivalric manners and determines to give up prostitution and pursue a more "honorable" occupation, only to return to her former business by obliging Butch in order to get Boon out of jail. Despite Lucius's noting in his narrative as a grandfather "what the advertisements call the shorts or scanties capable of giving women the freedom they need in their fight for freedom" (883), women's freedom in the text is suspect, and even when Everbe adopts male-dictated Arthurian strategies of chivalric honor, she emerges not as a liberated feminist (not a first-wave feminist, at least) but rather as a woman married and installed in the peripheral space of Jefferson, Mississippi.

The imperialism of the Arthurian quest in a southern context becomes most attenuated when Faulkner focuses on the problem of how poor whites become cavaliers and how the already-instated cavaliers respond to this transition. Such is the movement of *Absalom, Absalom!* The poor white Thomas Sutpen makes/experiences a King Arthur–like rise and fall from power as he attempts to scale the wall of class and race and achieve ultimate power. Like the Arthurian parallels in *Mayday,* those in *Absalom, Absalom!* imply Faulkner's wide reading in Arthurian literature, but in the latter novel the spooflike mediating influence of *Jurgen* gives way to a direct reconfiguration and critique of *Le Morte Darthur*'s tragic plot, tone, and style. The novel's very inception was Arthurian not only in its relation to Quentin and *The Sound and the Fury* but even more directly in its relation to Faulkner's unpublished story "Evangeline."[11] This story concisely presents Sutpen's story, describing Henry Sutpen and Charles Bon as "knights" and emphasizing "the old days" in language reminiscent of *Mayday.* The Arthurian origin of *Absalom, Absalom!* strengthens the significance of Faulkner's handful of explicit references to Arthurian characters and events and heightens the importance of equating the story of Sutpen to the story of Arthur.

Like the Arthurian legend, the legend of Sutpen must be pieced together from numerous, often conflicting accounts, achieving an impressively complex mythic layering. Like Malory, Faulkner provides an omniscient third-person narrator who combines stories of Sutpen as told by multiple sources. Just as the legend of Arthur gains in mass and inconsistency with passing years and narrators, so the narratives in *Absalom, Absalom!* manifest a mythologizing of Sutpen as the narrators grow more distanced in time and place from the man himself. Concerning this mythologizing process and the intrigues and problems it presents, Mr. Compson comments:

> We have a few old mouth-to-mouth tales; we exhume from old trunks and boxes and drawers letters without salutation or signature, in which men and women who once lived and breathed are now merely initials or nicknames out of some now incomprehensible affection which sound to us like Sanskrit or Choctaw; we see dimly people, the people in whose living blood and seed we ourselves lay dormant and waiting, in this shadowy attenuation of time possessing now heroic proportions, performing their acts of simple passion and simple violence, impervious to time and inexplicable . . . you bring them together again and again and nothing happens: just the words, the symbols, the shapes themselves, shadowy inscrutable and serene, against the turgid background of a horrible and bloody mischancing of human affairs. (80)

The omniscient narrator also comments on the mythmaking process, noting that when Quentin and Shreve discuss the Sutpen story at Harvard they are "creating between them, out of the rag-tag bob-ends of old tales and talking, people who perhaps had never existed at all anywhere, who, shadows, were not of flesh and blood which had lived and died but shadows in turn of what were . . . shades too" (243).

From the varied renditions of these narrators emerges a legend of Thomas Supten, beginning with his birth in western Virginia among lower-class mountain people. His family's moving to the wealthy Tidewater region of the state arouses his sense of himself as part of this lower class. As a result of the epiphany he has concerning his lower-class status when the black servant treats him as an inferior, Sutpen leaves home at age fourteen to realize his dream of becoming part of the planter class. He conceives a "design" to create his own empire and establish it for his lineage. Although he tries to accomplish this design first in Haiti with a sugar plantation, he finds that his son's blood is tainted by his wife's hitherto unrevealed partially "Negro" blood. He thus shuts his wife and child out of his life and starts working on his design all over again in Jefferson, Mississippi. He acquires a significant plot of the Cotton Kingdom of antebellum Mississippi, where he builds the largest plantation in the area and names it Sutpen's Hundred.

While building his plantation, Sutpen enlists the help of a Merlin-like French architect. In Geoffrey's, Wace's, and Lawman's presentations of Arthur's story, Merlin is as much an architect as he is a magician. Malory gives him less pronounced architectural abilities, but he shows his ability to change his and other people's appearances. Sutpen's French architect resembles both of these aspects of Merlin. He helps Sutpen "drag house and formal gardens violently out of the soundless Nothing and clap them down like cards upon a table" (8), an act that mixes architecture and magic. Later, when he attempts to escape Sutpen and his slaves, he "architects" himself beyond the reach of people who seek to hunt him down. He becomes, like Merlin, a magician who can transform himself into a raccoon who had "calculated stress and distance and trajectory and had crossed a gap to the next nearest tree that a flying squirrel could not have crossed and traveled from there on from tree to tree for almost half a mile before he put foot on the ground again" (1930). Later Mr. Compson describes the architect as coming "out of a cave (in which he was hiding) fighting like a wildcat [. . . and upon being offered whiskey he] took the bottle in one of his little dirty coon-like hands" (207). The architect's being in a cave further echoes Merlin's imprisonment in a great stone in *Le Morte Darthur*.

As he moves from poor white to aristocrat, Sutpen attempts to adopt at least the trappings of noblesse oblige. The house is "the half-acre gunroom of baronial splendor . . . the largest edifice in the country not excepting the courthouse itself," ultimately outfitted with "chandeliers and mahogany and rugs" (30–33). Ellen's air is "a little regal," and she is "chatelaine to the largest, wife to the wealthiest, mother of the most fortunate" (54). Sutpen "acted his role, too—a role of arrogant ease and leisure which, as the leisure and ease put flesh on him, became a little pompous" (57). Thus, they perform the roles of lord and lady of their Camelot. They have two children, Judith and Henry, the latter being particularly welcome to Thomas as a son to carry out his design.

When, after Sutpen and his family have lived in such a manner for many years, Henry goes to the University of Mississippi, Charles Bon appears and plays a number of Arthurian roles. On one hand, as has been suggested already, Bon represents the presence of the Moor, the Oriental whose body must be conquered and ordered. When he and Henry ride to New Orleans at Christmas to investigate Bon's past, Henry is in part riding with the enemy to make sure that he is not the enemy. They ride south to the Oriental space of New Orleans, where Henry is introduced to an entirely different lifestyle, one that is not Anglo-Saxon and one that he is not certain is not that of the dark Other enemy. Henry's fears are later confirmed in Bon's proclamation that "I'm the nigger that's going to sleep with your sister" (286).

But on the trip to New Orleans Bon emerges as a fellow crusader, come from France—the "silken and tragic Launcelot" (256). His "French" origins and name, "Charles the Good," harken back to Charlemagne and even Lancelot, who originated in the matter of France. He is "the youthful Roman consul making the Grand Tour of his day among the barbarian hordes which his grandfather conquered, benighted in a brawling and childish and quite deadly mud-castle household in a miasmic and spirit-ridden forest" (74). He befriends and fights alongside Henry in the Civil War just as Lancelot fights in company with Gawain in their various knightly exploits in *Le Morte Darthur*. But then, in the manner of Lancelot, Bon triggers destruction for Sutpen's Hundred. Bon causes Judith to fall in love with him, and he plans to marry her, but Henry kills him to save the family's honor: the marriage would mean both incest and bigamy, as Henry discovers that Bon is the offspring of Thomas's first marriage and that Bon already has a wife and child in New Orleans.

Bon also serves as a Mordred, since it is his insistence on marrying Judith that initiates the beginning of Thomas Sutpen's destruction. Like

Malory, Faulkner makes his story that of estranged sons destroying their father and his plan. While Bon is a Lancelot-like chivalric romancer, as Lothar Hönnighausen suggests when he writes that "Judith and Bon are conceived as characters from the Arthurian world of Tennyson and the Pre-Raphaelites" (*Faulkner* 171), Faulkner's own description of the tragedy in *Absalom, Absalom!* echoes the Maloryesque tradition of a man that "got too many sons—[and] his sons destroyed one another and then him" (*Faulkner in the University* 35). In effect, Bon parallels both characters that bring about the fall of Camelot.

The themes of family and incest and Malory's Arthurian connection to them inform the other explicit reference to the Arthurian legend in the novel. This reference occurs when Shreve McCannon responds to Quentin's admonishing him for referring to "Miss" Rosa as "Aunt" Rosa while they sit in their dormitory room at Harvard recounting and re-creating the Sutpen legend. Shreve says, "You mean she [Rosa] was no kin to you, no kin to you at all, that there was actually a Southern Bayard or Guinevere who was no kin to you? then what did she die for?" (142). This comment suggests that Quentin's preoccupation with incest as a possible vehicle to contain virginity and family honor (his central obsession in *The Sound and the Fury*) has spilled over into his discussions with Shreve. And, indeed, later Shreve and Quentin accentuate that real or imagined aspect of Sutpen's story. This theme of incest also evokes *Le Morte Darthur*, which turns on an act of incest.

Having killed Bon, Henry flees, and Thomas is left without a son upon whom to confer his grand design. Thus Thomas attempts to carry out his design again with his wife's sister, Rosa Coldfield. When that endeavor fails, he tries again with the white trash Wash Jones's granddaughter, Milly. When Milly has a daughter instead of a son and Sutpen rejects her, Jones kills him with a scythe. Thus Sutpen and his design fall, his plantation and legacy reverting to the jungle from which he had so violently torn it. Just as Mordred, the unchivalrous villain, finally kills Arthur, so Wash, lowly squatter, destroys Sutpen and his design. In a larger sense, though, Sutpen's sons have frustrated his design, so that, as the Lupacks point out, "the very dynasty Sutpen tries to create is soon destroyed; and, like Camelot, it is destroyed not from without but from within" (182).

In the novel's context the theme of falling from within is biblical and Greek as well as Arthurian and thus exhibits multiple mythic-imperial layers. Faulkner makes clear connections to the biblical story of King David's sons' attempting to destroy him and to Agamemnon's fall coming from within his family. As such scholars as Ralph Behrens, John V. Hagopian, and Maxine Rose have noted in discussing the novel's biblical connections, the title and plot come from the story of King David and his sons in 2 Samuel 11–18. When Amnon, one of David's sons (Charles Bon's counterpart), rapes his half-sister Tamar (Judith Sutpen), her brother Absalom (Henry Sutpen) kills Amnon. The novel's title echoes David's wail when Absalom is killed during his rebellion against his father: "Absalom, my son, my son." References to Greek literature abound, from Quentin Compson's description of Miss Rosa Coldfield as having an air "Cassandra like and humorless" (15) to mention of Pyramus, Niobe, Cerberus, and other such figures from Greek myth. Most importantly, Lynn Levins and Lennart Björk discuss similarities between *Absalom, Absalom!* and Aeschylus's *The Oresteia,* which Faulkner evokes in plot as well as in references and echoes, as when Sutpen names his mulatto daughter Clytemnestra.[12]

While these elements are individually significant, their greatest importance lies in Faulkner's Malory-like conflation of them. Malory also deepens literary/historical connections to the Arthurian legend, first by infusing it with biblical parallels that equate King Arthur with the Hebrew King David. Both M. Victoria Guerin and R. A. Shoaf have noted that the story of the rise and fall of King Arthur is a variation on the David story. Both David and Arthur must slay a giant to gain notoriety (1 Samuel 17; Malory, *Le Morte Darthur* 87–91). Just as David begets a child by Bathsheba, who is another man's wife (2 Samuel 11), so Arthur begets a child with Orkney's wife (Malory, *Le Morte Darthur* 21). Merlin's disguising himself as an old man to accuse Arthur of committing adultery with his sister and to prophesy that his illegitimate son will destroy him bears great resemblance to Nathan the prophet's similar accusation of and prophecy to David (2 Samuel 12:1–15; Malory, *Le Morte Darthur* 21–23). And just as Absalom attacks his father and commits adultery with his father's wives (2 Samuel 16:21–22), so Mordred rebels against Arthur and attempts to wed Guinevere (Malory, *Le Morte Darthur* 505). Guerin notes that Arthur's incest "would also echo Amnon's rape of his half-sister Tamar" (18), though Arthur and his sister's involvement transpires upon their most unhesitant mutual consent.

Furthermore, Malory employs dynamics of Greek tragedy to inform the story's sense of worldly loss. As Beverly Kennedy notes, the discovery of

Greek texts during Malory's time offered stories of myth development as well as fall from within (364). The appearance of characters throughout such works as the *Iliad* and the *Odyssey* served as examples of character development through numerous works. The fall of Troy featured not only a disaster caused by an extramarital affair but also conflicts within the Greek army as well as a literal fall from within wrought by the Trojan Horse ploy. Kennedy argues that *Le Morte Darthur* marks the return to Western literature of Greek-style tragedy of failed horizontal transcendence. She notes that the tragedy of Malory's Arthurian account lies not in a breakdown of vertical transcendence or the hope that "through appropriate action in the here and now, [one can] make this world a better place for future generations" (363), observing that Arthur resembles Agamemnon in his concern with preserving his power and legacy. She also designates Gawain and Lancelot as tragic heroes, with Gawain striving to preserve his family and Lancelot seeking to create "a truly just society of all men in a unified Christendom" (368–69).

Faulkner varies the elements in piecing them together, combining many of Malory's variations in his version of the Arthurian legend. Though Lancelot is the counterpart of the villainous Amnon, Malory presents him as a hero. Likewise, though Charles Bon's presence is destructive, Faulkner portrays his character ambiguously, at times even as heroic. Hagopian points out the fact that in the biblical account, "Tamar knows that Amnon is her half-brother . . . [but] Judith never learns that Bon is her half-brother" (133), just as Arthur does not know that Lot of Orkney's wife is his sister when he becomes involved with her. The tragic figures correspond in their struggle for horizontal transcendence. Sutpen, like Arthur and Agamemnon before him, concerns himself with preserving his power and legacy. Henry resembles Gawain in his struggle to preserve family by preventing Charles from marrying Judith in order to avoid bigamy and incest. And just as Lancelot wishes for unity, so Charles wants familial inclusion by means of "that instant of indisputable recognition [when Sutpen] would know for sure and forever . . . that [he, Charles, is] his son" (255). Faulkner himself stated that "the Greeks destroyed [Thomas Sutpen], the old Greek concept of tragedy [which Faulkner earlier identified to be, among other things, the desire to] establish a dynasty" (*Faulkner in the University* 35).

In addition to being part of Faulkner's larger treatment of the palimpsestic configurations of mythic place and imperials space, this very same conflation of literary material appears in *Mayday*. Besides being an Arthurian event, Sir Galwyn's encounter with Yseult parallels the same biblical and Greek elements present in *Absalom, Absalom!* Galwyn, noting Tristram's amorous designs on Yseult, thinks to himself, "And a would'be adulterer, also! Faith, and his vow of knighthood rests but lightly upon him who would make a Menelaus of his own uncle" (65). When Galwyn finally meets Yseult, she is bathing, thus echoing the similar story of David and Bathsheba. Faulkner's *Mayday* frontispiece further demonstrates this conflation in terms of his frequent evocation of Beardsley. Faulkner's picture features Pan in one corner and a satyr and nymphs frolicking in the upper left-hand corner. To these Greek elements Faulkner adds a nude female form, who represents Yseult but parallels Bathsheba. And to call attention to his reliance on Beardsley in the context of *Absalom, Absalom!* Faulkner describes Judith's visit to her family's graveyard in terms of a Beardsley drawing (157).[13] The most important point to note regarding this conflation of layers in *Absalom, Absalom!* is that Thomas Sutpen contains within the location of his mythic body King Arthur, Agamemnon, and David because all three of these figures are empire builders. All of these figures quest for power, control, and glory but in the end are victimizers victimized. Sutpen is a mythic hybrid, and Sutpen's Hundred is a mythic place that contains all the "glories" and "curses" of imperial space.

The hegemonic forces in *Absalom, Absalom!* are exclusively white and aristocratic. The Arthurian tone as well as the Arthurian parallels in the story of Sutpen are provided by narrators invested in Arthurian rhetoric: Quentin is still the half-baked Galahad, Rosa a "Guinevere," and every man a "Southern Bayard" (142). The speaking in the novel is largely in the voices of aristocratic white men dedicated to the chivalric defense of women; even Mr. Compson, nihilist that he is, cannot escape this rhetoric. The overwhelming male control of the novel's presentation created by the re-creation of Orientalist discourse dominates and indeed colonizes the perspectives of women and people of color in the novel. Stephen Ross notes the effect of what he calls "Southern oratory" on the novel. Noting that "although oratory is dialogical in that it presupposes an audience, it is also in the nature of oratorical discourse to dissimulate its dialogical relationship with the audience. Colloquial oratory with its relentless movement forward, its accretion of layer upon layer of assertion, its affirmation of and its appeal to accepted values—in these ways oratory adopts the pose of monological discourse. [. . .] Thus, it is in the nature of the oratorical to mask itself as monological even within a dialogical circumstance" ("Oratory" 77–78). Drawing on Bakhtin's concept of dialogical discourse's tendency to move toward a monological discourse, Ross asserts that "a complete analysis of the relationships among the voices in *Absalom* must begin with a recognition of just how great the pressure is to transform all the discourse in the text into the monological" (78). This movement renders "a monological 'overvoice' generated by the overdetermined, cumulative rhetoric" that "creates a tremendous *authority,* an implied and truth-uttering presence. The oratorical discourse, *as discourse,* re-presents Sutpen's authority as 'father' in the novel: Quentin may tell us that all the narrators [. . .] 'sound just like father' [. . .], but the word 'father' means a principle of authority far greater than Mr. Compson" (79).

Rosa also appropriates Arthurian rhetoric to speak against Sutpen, demonizing him as a symbol of the curse of the southern land. Yet, as Ross notes, equating "father" as the pervading omnipotent and omniscient "principle of authority" with Thomas Sutpen necessarily places that principle in the realm of and as a tool in colonization, since Sutpen, with his Design, represents the imperial force in the novel. The male narrators therefore carry on Sutpen's colonizing linguistic performance, with the current dominated objects being women and African Americans. Dominating and preserving the story of Thomas Sutpen, however, calls for extensive sleight of hand because the fact remains that of all the narrators, only Rosa actually knew Sutpen, which alone establishes her with authority, which Jenny Jennings Foerst acknowledges. Like Ross, Foerst evokes Bakhtin, noting that although "Faulkner's arrangement of the polyphonic texts composing *Absalom* suggests at least the *illusion* that Mr. Compson possesses an authority," he seizes this authority from Rosa (38). This colonization of language and perspective is all the more lethal, however, because it does not involve a simple failure to acknowledge Rosa's voice and perspective. Rather, the male narrators appropriate her perspective by "rendering Rosa a ghost [as Mr. Compson does all southern women . . . and] Mr. Compson and Quentin [and, it should be added, Shreve] become *ghost writers* themselves, editors corrupting what ostensibly announces itself as Rosa's text in chapter V" (45).

Thus, the narratives of Rosa and other would-be speakers in the text are obfuscated and subsumed in an overarching (and Orientalist-like authoritative) white and male narrative project. Where Rosa would use the Arthurian legend against itself by redefining Camelot as tinged with Sutpen's evil, the male voices reappropriate her appropriation to render Sutpen one of their aristocratic own. For in the mythic narratives of Mr.

Compson, Shreve, and Quentin, Sutpen surely becomes the aristocratic quester he was never able to be in life, and Sutpen's Hundred might indeed be the bright center of Camelot (brought down literally in a blaze) that its peripheral status to Jefferson and New Orleans prevented it from being during Sutpen's life. While Rosa's voice finds itself channeled into the voices of these male narrators, Clytie never gets to speak directly in the text. Finally, Jim Bond, the grandson of Charles Bon, cannot speak at all, registering the ultimate silencing of Sutpen's dark house even as it is given tireless (and tiring) verbal treatment in the chivalric rhetoric of the novel's controlling male narrators.

What *Absalom, Absalom!* does allow is for a poor white man to seize upon myth and place to transform himself into an aristocrat. In the novel, Faulkner seeks to recuperate and explore for the first time how the southern aristocrats became the aristocrats. In *Flags in the Dust* John Sartoris insists that in "the nineteenth century [. . .] chortling over genealogy anywhere is poppycock. But particularly here in America, where only what a man takes and keeps has any significance, and where all of us have a common ancestry and the only house from which we can claim descent with any assurance, is the Old Bailey" (96). In *Absalom, Absalom!* Faulkner presents the details of the change from criminal to aristocrat, for a very real difference exists between the Compsons (true aristocrats) and Thomas Sutpen, whom Rosa describes as being (unlike the Sartorises) "not even a gentleman [. . .] no younger son sent out from some old quiet country like Virginia or Carolina" (11). Indeed, Shreve very literally hopes to trace the progression from the first Sutpen, who came on a "ship from the Old Bailey" (180), to Thomas and his construction of his neo-Camelot.

Overt improvements of class status are not the only aims of poor white quests in Faulkner's canon. For example, the Bundrens in *As I Lay Dying* undertake a chivalric quest to bury Addie. It is easy to focus on the material gains the Bundrens seize at the end of their journey to Jefferson, but teeth, gramophones, and bananas are not necessarily more important to them than the fulfillment of honor. These material objects are not just symbolic; they are significant in the ways they are connected to and even contiguous with strategies of honor so impressionistic and abstract that they emerge as the antithesis of the codified "rules" of honor that haunt young Bayard when he must avenge his father's death. The Bundrens do not need to revise any aristocratic codes of honor. They adhere to but also fashion strategies of honor in their respective pursuits of material. Hence

Jewel's strict adherence to "rules" in his endeavor to buy a horse. He shirks neither the duties to his family nor the duties that will win him the horse, and in a strikingly knightly fashion the horse becomes not only the symbol of that honor but also an object whose significance is imbedded in the economy of duty and honor. In essence, sacrificing the horse parallels the acquiring of teeth, as both emerge as commodities in the economy of honor as embraced by the Bundrens.

But in *Absalom, Absalom!* Faulkner would begin his interrogation of the poor white project of building respectability as well as mansions. While the Bundrens operate within dynamic and developing strategies of honor, Sutpen struggles to grasp and then conform to aristocratic-defined strategies of honor. But he makes the typical mistake of seeing those fluid strategies as rigidly codified. He tries to become an aristocrat by moving through a formula but realizes that it is not enough—pulling the sword from the stone is not enough to make him the chivalric aristocratic knight. He must also have, according to Rosa, "respectability, the shield of a virtuous woman, to make his position impregnable even against the men who had given him protection on that inevitable day and hour when even they must rise against him in scorn and horror and outrage" (9).

Faulkner's exploration of the transition from poor white to aristocrat within the mythic rhetoric of the Arthurian legend continues on a large scale in the Snopes trilogy. In these novels, Faulkner juxtaposes the aristocratic Stevenses (both Gowan and Gavin are derived from Gawain) with the poor white Snopeses (whose ranks include a Launcelot) as he explores how the latter struggle to attain the position of the former.[14] Flem emerges as the Arthur figure in these novels, and the trajectory of his quest/career parallels Sutpen's in many ways. However, while Sutpen believes in the rigidity of the aristocratic code, Flem realizes that the code is in fact a strategy, and a thin mask of one at that, as he too seeks respectability but makes his project that of manipulating respectability and its expectations on his way to constructing his own Camelot. As he rises in power in Yoknapatawpha County, Flem analyzes and then appropriates codes of honor and conduct until he comes to occupy the space of the aristocrat, "the old De Spain house which he had remodeled into an ante-bellum Southern mansion" (*The Town* 316).

In the Snopes novels (as well as in *Knight's Gambit,* parts of which Faulkner incorporated into the trilogy), Gavin, like Gowan in *Sanctuary,* is a chivalric lover who fails to defend his ladies' honor. Unlike Sir

Gawain, neither Gavin nor Gowan achieves physical consummation in his love affairs. Indeed, the platonic nature of Gavin and Linda Snopes Kohl's relationship designates it as different, transcendent, and special in *The Mansion*. His resolute refusal to enter into sexual relations with Linda replaces a marked tension in his desired relationship with Eula in *The Town*. He rejects sex with Eula as well, but he also wishes *he* were her lover instead of Manfred de Spain. Like Quentin in *The Sound and the Fury,* Gavin loses his fight in defense of Eula. As Chick Mallison notes, it "should have been Mr. Snopes of course because he was the husband, the squire, the protector in the formal ritual. But it was Uncle Gavin and he wasn't any husband or squire or knight or defender or protector either except simply and quickly his own [. . .]. What he was doing was simply defending forever with his blood the principle that chastity and virtue in women shall be defended whether they exist or not" (66–67). In the end, Gavin is what Ratliff calls a "next-best" one of the others besides the "Helens and Juliets and Isoldes and Guineveres [. . . and] Launcelots and Tristrams and Romeos and Parises [. . .]. And being the next-best to Paris is jest a next-best too, but it aint no bad next-best to be. Not ever body had Helen, but then not ever body lost her neither" (89). On the other hand, Gavin does wind up with Melisandre Backus, "whose terrible power was that defenselessness and helplessness which conferred knighthood on any man who came within range" (157).[15]

The Snopeses too have Arthurian-chivalric names. Colonel Sartoris Snopes's chivalric name actually seems to inform his honorable decision to abandon the spiteful ways of his father, Ab, in "Barn Burning." A more problematic figure is Lump, or Launcelot, Snopes. The epitome of Snopes pragmatism, Lump not only runs the Ike and the cow-diddling show but also advises Mink to steal the money from Jack Houston's corpse. Alan and Barbara Tepa Lupack see Lump as a villain who "succeeds in ruining the one pure, natural, affectionate relationship in the novel [that of Ike and the cow]" and a figure who represents "the lack of heroic idealism in the modern world and [. . .] the degree to which such legendary ideals have been perverted or debased" (180–81). It is true that Lump's Arthurian parallel is ironic, that he "is no noble character but rather is thoroughly deromanticized" (Lupack and Lupack 181), but it should be acknowledged that Lump merely represents a stage in development away from the Old Bailey toward the establishment of Camelot.

In fact, the Snopeses are crusading knights; they represent the imperial project inherent in the Arthurian legend. A vivid illustration of a Snopes manipulation of Arthurian-chivalric rhetoric, narrative, and imagery appears in Clarence Egglestone Snopes's successful campaign for state senator. Just prior to the beginning of his campaign, Clarence had risen to the rank of "local Dragon or Kleagle" of the Ku Klux Klan (*The Mansion* 600), an organization rank with the stench of chivalry at its worst. Yet, in his campaign, "he came out publicly against the Ku Klux Klan [. . . going to] Jackson not as the successful candidate for a political office but as the dedicated paladin of a cause, walking (Charles's uncle said) into the legislative halls in an aura half the White Knight's purity and half the shocked consternation of his own kind whom he had apparently wrenched himself from and repudiated" (601). Clarence, who possesses the Snopes ability to sniff out deconstructions of the strategies of their *habitus,* first embraces the very personification of the South as Camelot, as developed by Thomas Dixon, and then turns that very rhetoric of mythic place against itself.

What is interesting is that this rhetoric of chivalry is the province of the periphery. Clarence's involvement with the Klan was the activity of one on Yoknapatawpha society's margin, as he initially only "boasted quietly of it—that he was a member of the Ku Klux Klan when it appeared in the county (it never got very far and didn't last very long; it was believed it wouldn't have lasted at all except for Clarence)" (600). But when Clarence turns against the Klan, he simply appeals to another marginal group, but this one stands across the gap of the cultural mainstream. In his quest "to destroy a dragon" he wins "the race by that scant margin of votes coming mostly from Jefferson itself—schoolteachers, young professional people, women—the literate and liberal innocents who believed that decency and right and personal liberty would prevail simply because they were decent and right" (601). Clarence actually mobilizes and unifies what would otherwise be a nonactive and disparate set of groups, "who until Clarence offered them one, had had no political unanimity and had not even bothered always to vote, until at last the thing they feared and hated seemed to have produced for them a champion" (601). Clarence recognizes that he can galvanize a new political force whose machinery does not differ from that of the Klan. These groups are not just schoolteachers, young professionals, and women; they are schoolteachers, young professionals, and women who believe in honor and so are just as peripheral and just as vested in chivalric rhetoric as members of the Klan, despite being opposites morally.

Actually, the Snopeses carry on an imperializing project that does not greatly differ from the Stevenses'. *The Town* opens with Chick explaining that Gowan's "father worked for the State Department, and all of a sudden the State Department sent his father to China or India or some far place" (3). Implicit in Gowan's father's position in a growing Western power is that power's relation to the East. In the very next paragraph, Chick echoes Ratliff's comments on Flem's imperial project, observing that at "first we thought that the water tank was only Flem Snopes's monument. We didn't know any better then. It wasn't until afterward that we realised that that object low on the sky above Jefferson, Mississippi, wasn't a monument at all. It was a footprint" (3). The only difference between the two groups is that the Stevenses carry on their project within a rhetoric of honor, whereas, initially at least, Flem Snopes does not.

But then it is only a matter of time until Flem too employs honor as a tool in his imperial project. Gavin ponders with some horror the one honorable Snopes—Eck—and the omnipotent marriage of honor and rapacity he introduces into the Snopes ethos:

> And then suppose, just suppose; suppose and tremble: one generation more removed from Eck Snopes and his innocence; one generation more until that innocent and outrageous belief that courage and honor are practical has had time to fade and cool so that merely the habit of courage and honor remain; add to that then that generation's natural heritage of cold rapacity as instinctive as breathing and tremble at that prospect: the habit of courage and honor compounded by rapacity or rapacity raised to the absolute *nth* by courage and honor: not horse boy but a lion or tiger boy: Genghis Khan or Tamerlane or Attila in the defenseless midst of indefensible Jefferson. (31–32)

Thus, as Gavin imagines such a scenario, chivalry weds rapacity in the Snopes imperial project, rendering it a formidable invading force. As it turns out, no next generation is needed, as Flem himself realizes the power of honor and actually positions himself against Eck and other Snopeses who might, would, or do threaten his takeover of Jefferson.

What the next generation of Snopeses does produce is another and different form of knight: a female one, Linda Snopes Kohl. By the end of World War II she has been transformed into Rosie the Riveter in a Pascagoula shipyard. Part of a new mythology seeking to realign female subjectivity, she signifies a new image, her body registering a new speaking woman, who quacks away in her deafness to all of Gavin's chivalric verbosity, draining *"all that magic passion excitement [into and] summed up & dismissed in that one bald unlovely sound,"* which is her speaking "that word" (*The Mansion* 546). Gavin describes the ways she signifies this woman-figure who disrupts the aristocratic white southern male's control of chivalric narrative, noting that

> her hands, fingernails, showed it: not bitten, gnawed down, but worn off. And now she had a fine, a really splendid dramatic white streak in her hair running along the top of her skull almost like a plume. A collapsed plume; in fact, maybe that was what it was, he thought: a collapsed plume lying flat athwart her skull instead of cresting upward first then back and over; it was the fall of 1945 now and the knight had run out of tourneys and dragons, the war itself had slain them, used them up, made them obsolete. (644)

Here Gavin recognizes that Linda exhibits the signs of the Arthurian legend normally used to objectify women; she has performed the same trick of appropriating the monological overvoice that the male narrators in *Absalom, Absalom!* perform. Indeed, her very inability to hear seems to negate Gavin's speaking, and as he writes on the pad full of ivory leaves, she continues to speak, her harsh and bald language turning Gavin into the blushing "woman" figure of chivalric rhetoric.

Another instance in which a woman appropriates and subverts male rhetoric of chivalry occurs in *Requiem for a Nun*. Temple, the Governor, and Gavin discuss the etymology of Nancy Mannigoe's name, the Governor asking Temple to tell him "about Nancy—Mannihoe, Mannikoe—how does she spell it?" Temple replies, "She doesn't. She cant. She cant read or write either. You are hanging her under Mannigoe, which may be wrong too." To which the Governor replies in turn, "Oh, yes, Manigault. The old Charleston name." And Gavin adds, "Older than that. Maingault. Nancy's heritage—or anyway her patronym—runs Norman blood" (103). Realizing the implications of empowerment (even though he ostensibly seeks some liberty and empowerment for Nancy), Gavin makes the careful distinction that her name, not her blood, positions her within the tradition of chivalry from the Arthurian tales through Scott and then Charleston and into the southern aristocratic chivalric tradition.

Later, Temple plays with her own role as Arthurian-chivalric lady. When she is offered a cigarette, she says, "No, thanks. Really," and then goes on to say, "You'll notice, I always remember to say that, always remember my manners,—'raising' as we put it. Showing that I really sprang from gentlefolks, not Norman knights like Nancy did, but at least people who dont insult the host in his own house, especially at two oclock in the morning. Only, I just sprang too far, where Nancy merely stumbled modestly: a lady again, see" (108). Daughter of a prominent judge in Jackson and wife to a man with a name derived from the Arthurian legend whose uncle also bears such a name, Temple embraces Arthurian-chivalric nomenclature in her attempts to forge a viable subject position even as she strikes at the core of that nomenclature with her irony.

For Flem, Clarence, Temple, Linda, and Nancy Mannigoe as described by Temple, as well as for Thomas Sutpen or Quentin Compson, Camelot is ultimately an in-between space, a mythic place in which to negotiate imperial and anti-imperial impulses. Within southern white aristocratic figuration, Camelot as a mythic place is a space containing multiple mythic-imperial layers that have equally important significance in southern aristocratic space and in establishing and operating within an imperial drive. At the same time, Camelot is a place beset, whether by Yankees or poor whites, the latter of whom are likely to move into that very space once its current occupants have been demoted and assert themselves as the new chivalric Arthurian knights. As a place where crusaders are either out from and/or sent to, Camelot emerges as a key metaphor for liminal space in Faulkner's South.

CONCLUSION

Rapacity Does Not Fail
Mythic Place, Imperial Space, and *A Fable*

In Valhalla's un-national halls the un-national shades, Frenchman and German and Briton, conqueror and unconquered alike—Immelman and Guynemer, Boelcke and Ball identical not in the vast freemasonry of death but in the closed select one of flying, would clash their bottomless mugs, but not for him.

—*A Fable*

A Fable provides a site for offering final comments and observations on mythic place and imperial space in Faulkner's cosmos. Of all Faulkner's novels, this one most explicitly proclaims its mythic and imperial nature; it is a fable, his most extensive meditation—along with *Light in August*—on Christ and the Crucifixion. Here Faulkner explores not only the imperial implications and impulses of what he regarded as the "fairy tale that has conquered the whole Western earth" but also the potentialities for anti-imperial expressions in that story. Dealing directly with World War I and the problems of space and place in the form of regionalism and nationalism, *A Fable* explores the interstices of occurrence and narrative as it details the literal actions and activities of imperial impulses and projects.

Faulkner makes the progression of mythic-imperial layers explicit in the novel, exposing them throughout the text and examining the processes of their formation. To begin with, the central event of the novel—the French corporal's compelling his regiment to refuse to participate in a suicidal attack—occurs against the backdrop of and in procession with

> the long heroic roster who were the milestones of the rise of man—the giants who coerced compelled directed and, on occasion, actually led

his myriad moil: Caesar and Christ, Bonaparte and Peter and Mazarin and Alexander, Genghis and Talleyrand and Warwick, Marlborough and Bryan, Bill Sunday, General Booth and Prester John, prince and bishop, Norman, dervish, plotter and khan, not for the power and glory nor even the aggrandisement: these were merely secondarily concomitant and even accidental; but for man: by putting some of him in one motion in one direction, by him of him and for him, to disjam the earth, get him for a little while at least out of his own way [. . .]. (833–34)

There is a marked slippage between imperialist and anti-imperialist in this litany of figures; as might be expected, the narratives that surround these individuals exhibit both perspectives. The Generalissimo explains the mechanics of this progression to his son, the corporal, in their final conversation, in which the old general offers him freedom and power.

The old general believes that whether one is wielding or subverting power, speech is the primary tool and discursiveness, with its forging of narrative, the supreme mode of negotiating imperial impulse. Envisioning a future mythic-imperial moment, he asserts: "I know that [man] has that in him which will enable him to outlast even his wars." Just as the subaltern might appropriate and use the currency of myth against itself, so, the old general predicts, humanity will "outlast even this next avatar of his servitude which he now faces: his enslavement to the demonic progeny of his own mechanical curiosity, from which he will emancipate himself by that one ancient tried-and-true method by which slaves have always freed themselves: by inculcating their masters with the slaves' own vices—in this case the vice of war and that other one which is no vice at all but instead is the quality-mark and warrant of man's immortality: his deathless folly" (992–93). The old general explains that even over the "two mechanical voices [of the two final machines fighting a final apocalyptic battle and] bellowing at each other polysyllabic and verbless patriotic nonsense" there will be heard the human's "puny inexhaustible voice still talking, still planning [. . .] his voice, planning still to build something higher and faster and louder [. . .] yet it too inherent with the same old primordial fault since it too in the end will fail to eradicate him from the earth" (994). Even though this future machine age transforms "the entire earth [into] one unbroken machined de-mountained dis-rivered expanse of concrete paving," this seemingly egalitarian space only facilitates an even greater and more solipsistic regionalism, as humans will merely live on wheels that scuttle around the planet—small mobile heterotopias (993). Thus perhaps even the seemingly recalcitrant topography is doomed to collapse while human voices carry on to the next imperial project.

The Generalissimo makes these comments to his son at an old Roman citadel, a trace of the Greco-Roman mythic-imperial layer in the novel. On one hand, the old general offers his son the imperial glory of Rome, explaining that he will use his power to "open another [window] for you on a world such as caesar nor sultan nor khan ever saw, Tiberius nor Kubla nor all the emperors of the East ever dreamed of" (988). But it is the image of Rome's demise that persists. Just before the general evokes the glory of Rome, he recollects its fall to the Germans, observing that the latter are "the best soldiers on earth today or in two thousand years, for that matter, since even the Romans could not conquer them" (984). More importantly, regarding the power of discursiveness and narrative in empire building, the priest later tells the corporal that it "wasn't He nor Peter, but Paul who, being only one-third dreamer, was two-thirds man and half of that a Roman, could cope with Rome. Who did more; who, rendering unto Caesar, conquered Rome. More: destroyed it, because where is that Rome now? What remains but that *rock,* that citadel" (1004). Paul thus emerges as the hybrid figure whose subversive capabilities breed the anti-imperial narrative that can bring the collapse of the pagan mythic layer. His presence also signals the beginning of the Arthurian/Christian imperial epoch.

And this Christian-informed Arthurian layer is omnipresent. The emblems of the Crusades are present in the emblems of the British colonel, who sits "martial and glittering in his red tabs and badges of rank and the chain-wisps symbolizing the mail in which the regiment had fought Crecy and Agincourt seven and eight hundred years ago" (922). And the hegemony of crusading pervades the novel even as it tries to marginalize itself. Meanwhile, a number of the soldiers in the novel negotiate Arthurian-informed strategies of honor. The most courtly of knight-type figures is the Generalissimo himself, but General Gragnon also maintains a chivalric fidelity to a code of honor. Even though his regiment mutinied against his command, he proceeds on a personal notion of transcendent justice. He maintains a cynical attitude toward the war machine that would churn out "candy stripes of valor" in order to propagate its own causes, gorging itself on its own manufactured sugar. Indeed, to the corps commander's assurance that his sacrifice will win him a ribbon, he responds: "I don't have enough rank to get the one they give for failures" (687). Later, when the group commander admits the voracious nature of war, Gragnon realizes his doom and fatalistically prepares to meet it, bitterly acknowledging that "there are rules [. . .]. Our rules. We shall enforce them, or we shall die—the captains and the colonels—no matter what the cost" (45).

The emblem of the narrative of honor in Gragnon's life is the book written by what the uncorrected text of *A Fable* describes as his "divisional Judge Advocate General" (37)—a title with overtones of Christ as advocate, judge, and deity.[1] Relentlessly seeking the narrative of courage in books, this divisional aide explains to Gragnon that he wants to find out about "being brave. About glory, and how men got it, and how they bore it after they got, and how other people managed to live with them after they got it; and honor and sacrifice, and the pity and compassion you have to have to be worthy of honor and sacrifice, and the courage it takes to pity, and the pride it takes to deserve the courage." "Courage, to pity?" asks Gragnon. And the aide replies, "Yes. Courage. When you stop to pity, the world runs over you. It takes pride to be brave" (707). Although Gragnon realizes the horrifying hegemony of war and the relentlessness of imperial impulse, he cannot fashion an anti-imperial perspective, voice, or narrative for himself. Instead, he silently faces the rules in which he has long been ensnared until he finally asserts himself at the moment of his execution by managing to get himself shot from in front rather than behind as the army's cover-up scheme has dictated.

In contrast to Gragnon's silent, quixotic awareness and ultimate attempt at resistance, Gerald David Levine thoroughly embraces the rules and values of war as he makes a selfish and debased attempt to realize the role of knight questing for martial glory. Another of Faulkner's David characters, Levine cares only for his own glory; hence the consistent use of his given, "Christian" name. He wants to enter "Valhalla's un-national halls" to be a part of the "vast freemasonry [. . .] of flying" (747). Whereas the flyers in *Pylon* might have been the progenitors of a race without region or empire, Levine sees flying as part of the glory of the old nationalism and regionalism. Indeed, much as the young Faulkner saw the glory of the cavalry transferred into the Royal Air Force, so Levine sees the position of airplane pilot as the glorious pinnacle of chivalric combat. While still in training, he fears that the war will end before he can gain glory. When he is assigned to the RAF instead of the RFC because the latter "had ceased to exist on April Fool's day, two days before his commission came through," he laments the fact that a "door had closed on glory; immortality itself had died in unprimered anti-climax: not his to be the old commission in the old glorious corps" (747), and later he seethes when he thinks that the war has ended before he can attain the acclaim he desires. Like Gragnon, Levine finds himself faced with the presence of the book, in this case the codified rules of warfare. Levine's relationship with the rules of war differs from Gragnon's because he would enact his own desires to gain selfish honor rather than the transcendent honor that Gragnon embraces. Terrified that he has again lost his chance to become a hero, Levine would evade the war machine's orders in order to create his own blaze of glory. But the adjutant tells him that "when they gave you those badges, they gave you a book of rules to go with them, to prevent you needing ever to rack your brains like this" (751). Confined to his quarters, Levine resorts instead to reading what is apparently a novel, *Gaston de la Tour,* whose title suggests a Scott-esque romance.

Ultimately, an eerily Arthurian implicit imperial impulse of united Christendom emerges in the novel, as the matters of Britain, France, Germany, and the United States, as it were, ally to further what Winston Churchill would later refer to (after the time of the novel's action) and had already referred to (at the time of Faulkner's writing) as "Christian civilization." In a maneuver of counterfeit Othering resembling that in *Absalom, Absalom!* the white male leaders of the armies rhetorically marginaize members of their own group to forge their own reconciliation romance. When the American, British, and French generals meet with the German general, the latter argues for the alliance of Germany, America, Britain, and France, "which will conquer the whole earth—Europe, Asia, Africa, the islands—to accomplish where Bonaparte failed, what Caesar dreamed of, what Hannibal didn't live long enough to do" (948). Although the Generalissimo sardonically asks the German general, "Who will be emperor?" (948), he later acknowledges that these parties met to achieve "the formal ["mutual" in the uncorrected text] ratification of [their] agreement" (952). This agreement continues the war, as these generals reconcile and form an alliance that ironically resumes the combat that had been halted: the German general, the bizarre "Other," who in his grotesque commitment to war shoots his own pilot (766), is brought into the fold of his very enemies. The alliance that results pits the four generals, the Christian nations they represent, and the machine of war against the soldiers of all armies who actually fight.

While the generals' alliance-of-war represents the corrupted, imperially driven layer of the Christian epoch, the runner's proposal of an alliance of peace marks a return to an earlier period in that mythic-imperial layer's development as the runner's inspiration comes from what he sees as the corporal's Christ-like marginal and subversive actions. The runner explains to Reverend Sutterfield that if

> all of us, the whole battalion, one unit out of the whole line to start it, to lead the way—leave the rifles and grenades and all behind us in the trench: simply climb barehanded out over the parapet and through the wire and then just walk on barehanded, not with our hands up for surrender but just open to show that we had nothing to hurt, harm anyone; not running, stumbling: just walking forward like free men—just one of us, one man; suppose just one man, then multiply him by a battalion; suppose a whole battalion of us, who want nothing except just to go home and get themselves into clean clothes and work and drink a little beer in the evening and talk and then lie down and sleep and not be afraid. And maybe, just maybe that many Germans who dont want anything more too, or maybe just one German doesn't want more than that, to put his or their rifles and grenades down and climb out too with their hands empty too not for surrender but just so every man could see there is nothing in them to hurt or harm either— (955)

The runner then attempts to create this alliance-of-peace, leading soldiers out of the trenches in peace toward the Germans, who in turn emerge from their trenches to meet their enemies in the middle, "a thin murmuring sound rising into the incredible silence like a chirping of lost birds" articulating the perspective of these victims of war (963). But the war-promulgating alliance of the generals proves too powerful for the war-oppressed: "both sides [. . .] get a barrage down on them" (967) and "German and the British, too" (963) shell the would-be peacemakers.

In the midst of these parallel alliances stands the common denominator between them and the catalyst of their formation—the corporal. The corporal represents another incarnation of the marble faun, as he, like Joe Christmas and Charles Bon, is a foreigner and a hybrid figure born of a "mountain woman" and the French Generalissimo. A man apparently of "middle-European nationality" (784), the corporal signals liminality as he unites the men around him in a manner that represents the ethics that Christ introduced to his disciples. The old porter first makes the connection between the corporal and Christ, telling the runner, "[O]ne [was] enough then to tell us the same thing all them two thousand years ago: that all we ever needed to do was just to say, Enough of this" (727). Like Christ's, the corporal's body is a resurrected one, and one that serves as the "trace" that threads through time and space as he appears as Boggan in the English army and Brzewski in the American army before returning as the corporal in the French army. Even though he is half a product of the French center, he preserves his marginality, rejecting the nationalism that promotes the war as he implicitly realizes what the group commander acknowledges to Gragnon, that it is "no abrogation of a ruler that will destroy [the army]. It's less. The simple effacement from man's memory of a single word will be enough[: the word . . .] Fatherland" (715–16). Rejecting his father's offers of rank, position, and power, the corporal refuses the power of the center. It is a bitter irony that the corporal's body should be turned into a monument of France, an act that presumably entraps him in the same bonds that confine the marble faun. It is also ironic that despite his loyalty to marginality, the corporal is the center of his twelve followers. In this reincarnation of Christ's anti-imperial narrative lie the seeds of the imperial narrative that is realized in the imperialism that drives this war and that the generals embrace and promote.

In fact, the corporal's very emergence as a body from the past, even the old general's past, signals the Egyptian mythic-imperial layer that haunts the text; the corporal represents the entombed mummy unwrapped and appearing to inform the glory of the present. The tomb-raiding/mummy-unwrapping motif informs the lives of the old general and the corporal and the interconnections between them. Sitting in his chair in the headquarters, the general resembles "a boy, a child, crouching amid the golden debris of the tomb not of a knight or bishop ravished in darkness but (perhaps the mummy itself) of a sultan or pharaoh violated by Christians in broad afternoon" (885). From out of his buried past comes his son, the mysterious corporal unwrapped and exposed in his half-sister's discussion with the general. The corporal then becomes a figure of ubiquitous death and resurrection; even after his execution the grave that is the silent monument of his sacrifice is raided and decimated by the reactivation of the war he had successfully stopped. And when the war is over for good, a party of soldiers exhumes his remains to rebury them in a tomb of the Unknown Soldier. The trope of the raided tomb thus reverses itself: Initially, the corporal's act and sacrifice represent a digging down through layers of narrative and bringing to the present surface the story of Christ's sacrifice as a means to counteract the hegemonic forces whose execution occurs in war. Yet this soldier's body later becomes the prime signifier of postwar remembrance that is admittedly a memorial to sacrifice, but one that confirms rather than transcends the state.

And his body is not the only one that becomes part of a monument: years later the site of the burial ground from which the soldiers originally exhumed remains for the tomb of the Unknown Soldier would become a cemetery, with

> a vast towered chapel [. . .] created out of gray stone not by a sculptor but by expert *masons*[, and . . .] facing it would be the slope white with the orderly parade of Christian crosses bearing the names and regimental designations of the bones which could be identified; and beyond it, that other slope ranked not with crosses but with rounded headstones set faintly but intractably oblique to face where Mecca was, set with a consistent and almost formal awryness and carved in cryptic and indecipherable *hieroglyph* because the bones here had been identifiable too which had once been men come this far from their hot sun and sand, this far from home and all familiar things, to make this last sacrifice in the northern rain and mud and cold, for what cause unless their leaders, ignorant too, could have explained some of it, a little of it to them in their own tongue. (1044, emphasis mine)

Here the crusaders and the moors, the empowered and the subaltern, lie joined together by a similar hieroglyph, the centerpiece (and likely their monuments as well) fashioned by the mysterious arts of ancient Egypt.

The Masonic presence in the novel informs yet another dynamic of a marginalized configuration of center and periphery. Before the sentry was a sentry, he was a groom, a Cockney come to America to take care of a famous and profitable racehorse. While in "an inaccessible valley in the East Tennessee mountains [. . .] remote not only from railroads but even telegraphs and telephones too [. . .] he joined, was received into, the order of Masons" (811). The sentry's positioning at this point is interesting: seen as "a small bandy-legged foreigner" in the United States (810), he moves into a patently peripheral space where he assumes the same mantle as that worn by the nation's founding fathers in an act that would seem to endow him with centeredness. As a "foreigner" in the United States and later in France, he parallels the French corporal; he also resembles the corporal in the way that he becomes a simultaneously marginal and centered figure around whom a group of men gather, as first "eleven privates in the battalion had made the man beneficiary of their soldiers' life assurance policies; by the time the colonel reached the war ministry, the number had increased to twenty" (718). Although his superiors speculate that soldiers flock to him because of their love for him (719), the runner later explains that "[e]very man in the battalion owes him his pay for weeks ahead, provided they live long enough to earn it and he lives long enough to collect it from them. He did it by making them all Masons or anyway making them believe they are Masons. He owns them, you see. They cant refuse him" (954). The runner sees the sentry as a sort of parallel Christ figure to the corporal, the person who has learned how to coerce a mob into action, and so the runner seeks to employ the sentry in his project of creating an alliance of peace.

The sentry's activities in Tennessee are, of course, part of a much larger treatment of American space in the novel, for right in the middle of the novel, the present action of which is set in Europe, Faulkner takes his narrative back to American southern spaces; indeed, the U.S. South appears at the very core of the novel. Once again, Faulkner's treatment of southern space exhibits a strong awareness of the interconnections between such global southern places as South America and such global northern places as the northern United States, whose convergence forms the U.S. South. In the very middle of the narrative of the corporal and the old general is the story of the horse thieves and their trek throughout marginal spaces in the United States. The events in the story revolve around a horse that apparently was born in England and then purchased by an "Argentine hide and-wheat prince" (805), who also brought the English groom (later the sentry) to South America, where the horse "before the groom came into its life, merely won races, but [. . .] after his advent began to break records" (806). Seeing the horse's greatness, a "United States oil baron" (128) buys the horse and ships it to New Orleans, where it is met by Tobe Sutterfield, an "old Negro, a preacher on Sunday and the rest of the week a groom and hostler in the new owner's Kentucky breeding and training stables" (806). On the train out of New Orleans the horse itself becomes Other as it with "the two grooms, the white one and the black one, plunged through a flood-weakened trestle: out of which confusion and mischance were born the twenty-two months [. . . when] the crippled horse and the English groom and the old Negro and [a] twelve-year-old child who rode [the horse traveled] up and down and back and forth through the section of the Mississippi watershed between Illinois and the Gulf of Mexico and Kansas and Alabama, where on three legs the horse had been running in remote back-country quarter-races and winning most of them [. . .]" (806–7).

This U.S. excursion brings some favorite Faulknerian haunts into the novel. Much like Midgleston, passing through New Orleans the horse becomes "darker," no longer the splendid toy of economic emperors but the apotheosis of a cause of subversion.[2] At the same time, these thieves, who anticipate the reivers in Faulkner's final novel, make their way through the Delta, fleeing through the New Egypt not so much in search of but creating their own Promised Land of freedom, for surely their following the Mississippi River also recalls the interracial freedom and fluidity of Huckleberry Finn, Jim, and their "English" guests. Sutterfield, the groom, and the boy form yet another three-way alliance in the novel, and this alliance contains all the vulnerabilities and failures of any alliance of the margin, as it eventually breaks up when the groom kills the horse to prevent its owners from taking "it back to the Kentucky farm and shut[ting] it up in a whorehouse where it wouldn't need any legs at all [. . .]. Fathering colts forever more" (816).

This story represents the adventures of the periphery and the ways the marginal narrative can be used to combat patriarchy's hegemony. The story's lone auditor is the runner, who uses its precepts to inform his own subversive actions, as he learns the mechanics of influencing and leading the mob from the New Orleans lawyer who tracks down the horse. The lawyer's rhapsody on the moments of marginal mobilization contains the seeds of the movement the runner envisions, as the former considers the power of

> no mere immobile mass of [the human], no matter how large nor apparently doing or about to do no matter what, nor even the mass of him in motion mounted on something which, not he but it, was locomotive, but the mass of him moving of itself in one direction, toward one objective by means of his own frail clumsily jointed legs and feet—not Ghengis' bone horns nor Murat's bugles, let alone the golden voice of Demosthenes or Cicero, or the trumpet-blast of Paul or John Brown or Pitt or Calhoun or Daniel Webster, but the children dying of thirst amid Mesopotamian mirages and the wild men out of the northern woods who walked into Rome carrying even their houses on their backs and

Moses' forty-year scavengers and the tall men carrying a rifle or an axe and a bag of beads who changed the color of the American race [. . .] neither in lust nor appetite nor greed lay wombed the potency of his threat, but in silence and meditation: his ability to move *en masse* at his own impulse [. . .]. (838–39)

The runner latches on to the machinations of the margin because he is already predisposed to do so: having risen to the rank of officer, he first demands and then finagles his way back to private and then becomes a battalion runner, thus preserving his occupancy in the margins of the military.

While the trek through the United States by Sutterfield et al. on some level represents movement through the periphery, the line between center and periphery remains predictably unstable. For example, the runner is stunned when he discovers that the African American youth (Sutterfield's grandson) who rode the horse speaks "the French of the Sorbonne, the Institute" (850). Sutterfield explains that he can speak French so well because his "mamma was a New Orleans girl" (850). Thus, while New Orleans might seem a marginal space in relation to Paris, France, it is also a liminal space that contains elements of cultural centeredness; hence, Sutterfield's explanation requires no elaboration. Meanwhile, Sutterfield himself may in his speech and style represent the American periphery, but he also has the "noble face of an idealized Roman consul" (798). In France he is no longer the Reverend Sutterfield but Monsieur Tooleyman, president of *Les Amis Myriades et Anonymes à la France Tout le Monde*. Moreover, the very peripheral places through which they pass during their racing spree might, as all spaces might, be reconfigured into centers, as Sutterfield and his companions "trod with their actual feet the hard enduring ground bearing the names of Louisiana and Missouri and Texas and Arkansas and Ohio and Tennessee and Alabama and Mississippi— words which until then had been as foundationless and homeless as the ones meaning Avalon or Astalot or Ultima Thune" (851). Highlighting the mythic quality of these places (evoking the returned King Arthur in the reference to Avalon), Faulkner exposes the flexibility of definitions of place.

Indeed, U.S. spaces just as easily align themselves with the novel's centers of power. The planter class shows up briefly in the reference to the fact that the father of the glory-seeking Levine manages "the London office of a vast American cotton establishment" (775). Additionally, there are the three American privates brought in to kill General Gragnon. The

Iowan is happy to visit Chaulnesmont to add it to the list of places seen that he keeps to show his girlfriend in much the same way that a rapacious big-game hunter might be glad to find another elephant to shoot. Buchwald is a bootlegger and "czar of a million-dollar empire covering the entire Atlantic coast from Canada to whatever Florida cove or sandspit they were using that night" (1011). The third private is Philip Manigault Beauchamp; although he is an African American, his name signifies the highest in Norman and aristocratic descent in Yoknapatawpha County, and he plans to go to Chicago after the war to become an undertaker. These three young men seem to represent a different type of American presence from that set forth in the story of the racehorse. They have no interest in challenging anything, maintaining instead a belief in national systems and a youthful, somewhat naive implicit confidence that the powers that be are taking care of them and that they need merely to do their duty.

What is problematic about the fluidity of centeredness and marginality in *A Fable*'s American spaces and representatives of those spaces is the ways that fluidity permits colonization of language. While Sutterfield's grandson might be able to move triumphantly from speaking "African American" to the most sophisticated French, Sutterfield's narrative is colonized, taken over by the third-person narrator, as if the African American presence registers some linguistic danger that must be controlled. Likewise, the second appearance of a U.S. southern space in the text features a complex linguistic mythic-imperialization. Trying to persuade his son to flee his execution, the old general tells the corporal the story of the hanged man and the bird. "It happened in America," the old general explains, "at a remote place called by an Indian name I think: Mississippi" (990). Just as the runner finds inspiration in the resistance of power for transcendent attainment in the poetics of the American periphery, the old general uses the principles of an event that occurs "at a remote place" to try to get his son out from under the thumb of the center's power as represented in the military. But this very space, Mississippi, bears a name taken from a lost and defeated people, a name that is the trace of a past mythic-imperial layer. The general, then, views the accumulation of such layers as inevitable, unstoppable. What *can* be preserved (at least in this case) is life: the general explains that the criminal protests his innocence when he hears a bird sing because "tomorrow, next year, there would be another bird, another spring, the same bough leafed again and another bird to sing on it, if [the man in Mississippi] is only here to hear it, can only remain" (992).

The haunting irony of the old general's telling this story is that he has in his own French language colonized this story of the periphery; he, the empowered, uses the poetics of the periphery to *grant* a marginalized person freedom from that power. The old general's maneuver is suspicious, almost grotesquely gratuitous, in that it installs a safety valve in its own infrastructure of power. For what resistance has been accomplished when the center has permitted that resistance? In fact, the corporal cannot act in any way that will actually affect the war, for the general is in control no matter what decision the corporal makes. Like much peripheral speaking, the story the general tells fails to do anything more than articulate the marginal perspective. That is, it fails to affect the war materially in the short run, although already in the novel the signs of more potent future forces of marginal resistance have appeared. Ultimately the elements of hope and despair in *A Fable* are cyclical and inescapable. In a typically modernist conception of world narrative, Christ returns as Boggan, then Brzewski, then the corporal, and then in the future someone else, all determined to subvert imperial impulse and all destined to become symbols of that impulse revived. Looming in the backdrop are the silent Senegalese soldiers and the subalterns of what the old general thinks will be the Third World. Already signs of situations that would occur in the latter half of the twentieth century appear in the novel: Levine would crash his airplane "before they can sell [it] to South America or the Levantine" (772), and the old general offers the corporal escape to "South America—Asia—the Pacific islands" (986). In short, already the next phase of speaking, subverting, and imperializing is assembling and positioning its components.[3]

Movement back and forth from center to periphery—this is the constant motion of the novel. The old general starts his career in France and then goes to Africa. The corporal begins his life in peripheral spaces only to wind up interred in the French tomb of the Unknown Soldier. The runner begins his career as a private, rises in rank, goes to a marginal space in the centered place of Paris to devise a ruse by which to be demoted back to the rank of private, becomes a runner, and then, scarred from his attempt at peacemaking, rushes into the old general's funeral procession to denounce him only to be cast into the gutter. Then there are the women, the corporal's family. Particularly interesting is the book's opening chapter, in which despite the overarching masculinity in the novel, Faulkner focuses first on the young woman, the corporal's wife. She first appears as an object who is trampled by the mob and must be picked up and fed. As she eats the bread and the lorries enter town carrying, among other people and things, the mutinied regiment, she attempts to speak but cannot "because there was not time to turn her head aside and void her mouth for speech, already screaming something at him through the spew and spray of mastication" (683). Not only does her own attempt at speech fail but the text restores her to object status in the same way that it colonizes Sutterfield's speech. The first chapter closes with a description of her as "a slight woman, not much more than a girl, who had been pretty once, and could be again, with sleep and something to eat and a little warm water and soap and a comb, and whatever it was out of her eyes, standing in the empty *Place,* wringing her hands" (683). Now she has become something of a doll, an object to be appraised for its potential beauty. Like so many people and principles swallowed up by the war in the novel, in this passage consumption gets in the way of speech, and the body finds itself colonized by patriarchal nomenclature of desire.

Not that the women connected with the corporal do not get to speak. Unlike Sutterfield's voice, which the third-person narrator colonizes to the point of obliteration, the corporal's sister Magda speaks with her own voice to the old general himself. She, in fact, actually carries the trace of the old general's past, the locket containing the picture of his mother. Magda tells the story of the general's other life, filling in the blanks left in the official narrative, revealing that even the old general cannot escape hybridity of experience (the hybridity in which, Bhabha claims, the empowered participate as much as the oppressed). And her voice does produce some effect, as it confirms for the general the fact that the corporal is his son and leads to the old general's offering him freedom from the military's retribution. But as has already been noted, even this nod to the poetics of the margin have no real material effect on the war itself. Ultimately, the only true auditors of her story, as well as the stories of the other marginal characters in the novel, are the novel's readers. And whatever hope of change may exist in the novel depends on what the readers attend.

Again, *A Fable* explores the Faulknerian cosmos more extensively than any other single novel. As in all of Faulkner's work, constantly shifting and overlapping configurations of center and periphery appear as characters travel throughout, to, and from the Americas, Asia, Africa, and Europe in their struggles to negotiate the intersections of centers and margins. In the end, however effective the voice of the periphery has been, it is the center that maintains its power as France mourns the death and celebrates the life of the old general, leaving those who would remember the sacrifice of the corporal relegated to the gutter in tears (1071–72). For discursiveness is finally nothing more nor less than an economy—as color-blind as paper currency—whether wielded by the empowered once unempowered and soon to be disempowered or by the unempowered perhaps someday to be empowered and finally to be disempowered in turn.[4] To the world's strata of narrative these groups simply add another layer as their voices drone on, inexpugnable and as without progress as the silent friezes on their respective urns.

NOTES

Introduction

1. I use the terms *space* and *place* throughout this volume, so a note on how they operate is in order. Much has been written on these two concepts and their interrelation in philosophical and geographical thought from the work of Plato and Aristotle to more recent texts such as Gaston Bachelard's *The Poetics of Space*; Edward S. Casey's *The Fate of Place*; Mike Crang's *Cultural Geography*; André C. Drainville's *Contesting Globalization*; Michel Foucault's "Of Other Spaces"; Henri Lefebvre's *The Production of Space*; J. E. Malpas's *Place and Experience*; E. Relph's *Place and Placelessness*; Edward W. Soja's *Postmodern Geographies*; and Yi-Fu Tuan's *Space and Place*. See also the essays in *Undoing Place? A Geographical Reader*, edited by Linda McDowell, and *Thinking Space*, edited by Mike Crang and Nigel Thrift. My argument proceeds with the fundamental understanding that, as Wesley A. Kort writes, the "notion that space is first of all general and without qualities and that particular places with qualities are secondary and temporary has proven to be too firmly a part of Western culture to be dislodged by the move from modernism to whatever one calls the culture that today we are in" (8). That is, *space* signals an abstraction, while *place* denotes a particularity. This approach reflects Joseph A. Kestner's discussion of space and his brief treatment of place in *The Spatiality of the Novel*. For other treatments of space in fiction, see, in addition to Kort, J. J. van Baak's *The Place of Space in Narration*; Leonard Lutwack's *The Role of Place in Literature*; Sharon Spencer's *Space, Time, and Structure in the Modern Novel*; and Raymond Williams's *Country and City in the Modern Novel*. However, while these two terms are in some ways distinct from each other, in my argument they are inextricable, tied together in a dynamic relationship. Tuan explains this relationship when he discusses the dialectic relationship between the actually fluid notions of space and place; he argues that

> the meaning of space often merges with that of place. "Space" is more abstract than "place." What begins as undifferentiated space becomes place as we get to know it better and endow it with value. Architects talk about the spatial qualities of place; they can equally well speak of the locational (place) qualities of space. The ideas "space" and "place" require each other for definition. From the security and stability of place we are aware of the openness, freedom, and threat of space, and vice versa. Furthermore, if we think of space as that which allows movement, then place

is pause; each pause in movement makes it possible for location to be transformed into place. (6)

In my argument, then, space and place signify abstraction and particularity, respectively, with the understanding that the two terms work together to define location in ways that I specify as this volume progresses.

2. John T. Matthews, in *The Play of Faulkner's Language*, persuasively applies Derrida's theories of *difference* to argue that Faulkner's work resists the notion of a center, deferring presence and basing meaning in language alone. Indeed, Faulkner realizes that even topography does not exist outside of language in a knowable way, but such passages as the above seem to confirm the presence, unknowable and unpossessable as it may be, of the land as an implacable and indomitable anterior substance.

3. See Urgo's *Faulkner's Apocrypha*. The Cowley quote comes from his introduction to *The Portable Faulkner*. See Cowley's *The Faulkner-Cowley File* regarding Faulkner's disagreements with Cowley about the nature of his creation.

4. See Charles Aiken, Calvin S. Brown, Robert Coughlan, Don H. Doyle, Elizabeth M. Kerr, Lewis Leary, Michael Millgate, and Ward L. Miner, as well as the less academic but equally important texts of this ilk by John Faulkner, John B. Cullen, and Murry C. Falkner. Walter Taylor early on offered the more subtle assertion that "the South" is for Faulkner simply "some cluster of images, experiences, and fantasies inherited from the world of his youth" that no amount of effort ever allowed him to escape (x), but William T. Ruzicka could safely assert in 1987 that "[s]tandard remark on Faulkner's region and landscape usually concerns itself with the inconsistencies of his Yoknapatawpha map or its parallels to Lafayette County" (5), and that observation has held true until very recently.

5. In fact, the explorations of space and place I undertake here are in part a response to Barbara Ladd's urging literary critics "to develop a vocabulary for the discussion of the way place animates a text, governs movement, and makes change possible" ("Dismantling the Monolith" 51). Building on Michael Kowalewski's championing of mappings that "put places into motion, making them move within their own history, both human and nonhuman" (181), Ladd asserts that "place can be a dynamic and vital force in literary study. More and more, place needs to be constructed not as a stable site of tradition and history within a progressive nation but as something more provisional, more fleeting, more subversive, and likewise more creative—a locus for economic, political, discursive, and more broadly cultural transactions, a site of memory and meaning both for the past and the future. Places, like memories, are always in transition, always redefined, resituated, by experience over time" (56).

6. While Charles Baker's *William Faulkner's Postcolonial South* represents an application of postcolonial theory to the U.S. South, the landmark volume that has done so much to position the region in hemispherical studies is *Look Away! The U.S. South in New World Studies*. In their introduction, editors Jon Smith and Deborah Cohn write that the U.S. South is

> a space unique within modernity: a space simultaneously (or alternately) center and margin, victor and defeated, empire and colony, essentialist and hybrid, northern and

southern (both in the global sense). While the U.S. South is no "happy medium," it is a zone where the familiar dichotomies of postcolonial theory—unstable enough since the early 1990s—are rendered particularly precarious. If there is such a thing as U.S. southern identity, white or black, it consists neither in those traits that have historically been identified as "southern" and oppressed by an imperial North, nor in those traits that make it clearly part of the hegemonic United States, an oppressor of those further south. [. . .] As the uncanny double of both the First and Third Worlds, the U.S. South of course calls attention to (and enables displacement of) the First World traits of putatively Third World writers and the Third World traits of the putatively First World. (9–10)

7. Certainly Brooks would examine spaces outside of Yoknapatawpha in *William Faulkner: Toward Yoknapatawpha and Beyond,* and a number of writers, such as Donald M. Kartiganer in his *Fragile Thread,* do not focus on place at all in their discussions of Faulkner's use of language and form and its negotiation of fragmentation. In his introduction to *Faulkner in America,* Urgo observes that the question "of how Mississippi is in America [. . .] has been begged for some time. [. . .] We now know that Faulkner spent his adult life and his literary career explaining how far north Mississippi extended: encompassing and overpassing the North, even to Alberta, Canada" (x–xi). Recently, the essays in the fall 2004 issue of the *Mississippi Quarterly* introduced subtle rethinkings of Faulknerian space and place. For example, Hortense J. Spillers examines "Faulknerian spatial practice in [its] demonstration of *topoi* as 1) psychic location, 2) material ground of identification, and 3) the site of creative intervention" (537), arguing that while "the modern novel broaches 'reality,' whose specialized analytical properties divide the human scene into disciplinary 'regions' that require space to stand apart from the speaking subject," in fact "modernist Faulkner seems to renegotiate the old split in a new way by generating a fictional discourse that 'speaks' place through character and character through place" (536). In another essay, Joseph Urgo observes that "Faulkner criticism continues to divide on the line between the abstract and the material" ("Yoknapatawpha Project" 646) and goes on to consider both aspects by discussing what he calls "the Yoknapatawpha project," which chronicles a "sense of dual lives, one material, one deeper, more profoundly inaccessible[, which] animates Yoknapatawpha" (648). In her essay, Catherine Gunther Kodat also sees a duality in Faulkner's writing, tracing "the two 'modes' of writing sex—the erotic and the pornographic—that spiral through Yoknapatawpha" (604) and asserting the connection between "the inner landscape ('the actual') and the work (the 'apocryphal') that emphasizes the sexual aspect—the sublimation—of the *copula* linking the two, and that takes that sexual dimension as one key to reading the arc of Faulkner's *oeuvre*" (614). Kodat concludes that the space of sexuality in writing is central to Faulkner (especially letter writing, which Kodat traces to Byron Snopes's pornographic letters in *Flags in the Dust*), observing that "the map of Yoknapatawpha is all over postings: a space made of letters, in letters, for letters" (615). See also the essays by Charmaine Eddy and Thomas L. McHaney.

8. Although he does not cite Bourdieu, Urgo argues in "Where Was That Bird?" the importance of understanding Faulkner's spaces, especially his construction of the United

States (whose very name, Urgo asserts, signals its performativity), as a performance. Urgo focuses on Faulkner's "performance" rather than on his "use" of sources in *A Fable*, stressing in particular the absence of the bird in the hanging story in *A Fable*, which Faulkner claims in his introductory note to the novel to have taken from James Street's *Look Away*—a strikingly prophetic reference in terms of the spatial models set forth in the recent volume of criticism *Look Away! The U.S. South in New World Studies*. Urgo writes that the "sheer impossibility of so much of *A Fable* is linked to the equivalent, historical impossibilities at the core of the existence of the United States, of Faulkner's America. The physical facts, the sources, the representational references are not traceable, and not as important to knowing the nation as are the performance [. . .]. Not the horse itself—you'll find a three-legged race horse in the same place where you'll find the story of the hanged man in the bird, which is no-place—but the performance of it, is what constitutes Faulkner's America: the 'we the people' part of American existence" (112).

9. Regarding the employment of myth and narrative by the oppressor, Louis Althusser's concept of the "ideological state apparatus" designates myth as a means of enforcing and propagating state power; Bruce Lincoln argues that myth often finds itself employed by racist imperialists; and Robert Lee Wolff observes that "[p]olitical theory and political action are difficult to disentangle; but surely, if practice initially gives birth to theory, then theory in turn may eventually dictate practice" (137). Spivak argues the power of narrative even over materiality most succinctly in a discussion with Geoffrey Hawthorn, Ron Aronson, and John Dunn published under the title "The Post-Modern Condition: The End of Politics?" (*Postcolonial Critic* 17–34).

10. Here I use the term *myth* in a very specific way. It might be argued that *narrative* is a more inclusive and appropriate term for the forms of communication I examine, for although all myth is narrative, all narrative is not myth. But *narrative* does not seem to carry the cultural significance that *myth* does. I therefore use *myth* not as a term describing narrative origin (that is, it does not, in my usage, address a narrative's veracity or lack thereof) but rather as one describing a narrative's cultural power. For my purposes, a narrative becomes a myth when a given cultural force (which either is an imagined community and/or is part of an imagined community) appropriates it to articulate its desires or values. In this volume *myth* denotes a narrative that is in some way charged with cultural significance—that is, employed by a cultural force in order to articulate that culture's attitudes, beliefs, etc. (even when the narrative is embraced and/or articulated by an individual for presumably individual reasons—again the macrocosm is present in the microcosm). This very transformation of narratives into myths appears in Faulkner's fiction as he works with his own "mythologized" narratives as well as those already furnished for him by ancient and modern cultures. Regarding the definition and cultural significance of myth and its relationship to and status of narrative, see Roland Barthes's *Mythologies* and the essays in Ohmann, *The Making of Myth,* and Sebeok, *Myth: A Symposium*.

11. Lest my assertions on the expansive capabilities of myth be read as implying universalism of imperial impulse, I would evoke (in addition to my already careful attempts to position these concepts within a discourse of material pragmatism) Spivak's notion of "strategic universalism" (see *Postcolonial Critic* 11). Imperial impulse, particularly, is (I

would again stress, in light of Kort's observations) an internalized ethos that is fundamental to perpetuating business as usual in capitalistic culture and ideology. I would note, too, at this point that while in this book I refer to past imperial projects (Greek, Roman, British, etc.), they are filtered through the lenses of modern, capitalist-driven imperial dynamics, as seems appropriate for discussing Faulkner's time and texts. Discussing vastly different imperial projects from vastly distant epochs runs the risk of being, in Terry Eagleton's words, "hair-raisingly unhistorical" (95), and Faulkner's own tendencies to the ahistorical have been well documented, but I do want to historicize his own moment. Meanwhile, a comparison of the specific ways that imperial projects produce and are the result of imperial impulses in different epochs, although interesting and important, lies beyond the scope of my argument. One final note: I use the term *imperial project* rather than *empire* because the former term provides flexibility for describing the various systems and forms of domination I identify in Faulkner's cosmos. On the terms *imperialism* and *empire* and imperial and anti-imperial thought, see Hardt and Negri; and Feuer.

12. Numerous scholars have discussed the ways Faulkner develops multiperspectived polyvocality in his texts. John N. Duvall and Philip M. Weinstein, in *Faulkner's Marginal Couple* and *Faulkner's Subject,* respectively, note the presence of countercultures, perspectives, and communities in Faulkner's world. Weinstein observes, for example, that the "self-ratifying [Faulkner] and his white male protagonists require collides with and shatters against the alterities that make up both his inner and his outer world—alterities that I shall examine most fully in the form of women and blacks" (2–3). And Duvall argues that at "the boundaries of the community, outcast individuals tend to form couples whose relationships defy communal norms. These 'deviant' couples point to a possibility that is neither isolation nor agrarian community. [. . .] Very often, [. . .] dialogue merely confirms the larger community's norms. And yet the above model [of "two people sharing a code or communication circuit"] suggests that a counterforce to the hegemonic community requires only two people" (xiv–xv). More recently, Davis examines the ways games function to enact and voice subversive maneuvers and ideas in *Go Down, Moses* (see *Games of Property*), and Faulkner's inclusion of oppositional voices and ideologies are discussed by Ted Atkinson and Charles Hannon, respectively.

13. Faulkner's comment upon being relieved of duty at the University of Mississippi post office. See Blotner 118.

14. The essay is reprinted in *Essays, Speeches, and Public Letters* but without the accompanying photographs, introduction, and the palpable *Zeitgeist* of the surrounding material in *Holiday.* Quotations are from the *Holiday* text.

15. As part of this mainstreaming, the program features Faulkner presenting his Lafayette County High School graduation speech in a re-creation of the actual event but omits Faulkner's critique of democracy as a system equal in its purpose and effect to communism.

16. As with conceptions of myth and place, many writers have theorized cosmos. In fact, the history of the term *cosmos* exhibits hybridity and a privileging of place. Analyzing various ancient creation narratives, Edward S. Casey notes that they signal the act of division of previously existing matter into parts (always at least two, highlighting again

the fundamental binary nature of thought about space and place, oppression and subversion). *Cosmos,* in fact, "implies the particularity of place; taken as a collective term, it signifies the ingrediency of places in discrete place-worlds. [. . .] The limit of a place is specified by what a body can do in that place, that is, by its sensory activity, its legwork, its history there" (78). This notion of cosmos is a significant one in modern thought, distinguishing it from the universalism of post-Greek thinking, in which the "universe is the passionate single aim of Roman conquest, Christian conversion, early modern physics, and Kantian epistemology. [. . .] where the universe calls for objective knowledge in the manner of a unified physics or theology, the cosmos calls for the experience of the individuated subjects in its midst." And, as Casey further states, to "have substituted the spatial infinity of the universe for the placial finitude of the cosmos is to have effected the fateful transition from ancient to modern thinking in the West" (78). The universe as an abstract contained in imperial impulse remains very much alive and operative in Faulkner's cosmos, but Faulkner also seeks to understand how the placedness of cosmos might subvert universalism at the same time that a place encodes universalism's hegemony.

One. Here Pan's Sharp Hoofed Feet Have Pressed

1. Crook details the origins and development of the Greek revival in Britain in *The Greek Revival.* Regarding the American context, see, in addition to Hamlin, W. Barksdale Maynard's *Architecture in the United States, 1800–1850;* and Peggy McDowell and Richard E. Meyer's *The Revival Styles in American Memorial Art.*

2. For a treatment of Greek Revival architecture in the South, see Mills Lane's *Architecture of the Old South.*

3. Other very helpful discussions of *The Marble Faun,* of its sources and its spaces, include H. Edward Richardson's *William Faulkner* and Judith L. Sensibar's *The Origins of Faulkner's Art.*

4. Faulkner rewrites the economic center-periphery relationship of U.S. baseball in "Mississippi," just as he rewrites the map scene from *The Unvanquished.*

5. The comment on *Sanctuary* is taken from Faulkner's introduction to the novel, included in the textual apparatus in the Vintage International edition (pp. 321–24).

6. Clark Gable once asked Faulkner, "Do you write?" to which Faulkner replied, "Yes, Mr. Gable. What do you do?" See Blotner 309–10. Regarding this event and others in Faulkner's biography, see also Gray; Karl; Minter; and Parini.

7. Indeed, falling into the trap of identifying Faulkner as a youthful romantic is to commit the same error that Stone made, and Stone's notions of who Faulkner was were notoriously inaccurate. See, along with Blotner, Susan Snell's *Phil Stone of Oxford.*

8. Carvel Collins has suggested that Faulkner may have played only a minimal role in this enterprise. But despite his being a suspect source, John Faulkner's offhand mention of the "company" and his brother's role in it suggests that Count No-Count (as some Oxfordians called the sartorial young Faulkner) was very much invested in the humor of the prank. On Faulkner's various poses, see James Gray Watson's *William Faulkner: Self-Presentation and Performance.*

9. Lord Elgin, a British ambassador to Constantinople, had brought the marbles from

Greece to London. An act regarded by many as imperial theft, Elgin's taking the marbles from their native locations sparked great controversy, the most well known critic being Lord Byron. Crook observes that the "Elgin episode made the Greek Revival" (37). See also William St. Clair's *Lord Elgin and the Marbles* and Theodore Vrettos's *The Elgin Affair*.

10. The urn as a usable object first in a Greek and then in a British context conforms to Lévi-Strauss's definition of "the significant images of myth, the materials of the bricoleur, [which] are elements which can be defined by two criteria: they have *had a use*, as words in a piece of discourse which mythical thought 'detaches' in the same way as a bricoleur, in the course of repairing them, detaches the cogwheels of an old alarm clock; and *they can be used again* either for the same purpose or for a different one if they are at all diverted from their previous function" (35).

11. Further discussion of these figurations of Satan, goats, and blackness may be found in *A History of the Devil and the Idea of Evil*, by Paul Carus; *The Devil in the New World*, by Fernando Cervantes; *A History of the Devil*, by Gérald Messadié; and William Woods's book with the same title. On racist assignment of signifiers of blackness, see George M. Fredrickson's *The Black Image in the White Mind*; Robert E. Hood's *Begrimed and Black*; Winthrop D. Jordan's *The White Man's Burden*; and Peter Rigby's *African Images*. And on the development of concepts of blackness in America from the goat/Satan/blackness figuration to the "Black Beast" and twentieth-century depictions, see Bruce Dain's *A Hideous Monster of the Mind*; Adam Lively's *Masks*; Mason Stokes's *The Color of Sex*; and the essays in Seymour L. Gross and John Edward Hardy's *Images of the Negro in American Literature* and Janis Faye Hutchinson's *Cultural Portrayals of African Americans*.

12. The term *Negro* is employed here in the same sense that it is employed by Thadious Davis, who notes that Faulkner understood African Americans not as "black" but as "Negro," with all of that term's various stereotypical overtones (see *Faulkner's "Negro"*).

13. My inspiration for the term *counterfeit Other* is the following passage from Diane Roberts:

> The epiphany of powerlessness that comes when the young girl finds she is not the adored heiress of the house but a slave is titillating to a white audience not encouraged to think of real white women being raped. Counterfeit white women are another matter. The mulatta's sexuality—the core of her identity—is disguised in whiteness, making it all the more thrilling. There is fear not only of the hidden Other, the alien "blackness" lurking inside the mulatta's fair form, but a terror of *sameness* that implicates white culture, producing its overinsistent stories. To borrow a phrase from Jonathan Dollimore, "the Other is inscribed in the self-same." The mulatta is doubly threatening for being both unbearable things at once: black and female, yet "like" whites as well. The tension produced by this collapsing of absolutes creates the suppression of the black and the feminine in texts that simultaneously attempt to demystify race and deny female sexuality. (78)

14. See Trefzer regarding hybridity and colonial/cultural contact in Faulkner's treatment of Native Americans. See also Lewis M. Dabney's *The Indians of Yoknapatawpha*.

15. "Black Music" does not appear on Faulkner's list of short stories submitted for publication until 1931, but Blotner and Skei both date its composition in 1926, the same year that Faulkner wrote "Carcassonne." Quotations are from *Collected Stories*.

16. On journalistic attacks on the Standard Oil Company at the time and their enduring impact on the public's perception of it, see Roger M. Olien and Diana Davids Olien's *Oil and Ideology*.

17. See Davis's *Faulkner's "Negro."* Blotner connects the story to Anderson, noting that just as Wilfred Midgleston has his vision in the mountains of Virginia, "[w]hen Faulkner had seen Sherwood Anderson in early 1926, Anderson had just bought a farm in the ruggedly beautiful, isolated region of southwest Virginia close to Marion" (254).

18. Eiko Owada too notes the connections between the Van Dymings' project and Jefferson's Monticello, noting also that "Faulkner's text evokes the historical background of US imperialism" (139).

19. In fact, the novel's third-person narrator often refers to Margaret Powers as the "black woman" in the same way that Faulkner has himself referred to as a "little black man" in *Mosquitoes* and that Popeye is referred to as a "black man" in *Sanctuary*. Also, the Latin Americans in "Black Music" form the backdrop for the actions of Midgleston.

20. Karl Zender notes the significance of silence in World War I, especially in *A Fable*.

21. That Donald is an icon becomes clear in the way Cecily's little brother Robert sees Donald as an emblem of a glorified notion of war. Donald's iconographic quality also affects Julian Lowe, who has no wound to show for, and thus cannot participate in, the overarching narrative of military glory.

22. See *Father Abraham*.

23. Note again Faulkner's connecting Babe Ruth with imperial impulse. Also, regarding Paul Rainey, John B. Cullen claims that "Rainey and Colonel Stone had a club house over in Panola County on section 16" and that on one hunt in the Delta with Faulkner they "camped close to Rainey. He had the reputation of an autocrat, but judging by the way he treated us, he was one of the finest and most courteous sportsmen who ever hunted in the Delta. [. . .] He] told us where he would drive and that we were welcome to have any bear we killed in front of his dogs" (26–27). Phrases like "one of the finest and most courteous" appear suspiciously often in Cullen's text, but the propinquity of the sportsman seems significant. I am also indebted to Tommy Covington for information on Rainey, including a copy of an anonymously authored article entitled "A Look at Paul Rainey—The Man."

24. The novel opens with the "Centaur in Brass" episode, which recalls "Black Music" when Mr. Harker explains to Gowan that Tom Tom and Tomey's Turl looked like "them double-jointed half-horse fellers in the old picture books [. . .] a centawyer running on its hind legs and trying to catch up with itself with a butcher knife about a yard long in one of its extry front hoofs until they run out of the moonlight again into the woods" (23). Like the marble faun, this hybrid creature from pagan myth flees the power of Flem by running to the woods, although together they cannot succeed in stopping Flem's imperial march, as the water tower with the brass in it stands as "his own monument, some might

have thought. Except that it was not a monument: it was a footprint. A monument only says *At least I got this far* while a footprint says *This is where I was when I moved again*" (25–26). Charles Mallison's mythic-spatial configuration in this observation provides the hybrid double function of the monument as the trace on the otherwise transparent mythic layer: the monument encodes the past while furthering the imperial designs of the present.

25. This Keatsian treatment of Eula recalls Horace Benbow's working out the essence of his sister Narcissa in his own "urn" in *Flags in the Dust*. Himself by name a trace of Roman achievement in literature, Horace after "four mishaps produced one almost perfect vase of clear amber, larger, more richly and chastely serene and which he kept always on his night table and called by his sister's name in the intervals of apostrophising both of them impartially in his moments of rhapsody over the realization of the meaning of peace and the unblemished attainment of it, a Thou still unravished bride of quietude" (190–91).

Two. A Tearing of Endless Silk

1. This brief outline of the history of New Orleans is based primarily on the following: Herbert Asbury's *The French Quarter*; Grace King's *New Orleans*; Mel Leavitt's *A Short History of New Orleans*; Robert C. Reinders's *End of an Era*; Lyle Saxon's *Fabulous New Orleans*; and the essays in Arnold R. Hirsch and Joseph Logsdon's *Creole New Orleans*.

2. The chief engineer's name resembles that of the Frenchman Le Blonde de Vitry, who accompanies Sam Fathers's father, Ikkemotubbe, from New Orleans to Mississippi.

3. Evelyn Scott develops a similar picture of New Orleans's situation, writing that in the Northern soldier Parker's "antagonism to the city, it had appeared to him that the very architecture, with the habits of life implied [immorality and 'Catholicism'], defied the just prerogatives of *conquerors* and was designed to keep him on the alien fringe of the *native* life" (120, emphasis mine). Scott also describes New Orleans's aristocrats as having "Oriental" trappings, the Creole Eloise, for example, wearing "her India foulard with the spots on it" (137) prior to Butler's proclamation, the text of which Scott includes in full. In a very different treatment of this chapter of New Orleans history, William Wells Brown offers a defense of Butler and a condemnation of New Orleans's white aristocratic women in *Clotelle*.

4. Regarding writers and their connections to the city, see the essays in *Literary New Orleans in the Modern World* and *Literary New Orleans: Essays and Meditations*, both edited by Richard S. Kennedy.

5. Describing a quadroon ball, Mr. Compson says that the young men who would claim quadroon or octoroon women as mistresses are "goatlike" (89).

6. Actually, the notion that anyone can be anything other than hybrid seems tenuous. Quentin notes that the original settlers themselves came from "the Old Bailey" (180), and Shreve suggests that the "taint" of miscegenation is ubiquitous in his assertion that "the Jim Bonds are going to conquer the western hemisphere," that "even as they spread toward the poles they will bleach out again [. . . but] still be Jim Bond[s]; and so in a few thousand years, I who regard you will also have sprung from the loins of African kings" (302).

7. Regarding the Hegelian implications of this scene, see Godden's *"Absalom, Absalom!"* For postcolonial readings of *Absalom, Absalom!* see Ramón Saldívar's "Looking for a Master Plan"; and Maritza Stanchich's "The Hidden Caribbean 'Other' in William Faulkner's *Absalom, Absalom!"*

8. Without being superfluous, it seems appropriate to recall that Joe Christmas is left on the threshold of the orphanage on Christmas Eve.

9. On Faulkner's women and subversion, see Duvall's *Faulkner's Marginal Couple* and Weinstein's *Faulkner's Subject,* along with Deborah Clarke's *Robbing the Mother;* Doreen Fowler's *Faulkner;* Minrose Gwin's *The Feminine and Faulkner;* and David Williams's *Faulkner's Women.*

10. Ingomar's name is particularly provocative in terms of mythic place and imperial space because the Colonel named one of the stations on his railroad after him, and Ingomar remains the name of the hamlet that sprung up around the station.

11. On Faulkner's military role playing, see chap. 2 of James Gray Watson's *William Faulkner.* For John Faulkner's descriptions of William's airplane interests, see *My Brother Bill.* Regarding Faulkner's RAF experience, see Cowley's *The Faulkner-Cowley File,* 71–91.

12. Faulkner bases this mural on the actual mural in the real-life Shushan Airport in New Orleans. The mural actually presents a simultaneity of mythic layers, as Susie Paul Johnson quotes from the commemorative pamphlet of the fiftieth anniversary of the Lakefront [Shushan] Airport that eight murals "depict eight different sections of the world with the arrival of the airplane as their unifying factor" (41).

13. Note that the traditional punctuation vanishes in the experimentally futuristic construction of the sentence.

14. Again, in the spirit of hybridity that characterizes the novel, Faulkner removes the conventional punctuation. He later undercuts this attempt at freshness, however, by endowing the maid with traditional African American dialect, a maneuver that hints at a more dangerous, hidden side to Faulkner's experiment at racial rebirth, which will be discussed shortly.

15. Although *Pylon* does not have an explicit military context, it is perhaps noteworthy that on the back of one of the manuscript pages of the novel Faulkner drew a picture of a soldier in World War I garb aiming a rifle. University of Mississippi, Oxford, John Davis Williams Library, Special Collections, Rowan Oak Papers, box 3, folder 1.

16. These two images, of ranch life and hunt clubs, evoke two different depictions of the frontier as narrated by Buffalo Bill and Frederick Jackson Turner. As Richard White writes, "Cody's Wild West told of violent conquest, of wresting the continent from the American Indian peoples who occupied the land," while "Turner's history was one of free land, the essentially peaceful occupation of a largely empty continent" (9). Iconographically, these two stories generated the media images of the cowboy and the homestead, respectively—or, in Faulkner's terms, the "horse and spur" and the "posed countrylife." Regarding the imperialism, the American West, and the cowboy in media, see also Richard Slotkin's *Gunfighter Nation* and Patricia Nelson Limerick's *The Legacy of Conquest.*

17. On ideology and advertising, see the essays in Cross's *Advertising and Culture,* as well as John B. Thompson's *Ideology and Modern Culture* and Jackson Lears's *Fable*

of Abundance. Faulkner shows this "precession of simulacra" in other instances in the novel. For example, when Jiggs buys the boots at the beginning of the novel, he "puts his hand into his pocket [and the clerks] could follow it, fingernail and knuckle, the entire length of the pocket like watching the ostrich in the movie cartoon swallow the alarm clock" (781). Here the natural event—Jigg's putting his hand in his pocket—is compared to a representation—the movie-cartoon ostrich swallowing the alarm clock—whereas normally the representation follows the actual act; in other words, according to the conventional order of representation, the action of the movie-cartoon ostrich should more naturally represent and imitate the movement of a hand in a tight pocket. Here Faulkner actually achieves a doubly removed representation, as the ostrich he describes is not a real ostrich captured on film but rather a cartoon one. Toward the end of the novel, Faulkner dramatizes the results of this empowerment in another comment on film when Laverne takes her son to live with Roger Shumann's parents in Myron, Ohio. The child's grandparents' house is "a bungalow, a tight flimsy mass of stoops and porte-cochères and flat gables and bays not five years old and built in that colored mud-and-chickenwire tradition which California moving picture films have scattered across North America as if the celluloid carried germs" (984). Here Faulkner replaces the benign cartoon image of the ostrich with a much more potent illustration of film representation's capabilities for adverse influence. Built within the past five years, this house stands as the very natural incarnation of a typical midwestern home as disseminated by Hollywood, and such a house emerges as a symptom of a "disease" of representation originating in California.

18. Designating the barnstormers as the new cowboys is problematical because the application of this imperial iconography does not so much accurately identify the barnstormers themselves as colonizers as it points to the ways that imperial ideology colonizes the barnstormers. Jiggs himself embodies this problem: although he transforms into a similar hybrid figure, both cowboy and airplane mechanic, a person associated with the air who nevertheless remains earthbound throughout the novel, his boots do not fit over his tennis shoes, suggesting that overlaying the activities of the barnstormers with the imperial cowboy ideology represents a combining of two iconographies that do not harmonize. This opening scene thus anticipates and dramatizes the ways that media colonizes the flyers throughout the novel by endowing them with ideologies not necessarily their own and packaging narratives of their actions to appeal to whatever consumers those who stand to gain from the flyers' activities imagine.

19. Regarding this voice, Joshua Gaylord suggests that while critics see it "as the unmoored consciousness of modernity, we might also view it as the alienated/alienating godlike voice of artistic creation itself" (177). Indeed, like the voice of the Wizard of Oz, the voice of the announcer seems larger and more potent than the announcer himself, who "stood hiphigh among the caps and horns of the bandstand below the reserved seats, bareheaded, in a tweed jacket even a little oversmart" (*Pylon* 795), while his voice seems transformed by the amplifiers into something with its own volition and prescience, "as if it possessed some quality of omniscience beyond even vision" (796). John N. Duvall writes of "the gap between the power of the voice and the impotence of the man through whom the voice passes," explaining that it is "easier to identify whom the voice doesn't represent. It is not the man who owns the voice" ("Paternity in *Pylon*" 45).

20. Regarding the ways that media embeds pastoral within technology, see Martin Green's essay "Some Versions of the Pastoral: Myth in Advertising; Advertising as Myth," in Cross, *Advertising and Culture*.

21. John Matthews writes that this "description is a little less clinical than symbolic, and I suggest that its context is the grotesque exaltation of the phallus in carnival [as explained by Bakhtin]" ("Autograph of Violence" 256). Regarding the pylon as phallus, the reporter makes the following observations concerning Roger, Laverne, and Jack's relationship: "No; there aint any pylon [. . .]. Yair, it was a pylon only it was pointed down and buried at the time [. . .]; yair, two buried pylons in the one Iowadrowsing womandrowsing pylondrowsing" (*Pylon* 849).

22. It might be noted too that although *Pylon*'s systems of signification and communication differ in certain ways from those of Faulkner's Yoknapatawpha novels, the controllers of ideology basically correspond. Kevin Railey traces the centrality of racially charged paternalism and its conflicts with liberalism in Faulkner's Mississippi novels in *Natural Aristocracy*. *Pylon* shows more similarities than dissimilarities to the Yoknapatawpha novels in this respect because in the novel Faulkner locates the control of language and the power of generation in the domain of the masculine. A fierce paternalism pervades the novel, from Jack Holmes's "protection" of Laverne to the reporter's attraction to her to Shumann's father's treatment of his wife and Laverne and his assuming the role of the grandfather. Indeed, Marta Paul Johnson has shown how Laverne struggles with male-dominated narrative forms throughout the novel; and Duvall, in "Paternity in *Pylon*," traces the hegemony of patriarchy in the narrative. Furthermore, so much of the media rush to define in the novel concerns the problems of understanding a new "race," its needs, its desires, its past, and its future.

23. It is important to remember that Faulkner always maintained a dubious view of his characterization as a regionalist, even when he stood to gain the most from it.

24. Regarding the South as Orient, Diane Roberts notes that it is "surely no coincidence that one of the most popular works in the antebellum South was Thomas Moore's orientalist fantasy *Lalla Rookh*" (73), and she recognizes that "Harriet Beecher Stowe depicts the slave South as orientalized" (95).

Three. Sold into Egypt

1. Trafton discusses the influence of Freemasonry on the Egyptian iconography of U.S. emblems. See also Steven C. Bullock's *Revolutionary Brotherhood;* Joseph Campbell and Bill Moyers's *The Power of Myth;* and *Valley of the Craftsmen*, edited by William L. Fox. Freemasonry maintains an especially pertinacious connection with space and place because it focuses on the construction of buildings (spaces and places) and posits as its focus the Great Architect of the Universe, which is the "title applied in the technical language of Freemasonry to the Deity" (Mackey 310).

2. On Egypt in black figuration, see George M. Fredrickson's *Black Liberation;* Eddie S. Glaude Jr.'s *Exodus!* Cornel West's *Prophesy Deliverance!* and Gayraud S. Wilmore's *Black Religion and Black Radicalism*. On the function of spirituals, see Samuel A. Floyd

Jr.'s *The Power of Black Music;* Eileen Southern's *The Music of Black Americans;* and Jon Michael Spencer's *Protest and Praise.*

3. In *The Founding of Memphis* James Roper notes that "[a]ccording to his own statement to historian Charles Cassedy, [James Winchester] bestowed the name Memphis on the new town. His landing on the Cumberland near Cragfont was called Cairo, but it is doubtful whether this fact should be held to show his pro-Egyptian leanings in his nomenclature. He had originally named the place 'Ça Ira!' in honor of the French Revolution, but his backwoods neighbors soon triumphed over the cedilla and other Gallic niceties" (45). However tenuous Roper's observation may be regarding the metamorphosis of the name Cairo, it should be noted that he goes on to point out that Winchester "was a staunch republican of the old Roman breed, with sons named Marcus Brutus, Lucilius, and Valerius Publicola—not to mention a Napoleon" (46). Regarding Memphis history, see Gerald M. Capers Jr.'s *Biography of a River Town* and Shields McIlwaine's *Memphis.*

4. The region referred to officially as the Mississippi Delta is actually the Yazoo-Mississippi Delta, a delta-shaped swath of land stretching from Memphis to Vicksburg. Although New Orleans is not located in the Yazoo-Mississippi Delta, I include it later in the discussion because of its cultural and economic connections to the region. On the Delta and its culture, see James C. Cobb's *The Most Southern Place on Earth.*

5. One is reminded of Henry Adams's shock at Britain's supporting the southern states, as slavery had already been abolished in Britain. Frederick Engels explains in *The Condition of the Working Class in England* that with Britain's capacity to work more cotton, resulting from Hargreave's spinning jenny, and the South's ability to grow high-quality cotton with slave labor and to prepare more of it with Whitney's gin, the cotton industry in England exploded, initiating the industrialization of Britain. In 1859 and 1860 the South was England's primary supplier, exporting 2,555,000 pounds of cotton; India was second, exporting 563,000 pounds to Britain (Crawford 139–41).

6. On the history of cotton, see Crawford's *The Heritage of Cotton;* George Bigwood's *Cotton;* and Stephen Yata's *Cotton.*

7. On the history of modern Egypt and cotton, see Edward Roger John Owen's *Cotton and the Egyptian Economy;* and volume 2 of *The Cambridge History of Egypt,* edited by M. W. Daly. For a specific discussion of the U.S. South, Egypt, and cotton production and exportation, see Edward Mead Earle's "Egyptian Cotton and the American Civil War."

8. On the history of American-Egyptian cotton, see Joseph Clarence McGowan's *History of Extra-Long Staple Cottons.* The anonymously penned article "Arizona Ranks Second in Yield per Acre" discusses cotton in Native American history and the development of Yuma cotton. For a concise history of Pima cotton, see "History of Pima Cotton."

9. See Bigwood, *Cotton;* as well as "Cotton: The Perennial Patriot," an excellent description of cotton as a factor in the development of U.S. power. The article is part of "Cotton Counts," described as "a National Cotton Council of America campaign carried out by the National Cotton Women's Committee. The goal is to improve Americans' perceptions of the U.S. cotton industry. The primary focus is on helping students

better understand and appreciate cotton's significance in their daily lives and the industry's contributions to the nation's economic health." http://www.cotton.org/pubs/cottoncounts/index.cfm.

10. On the Cotton Carnival, Egypt, and Memphis, see John E. Harkins's *Metropolis of the American Nile*. Harkins notes that a pyramid was built in Nashville during the city's centennial celebration in the 1890s.

11. "Est le scribe au pays des ombres. Pour un peu on le prendrait pour un avatar clownesque de Thoth, le dieu égyptien de l'écriture et de la mort" (*"Pylon"* 446; the English translation in the text is mine). It should also be noted that Egypt is one of the sections of the world pictured in the airport mural. Susie Paul Johnson observes that the "real focal point of each of the murals I have seen and those reproduced in the commemorative pamphlet is a huge manmade monument like an Egyptian or Hindu temple, a Mayan pyramid, the Eiffel Tower, or the Brooklyn Bridge, which dwarfs the airplanes included in the paintings" (41).

12. Another Faulknerian liberator cast in the vein of George Washington is Wash Jones in *Absalom, Absalom!*—a poor white who converses with and ultimately murders the poor white/aristocrat hybrid, Sutpen. Jones's cutting Sutpen down with a scythe evokes the class conflict associated with the Communist imagery of the hammer and sickle, but it is also important to note that Jones's action evokes the American myth of George Washington and the cherry tree. Wash cannot abide by the lie that is Sutpen's social pretension when its effects lead to his own granddaughter's hardship and so cuts down Sutpen-as-cherry-tree, liberating himself and the world, as he thinks, from Sutpen and his kind.

13. On Moses's hybridity, see Trafton's *Egypt Land* and Freud's *Moses and Monotheism*.

14. Quotations from the Compson Appendix are taken from the text in *The Portable Faulkner*.

15. The lack of racial markers resembles Sam Fathers's calling the Chickasaws "The People" in "The Old People."

16. Vashtar's architecture must be executed in stone, making him a sort of mason. Such imperial upward mobility of Masons appears in *The Town*, when Ratliff observes that Eck Snopes's job was obtained for him because he was a Mason (381). Bruce F. Kawin notes "the similarities between *Land of the Pharaohs* and *Absalom, Absalom!*: Pharaoh's plans for the great pyramid obsesses him precisely as Sutpen's 'design' does him, and in both cases the overreachers are destroyed by their compulsions" (123–24). Kawin goes on to note that the "evil princess (Joan Collins) [. . .] arose more from Faulkner's nightmare of 'abomination and bitchery' *(Light in August)* than from Hawks's views of women" (124).

17. Faulkner recognized this flexibility, although in a slightly different manner. When asked about the film, he replied, "*Land of the Pharaohs* is nothing new [. . .]. It's the same movie Howard (Producer-Director Howard Hawks) has been making for 35 years. It's *Red River* all over again. The Pharaoh is the cattle baron, his jewels are the cattle, and the Nile is the Red River." *(Conversations* 117–18).

18. It might be added that Darl uses markedly Masonic imagery to describe Dewey Dell's "leg coming long from beneath her tightening dress: that lever which moves the world; one of that caliper which measure the length and breadth of life" (104).

19. The passage from his great-grandfather's *White Rose of Memphis* cited earlier is just such an example. On the functions of reconciliation romance, see Paul H. Buck's *The Road to Reunion;* Karen A. Keely's "Marriage Plots and National Reunion"; and Nina Silber's *The Romance of Reunion.*

20. Zora Neale Hurston uses the mule as a trope to articulate African American female experience, and it fits well with African American biblical figuration. Faulkner presents a scene that includes African Americans, mules, and Egypt simultaneously in *Soldiers' Pay:* "Monotonous wagons drawn by long-eared beasts crawled past. Negroes humped with sleep, portentous upon each wagon and in the wagon bed itself sat other Negroes upon chairs: a pagan catafalque under the afternoon. Rigid, as though carved in Egypt ten thousand years ago. Slow dust rising veiled their passing, like Time; the necks of mules limber as rubber hose swayed their heads from side to side, looking behind them always" (125–26).

Four. Fabulous Immeasurable Camelots and Carcassonnes

1. Examples include Elmo Howell's "Faulkner and Scott and the Legacy of the Lost Cause"; Lynn Gartrell Levins's *Faulkner's Heroic Design;* Richard Milum's "Faulkner and the Cavalier Tradition"; and William Schulz's "Just Like Father." Noteworthy exceptions appear in Richard P. Adams's *Faulkner* (which does note a few Arthurian as well as generally chivalric elements) and in Alan Lupack and Barbara Tepa Lupack's *King Arthur in America.* A recent work is Lorie Watkins Fulton's "William Faulkner's Southern Knights."

2. As both Thomas J. Heffernan and Antonia Gransden argue, historians and hagiographers in the Middle Ages concerned themselves first with a communal understanding (including legendary reports) of the truth about a person or given incident and then added details, rather than building up details to determine the truth. This strikingly postmodernlike privileging of discursiveness makes their historical veracity suspect but revealing regarding the development of cultural narratives.

3. The documents cited below in this paragraph are collected in Richard Brengle's *Arthur, King of Britain.* How much Faulkner knew of the Arthurian legend's development is unknown. He could have read a detailed description in John Rhys's introduction to J. M. Dent's edition of Sir Thomas Malory's *Le Morte Darthur,* a text with which Faulkner was acquainted and which is discussed later in this chapter.

4. Discussions of *Mayday* include, in addition to Brooks's article, Blotner's biography; Carvel Collins's introduction to *Mayday;* Gail Moore Morrison's "Time, Tide, and Twilight"; and Michael Salda's "William Faulkner's Arthurian Tale."

5. On the Albigensian Crusade, see Zoe Oldenbourg's *Massacre at Montsegur: A History of the Albigensian Crusade* and Jonathan Sumption's *The Albigensian Crusade.*

6. For additional discussions of "Carcassonne," see James B. Carothers's *William Faulkner's Short Stories;* David Minter's *Faulkner's Questioning Narratives;* and Polk's "William Faulkner's 'Carcassonne.'"

7. Further evoking the Arthurian legend, Boon later observes that "anybody that turns

his back on [Otis] had sho enough better be wearing one of them old-time iron union suits like you see in museums" (882–83).

8. In addition to Lucius's grandfather's ideas about what it means to be a "gentleman," it might be noted that the family must deck out in riding attire that includes "gauntlet gloves" (747).

9. This seemingly fraternal situation, however, also suggests the paternalism that Kevin Railey describes in *Natural Aristocracy,* in which aristocratic whites ally with "sympathetic" African Americans against rebellious blacks and poor whites.

10. Regarding the subversive effects of games, see Davis's *Games of Property.* Lucius observes that "we had everything else that any track had, but we had democracy too" (914).

11. See *Uncollected Stories of William Faulkner,* 583–609.

12. Kestner notes that one "may therefore read the accounts of David (Sutpen), Absalom (Henry), Tamar (Judith), and Amnon (Bon) as a palimpsest for *Absalom, Absalom!*" (164), but he does not discuss the Arthurian and Greek layers that also inform the text.

13. Faulkner conflated such material in other novels as well. The protagonist of "Carcassonne" is a David-artist figure (regarding the artist figure and the story's connection to *Absalom, Absalom!* see Hönighausen's "Pegasusrider and Literary Hack." In *Mosquitoes,* David encounters Patricia while she swims naked, and they subsequently elope from the yacht, which is named *Nausikka.* Later, in *If I Forget Thee, Jerusalem,* Charlotte Rittemeyer swims nude each morning after eloping with Harry. In *The Sound and the Fury,* while the biblical element is perhaps less explicit, Quentin's incestuous obsession with Caddy informs his reconstruction of Bon and Judith's relationship in *Absalom, Absalom!* At the same time, a Greek strain of tragedy runs throughout the work, appearing in numerous allusions and in such names as *Jason* Compson. Faulkner would have seen how these elements might fit together in *Jurgen.* Greek elements permeate the novel, and a biblical connection emerges when Jurgen states that Arthur "reminds me in all things of David of Israel, who was so splendid and famous, and so greedy, in ancient ages. For to these forest and island necks and other possessions, this Arthur Pendragon must be adding my one ewe lamb; and I lack a Nathan to convert him to repentance" (81).

14. Marta Powell Harley discusses Faulkner's use of *Sir Gawain and the Green Knight* in *Mayday,* "The Bear," and the character Gavin Stevens in the Snopes trilogy and *Knight's Gambit.*

15. Interestingly, Flem does not himself participate in a battle for a courtly lover—he is, in fact, the nonchivalric husband, whose presence often poses the least threat in chivalric literature—as he has not yet begun to operate within the sphere of knights.

Conclusion

1. The corrected text says that "the aide was his divisional JAG" (706).

2. On hybridity in *A Fable,* see Barbara Ladd's "William Faulkner, Edouard Glissant, and a Creole Poetics of History and Body in *Absalom, Absalom!* and *A Fable.*"

3. As Keen Butterworth asserts, "The novel recognizes that violence and conflict, no matter how regrettable, are unavoidable as long as man remains man" (16), which agrees

with Faulkner's own description of his project in the never-used blurb written for the novel's dust jacket. Noting a series of opposites in the novel, Heinrich Straumann observes that the "dualism that Faulkner attributes to the whole world order belongs to that concept of tragedy which rests on the irresolvable contrasts of existence" (371).

4. Polk suggests that *A Fable* (like Barthes's *Mythologies*) is Faulkner's response "to the postwar ideological scramble in which the cold war, the mass media, and modern technology combined in ways that drove the wedge between the powerful and the powerless, the individual and the masses, the illusioned and the disillusioned, even more deeply than the war had" ("Polysyllabic" 323).

WORKS CITED

Adams, Henry. *The Education of Henry Adams: An Autobiography.* Vol. 1. New York: Time, 1964.
Adams, Richard P. *Faulkner: Myth and Motion.* Princeton: Princeton UP, 1968.
Aeschylus. *The Oresteia.* Trans. Robert Fagles. New York: Penguin, 1977.
Aiken, Charles S. "Faulkner's Yoknapatawpha Country: A Place in the American South." *Geographical Review* 69 (1979): 331–48.
———. "A Geographical Approach to William Faulkner's *The Bear*." *Geographical Review* 71 (1981): 446–59.
The Alliterative Morte Arthure: A New Verse Translation. Trans. Valerie Krishna. Washington, DC: UP of America, 1983.
Althusser, Louis. "Ideology and Ideological State Apparatuses (Notes towards an Investigation)." *Lenin and Philosophy, and Other Essays.* Trans. Ben Brewster. New York: Monthly Review P, 1971.
Ammons, Elizabeth, and Valerie Rohy. *American Local Color Writing, 1880–1920.* New York: Penguin, 1998.
Anderson, Benedict. *Imagined Communities: Reflections on the Origin and Spread of Nationalism.* New York: Verso, 1983.
"Arizona Ranks Second in Yield per Acre." *Cotton Trade Journal* (international ed.) 12.1 (1932): 17–18.
Asbury, Herbert. *The French Quarter: An Informal History of the New Orleans Underworld.* New York: Knopf, 1936.
Atkinson, Ted. *Faulkner and the Great Depression: Aesthetics, Ideology, and Cultural Politics.* Athens: U of Georgia P, 2006.
Azer, Anis. "Egyptian Cotton States Its Case." *Cotton Trade Journal* (international ed.) 24.9 (1943–44): 50, 69.
Bachelard, Gaston. *The Poetics of Space.* Trans. M. Jolas. 1964. Boston: Beacon, 1969.

Baker, Charles. *William Faulkner's Postcolonial South*. New York: Peter Lang, 2000.
Bakhtin, Mikhail. *Rabelais and His World*. Trans. Helen Iswolsky. Bloomington: Indiana UP, 1984.
Barthes, Roland. *Mythologies*. Trans. Annette Lavers. New York: Hill and Wang, 1972.
———. *The Pleasure of the Text*. Trans. Richard Miller. New York: Hill and Wang, 1975.
Baudrillard, Jean. "Simulacra and Simulations." *Selected Writings*. Ed. Mark Poster. Stanford: Stanford UP, 1988.
Bauer, Margaret Donovan. *William Faulkner's Legacy: "What Shadow, What Stain, What Mark."* Gainesville: UP of Florida, 2005.
Beardsley, Aubrey. *Beardsley's Illustrations for "Le Morte Darthur": Reproduced in Facsimile from the Dent Edition of 1893–94*. Arr. Edmund V. Gillon Jr. New York: Dover, 1972.
Beck, Warren. *Man in Motion: Faulkner's Trilogy*. Madison: U of Wisconsin P, 1961.
Behrens, Ralph. "Collapse of Dynasty: The Thematic Center of *Absalom, Absalom!*" *PMLA* 89 (1974): 24–33.
Bentley, Nancy. "Slaves and Fauns: Hawthorne and the Uses of Primitivism." *ELH* 57.4 (1990): 901–37.
Bhabha, Homi K. *The Location of Culture*. London: Routledge, 1998.
Bigwood, George. *Cotton*. New York: Holt, 1919.
Björk, Lennart. "Ancient Myth and the Moral Framework of Faulkner's *Absalom, Absalom!*" *American Literature* 35 (1963): 196–204.
Black, Dorothy Lee. "Birthplace of Cotton Research." *Cotton Trade Journal* (international ed.) 24.9 (1943–44): 94–95.
Bleikasten, André. *The Ink of Melancholy: Faulkner's Novels from "The Sound and the Fury" to Light in August*. Bloomington: Indiana UP, 1990.
———. "*Pylon*, ou L'Enfer des signes." *Études Anglaises* 29 (1976): 437–47.
Blotner, Joseph. *Faulkner: A Biography*. New York: Random House, 1984.
Boccaccio, Giovanni. *The Decameron*. Trans. G. H. McWilliam. Harmondsworth: Penguin, 1972.
Bourdieu, Pierre. *Outline of a Theory of Practice*. Trans. Richard Nice. Cambridge: Cambridge UP, 1977.
Brengle, Richard L. *Arthur, King of Britain: History, Romance, Chronicle, and Criticism*. Englewood Cliffs, NJ: Prentice-Hall, 1964.
Brickhouse, Anna C. "'I Do Abhor an Indian Story': Hawthorne and the Allegorization of Racial 'Commixture.'" *ESQ: A Journal of the American Renaissance* 42.4 (1996): 233–53.
Brooks, Cleanth. "The Image of Helen Baird in Faulkner's Early Poetry and Fiction." *Sewanee Review* 85 (1977): 218–34.

———. *William Faulkner: The Yoknapatawpha Country.* New Haven: Yale UP, 1963.

———. *William Faulkner: Toward Yoknapatawpha and Beyond.* New Haven: Yale UP, 1978.

Brown, Calvin S. "Faulkner's Geography and Topography." *PMLA* 77 (1962): 652–59.

Brown, William Wells. *Clotelle; or, The Colored Heroine. A Tale of the Southern States.* 1867. Miami, FL: Mnemosyne, 1969.

Buck, Paul H. *The Road to Reunion, 1865–1900.* New York: Vintage, 1937.

Bullock, Steven C. *Revolutionary Brotherhood: Freemasonry and the Transformation of the American Social Order, 1730–1840.* U of North Carolina P, 1996.

Butterworth, Keen. *A Critical and Textual Study of Faulkner's "A Fable."* Ann Arbor: UMI Research, 1983.

Cabell, James Branch. *Jurgen: A Comedy of Justice.* New York: McBride, 1923.

Cable, George Washington. *The Grandissimes.* New York: Penguin, 1988.

Campbell, Joseph. *The Hero with a Thousand Faces.* New York: Meridian, 1949.

Campbell, Joseph, and Bill Moyers. *The Power of Myth.* New York: Doubleday, 1988.

Cantwell, Robert. Introduction. *The White Rose of Memphis.* By William C. Falkner. New York: Coley Taylor, 1953. v–xxvii.

Capers, Gerald M., Jr. *The Biography of River Town: Memphis, Its Heroic Age.* Chapel Hill: U of North Carolina P, 1939.

Carothers, James B. *William Faulkner's Short Stories.* Ann Arbor: UMI Research, 1985.

Cartwright, Keith. *Reading Africa into American Literature: Epics, Fables, and Gothic Tales.* Lexington: UP of Kentucky, 2002.

Carus, Paul. *The History of the Devil and the Idea of Evil from the Earliest Times to the Present Day.* New York: Bell, 1969.

Caruthers, William Alexander. *The Cavaliers of Virginia.* New York: Harper, 1835.

———. *The Kentuckian in New York.* New York: Harper, 1834.

———. *The Knights of the Horseshoe.* New York: Burt, 1928.

Casey, Edward S. *The Fate of Place: A Philosophical History.* Berkeley and Los Angeles: U of California P, 1997.

Cash, W. J. *The Mind of the South.* New York: Knopf, 1941.

Certeau, Michel de. *The Practice of Everyday Life.* Trans. Steven F. Rendall. Berkeley and Los Angeles: U of California P, 1984.

Cervantes, Fernando. *The Devil in the New World: The Impact of Diabolism in New Spain.* New Haven: Yale UP, 1994.

Chaucer, Geoffrey. *The Canterbury Tales. The Riverside Chaucer.* Ed. Larry D. Benson. 3rd ed. Boston: Houghton Mifflin, 1987. 3–328.

Chopin, Kate. *The Awakening.* New York: Capricorn, 1964.

———. "Désirée's Baby." *The Literature of the American South: A Norton Anthology.* Ed. William L. Andrews et al. New York: Norton, 1998. 301–5.

Chrétien de Troyes. *The Complete Romances of Chrétien de Troyes.* Trans. David Staines. Bloomington: Indiana UP, 1990.

Clarke, Deborah. *Robbing the Mother: Women in Faulkner.* Jackson: UP of Mississippi, 1994.

Cobb, James C. *The Most Southern Place on Earth: The Mississippi Delta and the Roots of Regional Identity.* New York: Oxford UP, 1992.

Collins, Carvel. Introduction. *Mayday.* By William Faulkner. South Bend, IN: U of Notre Dame P, 1976.

———. Introduction. *New Orleans Sketches.* By William Faulkner. Jackson: UP of Mississippi, 2002.

"Cotton: The Perennial Patriot; Since 1607 an American Patriot Yesterday Today and Tomorrow." Cotton Counts. National Cotton Council of America. 21 January 2005. http://www.cotton.org/pubs/cottoncounts/upload/Cotton-The-Perennial-Patriot.pdf.

Coughlan, Robert. *The Private World of William Faulkner.* New York: Avon, 1953.

Cowley, Malcolm. *The Faulkner-Cowley File: Letters and Memories, 1944–1962.* New York: Viking, 1966.

———. Introduction. *The Portable Faulkner.* Ed. Malcolm Cowley. New York: Penguin, 1977.

Crang, Mike. *Cultural Geography.* London: Routledge, 1998.

Crang, Mike, and Nigel Thrift, eds. *Thinking Space.* London: Routledge, 2000.

Crawford, Morris De Camp. *The Heritage of Cotton: The Fibre of Two Worlds and Many Ages.* New York: Grosset and Dunlap, 1924.

Crook, J. Mordaunt. *The Greek Revival: Neo-Classical Attitudes in British Architecture, 1760–1870.* London: Murray, 1972.

Cross, Mary, ed. *Advertising and Culture: Theoretical Perspectives.* Westport, CT: Praeger, 1996.

Cullen, John B. *Old Times in the Faulkner Country.* Chapel Hill: U of North Carolina P, 1961.

Dabney, Lewis M. *The Indians of Yoknapatawpha: A Study in Literature and History.* Baton Rouge: Louisiana State UP, 1974.

Dain, Bruce. *A Hideous Monster of the Mind: American Race Theory in the Early Republic.* Cambridge, MA: Harvard UP, 2002.

Daly, M. W., ed. *The Cambridge History of Egypt.* Vol. 2, *Modern Egypt, from 1517 to the End of the Twentieth Century.* Cambridge: Cambridge UP, 1998.

Davis, Thadious M. *Faulkner's "Negro": Art and the Southern Context*. Baton Rouge: Louisiana State UP, 1983.

———. *Games of Property: Law, Race, Gender, and Faulkner's "Go Down, Moses."* Durham, NC: Duke UP, 2003.

Derrida, Jacques. *Of Grammatology*. Trans. Gayatri Chakravorty Spivak. Baltimore: Johns Hopkins UP, 1976.

———. *Writing and Difference*. Trans. Alan Bass. Chicago: U of Chicago P, 1978.

Dixon, Thomas, Jr. *The Clansman: An Historical Romance of the Ku Klux Klan*. Armonk, NY: Sharpe, 2001.

Dobbs, Cynthia. "Flooded: The Excesses of Geography, Gender, and Capitalism in Faulkner's *If I Forget Thee, Jerusalem*." *American Literature: A Journal of Literary History, Criticism, and Bibliography* 73 (2001): 811–35.

Doyle, Don H. *Faulkner's County: The Historical Roots of Yoknapatawpha, 1540–1962*. Chapel Hill: U of North Carolina P, 2001.

Drainville, André C. *Contesting Globalization: Space and Place in the World Economy*. London: Routledge, 2004.

Du Bois, W. E. B. *The Souls of Black Folk*. New York: Penguin, 1996.

Duclos, Donald P. *Son of Sorrow: The Life, Works, and Influence of Colonel William C. Falkner, 1825–1889*. San Francisco: International Scholars Publications, 1998.

Duvall, John N. *Faulkner's Marginal Couple: Invisible, Outlaw, and Unspeakable Communities*. Austin: U of Texas P, 1990.

———. "Paternity in *Pylon*: 'Some Little Sign.'" *Faulkner Journal* 3.1 (1987): 39–51.

Eagleton, Terry. *Literary Theory: An Introduction*. 2nd ed. Minneapolis: U of Minnesota P, 1996.

Earle, Edward Mead. "Egyptian Cotton and the American Civil War." *Political Science Quarterly* 41 (1926): 520–45.

Eddy, Charmaine. "Labor, Economy, and Desire: Rethinking American Nationhood through Yoknapatawpha." *Mississippi Quarterly: The Journal of Southern Cultures* 57 (2004): 569–92.

Engels, Frederick. *The Conditions of the Working Class in England in 1844*. London: George Allen and Unwin, 1926.

Falkner, Murry C. *The Falkners of Mississippi: A Memoir*. Baton Rouge: Louisiana State UP, 1967.

Falkner, William C. *The White Rose of Memphis*. New York: Dillingham, 1881.

Faulkner, John. *My Brother Bill: An Affectionate Reminiscence*. New York: Pocket Books, 1964.

Faulkner, William. *Absalom, Absalom! The Corrected Text*. New York: Vintage International, 1990.

———. *As I Lay Dying: The Corrected Text*. New York: Vintage International, 1990.

———. *Collected Stories*. New York: Vintage, 1977.
———. *Conversations with William Faulkner*. Ed. M. Thomas Inge. Jackson: UP of Mississippi, 1999.
———. *Early Prose and Poetry*. Ed. Carvel Collins. London: Cape, 1962.
———. *Essays, Speeches, and Public Letters*. Ed. James B. Meriwether. New York: Modern Library, 2004.
———. *A Fable*. 1954. New York: Vintage, 1978. (Uncorrected text.)
———. *A Fable*. 1954. *William Faulkner: Novels, 1942–1954*. New York: Library of America, 1994. 665–1072.
———. *"Father Abraham": Holograph Manuscript, Typescripts, and Miscellaneous Pages; and "The wishing tree": Ribbon and Carbon Typescripts*. Ed. Thomas L. McHaney. New York: Garland, 1987.
———. *Faulkner in the University: Class Conferences at the University of Virginia, 1957–1958*. Ed. Frederick L. Gwynn and Joseph L. Blotner. New York: Vintage, 1965.
———. *Flags in the Dust*. Ed. Douglas Day. New York: Random, 1973.
———. *Go Down, Moses, and Other Stories*. 1942. New York: Vintage International, 1990.
———. *The Hamlet*. 1940. *William Faulkner: Novels, 1936–1940*. New York: Library of America, 1990. 727–1075.
———. *If I Forget Thee, Jerusalem [The Wild Palms]*. 1939. New York: Vintage, 1995.
———. *Intruder in the Dust*. 1948. *William Faulkner: Novels, 1942–1954*. New York: Library of America, 1994. 283–470.
———. *Knight's Gambit*. New York: Random House, 1949.
———. *Light in August: The Corrected Text*. New York: Vintage International, 1990.
———. *The Mansion*. 1959. *William Faulkner: Novels, 1957–1962*. New York: Library of America, 1999. 327–721.
———. *"The Marble Faun" and "A Green Bough."* New York: Random House, 1965.
———. *Mayday*. 1926. Ed. Carvel Collins. South Bend, IN: U of Notre Dame P, 1976.
———. "Mississippi." *Holiday*, April 1954, 34–47.
———. *Mosquitoes*. 1927. New York: Liveright, 1997.
———. *New Orleans Sketches*. 1958. Jackson: UP of Mississippi, 2002.
———. *The Portable Faulkner*. Ed. Malcolm Cowley. New York: Penguin, 1977.
———. *Pylon*. 1935. *William Faulkner: Novels, 1930–1935*. New York: Library of America, 1985. 775–992.
———. *The Reivers*. 1962. *William Faulkner: Novels, 1957–1962*. New York: Library of America, 1999. 723–971.
———. *Requiem for a Nun*. 1952. *William Faulkner: Novels, 1942–1954*. New York: Library of America, 1994. 471–664.

———. *Sanctuary: The Corrected Text*. New York: Vintage International, 1993.
———. *Selected Letters of William Faulkner*. Ed. Joseph Blotner. New York: Random, 1977.
———. *Soldiers' Pay*. New York: Liveright, 1970.
———. *The Sound and the Fury: The Corrected Text*. New York: Vintage International, 1990.
———. *Thinking of Home: William Faulkner's Letters to His Mother and Father, 1918–1925*. Ed. James G. Watson. New York: Norton, 2000.
———. *The Town*. 1957. *William Faulkner: Novels, 1957–1962*. New York: Library of America, 1999. 1–326.
———. *Uncollected Stories of William Faulkner*. Ed. Joseph Blotner. New York: Vintage, 1997.
———. *The Unvanquished: The Corrected Text*. New York: Vintage International, 1991.
Feuer, Lewis. *Imperialism and the Anti-Imperialist Mind*. Buffalo, NY: Prometheus Books, 1986.
Floyd, Samuel A., Jr. *The Power of Black Music: Interpreting Its History from Africa to the United States*. New York: Oxford UP, 1995.
Foerst, Jenny Jennings. "The Psychic Wholeness and Corrupt Text of Rosa Coldfield, 'Author and Victim Too' of *Absalom, Absalom!*" *Faulkner Journal* 4.1–2 (1988–89): 37–53.
Foucault, Michel. *Discipline and Punish: The Birth of the Prison*. Trans. Alan Sheridan. New York: Vintage, 1995.
———. "Of Other Spaces." Trans. Jay Miskowiec. *Diacritics* 16.1 (1986): 22–27.
Fowler, Doreen. *Faulkner: The Return of the Repressed*. Charlottesville: UP of Virginia, 1997.
Fox, William L., ed. *Valley of the Craftsmen: A Pictorial History. Scottish Rite Freemasonry in America's Southern Jurisdiction, 1801–2001*. Washington, DC: Supreme Council, Scottish Rite of Freemasonry, Southern Jurisdiction, 2001.
Frazer, James George. *The Golden Bough*. New York: Macmillan, 1940.
Fredrickson, George M. *The Black Image in the White Mind: The Debate on Afro-American Character and Destiny, 1817–1914*. Middletown, CT: Wesleyan UP, 1987.
———. *Black Liberation: A Comparative History of Black Ideologies in the United States and South Africa*. New York: Oxford UP, 1995.
Freud, Sigmund. *Moses and Monotheism: Three Essays. Standard Edition of the Complete Psychological Works of Sigmund Freud*. Trans. James Strachey. Vol. 23. London: Hogarth, 1959. 2–137.
Froehlich, Peter Alan. "Faulkner and the Frontier Grotesque: *The Hamlet* as Southwestern Humor." *Faulkner in Cultural Context: Faulkner and Yokna-*

patawpha, *1995*. Ed. Donald M. Kartiganer and Ann J. Abadie. Jackson: UP of Mississippi, 1997. 218–40.

Fulton, Lorie Watkins. "William Faulkner's Southern Knights: *Sir Gawain and the Green Knight*, Sir Galwyn of Arthgyl, and Gavin Stevens." *Modern Philology: Critical and Historical Studies in Literature, Medieval through Contemporary* 103 (2006): 358–84.

Gaylord, Joshua. "The Radiance of the Fake: *Pylon*'s Postmodern Narrative of Disease." *Faulkner Journal* 20.1–2 (2004–5): 177–95.

Genette, Gérard. *Palimpsests: Literature in the Second Degree*. Lincoln: U of Nebraska P, 1997.

Geoffrey of Monmouth. *The History of the Kings of Britain*. Trans. Lewis Thorpe. London: Penguin, 1966.

Gittes, Katharine S. *Framing the "Canterbury Tales": Chaucer and the Medieval Frame Narrative Tradition*. New York: Greenwood, 1991.

Glaude, Eddie S., Jr. *Exodus! Religion, Race, and Nation in Early Nineteenth-Century Black America*. Chicago: U of Chicago P, 2000.

Glissant, Edouard. *Faulkner, Mississippi*. Trans. Barbara Lewis and Thomas C. Spear. Chicago: U of Chicago P, 1999.

Godden, Richard. "*Absalom, Absalom!* Haiti and Labor History; Reading Unreadable Revolutions." *ELH* 61.3 (1994): 685–72.

———. *Fictions of Labor: William Faulkner and the South's Long Revolution*. Cambridge: Cambridge UP, 1997.

Gramsci, Antonio. *Selections from the Prison Notebooks of Antonio Gramsci*. Ed. and trans. Quintin Hoare and Geoffrey Nowell Smith. New York: International Publishers, 1971.

Gransden, Antonia. *Historical Writing in England, c. 550 to c. 1307*. Ithaca: Cornell UP, 1974.

Gray, Richard. Foreword. *South to a New Place: Region, Literature, Culture*. Ed. Suzanne W. Jones and Sharon Monteith. Baton Rouge: Louisiana State UP, 2002. xiii–xxiii.

———. *The Life of William Faulkner: A Critical Biography*. Oxford: Blackwell, 1994.

Gross, Seymour L., and John Edward Hardy, eds. *Images of the Negro in American Literature*. Chicago: U of Chicago P, 1966.

Gruesz, Kirsten Silva. "Delta *Desterrados:* Antebellum New Orleans and New World Print Culture." *Look Away! The U.S. South in New World Studies*. Ed. Jon Smith and Deborah Cohn. Durham, NC: Duke UP, 2004. 52–79.

Guerin, M. Victoria. "The King's Sin: The Origins of the David-Arthur Parallel." *The Passing of Arthur*. Ed. Christopher Baswell and William Sharpe. New York: Garland, 1988. 15–30.

Gwin, Minrose C. *The Feminine and Faulkner: Reading (beyond) Sexual Difference*. Knoxville: U of Tennessee P, 1990.

———. "Feminism and Faulkner: Second Thoughts; or, What's a radical feminist doing with a canonical male text anyway?" *Faulkner Journal* 4.1–2 (1988–89): 55–65.

Hagopian, John V. "The Biblical Background of Faulkner's *Absalom, Absalom!*" *William Faulkner's "Absalom, Absalom!" A Critical Casebook*. Ed. Elisabeth Muhlenfeld. New York: Garland, 1984. 131–34.

Hamblin, Robert W. "Carcassonne in Mississippi: Faulkner's Geography of the Imagination." *Faulkner and the Craft of Fiction: Faulkner and Yoknapatawpha, 1987*. Ed. Doreen Fowler and Ann J. Abadie. Jackson: UP of Mississippi, 1989. 148–71.

Hamblin, Robert W., and Ann J. Abadie. *Faulkner in the Twenty-first Century: Faulkner and Yoknapatawpha, 2000*. Jackson: UP of Mississippi, 2003.

Hamlin, Talbot. *Greek Revival Architecture in America: Being an Account of Important Trends in American Architecture and American Life prior to the War between the States*. London: Oxford UP, 1944.

Hannon, Charles. *Faulkner and the Discourses of Culture*. Baton Rouge: Louisiana State UP, 2005.

Hardt, Michael, and Antonio Negri. *Empire*. Cambridge, MA: Harvard UP, 2000.

———. *Multitude: War and Democracy in the Age of Empire*. New York: Penguin, 2004.

Harkins, John E. *Metropolis of the American Nile: An Illustrated History of Memphis and Shelby County*. Oxford, MS: Guild Binder, 1991.

Harley, Marta Powell. "Faulkner's Medievalism and *Sir Gawain and the Green Knight*." *American Notes and Queries* 21 (1982–83): 111–14.

Harris, Joel Chandler. *Uncle Remus: His Songs and His Sayings*. New York: Appleton, 1895.

Harrison, Robert. *Aviation Lore in Faulkner*. Amsterdam: John Benjamins, 1985.

Hawthorne, Nathaniel. *The Marble Faun; or, The Romance of Monte Beni*. New York: Signet, 1961.

Heffernan, Thomas J. *Sacred Biography: Saints and Their Biographers in the Middle Ages*. New York: Oxford UP, 1988.

Hicks, Gina L. "Reterritorializing Desire: The Failure of Ceremony in *Absalom, Absalom!*" *Faulkner Journal* 12.2 (1997): 23–39.

Hirsch, Arnold R., and Joseph Logsdon, eds. *Creole New Orleans: Race and Americanization*. Baton Rouge: Louisiana State UP, 1992.

"History of Pima Cotton." *Supima: World's Finest Cottons*. 27 January 2005. http://www.supimacotton.org/history/.

Hönnighausen, Lothar. *Faulkner: Masks and Metaphors*. Jackson: UP of Mississippi, 1997.

———. "'Pegasusrider and Literary Hack': Portraits of the Artist in Faulkner's Short Fiction ('Carcassonne' and 'Artist at Home')." *William Faulkner's Short Fiction: An International Symposium*. Ed. Hans H. Skei. Oslo: Solum Forlag, 1997. 275–88.

Hood, Robert E. *Begrimed and Black: Christian Traditions on Blacks and Blackness*. Minneapolis: Fortress, 1994.

Howell, Elmo. "Faulkner and Scott and the Legacy of the Lost Cause." *Georgia Review* 26 (1972): 314–25.

Hurston, Zora Neale. *Their Eyes Were Watching God*. New York: HarperPerennial, 1990.

Hutchinson, Janis Faye, ed. *Cultural Portrayals of African Americans: Creating an Ethnic/Racial Identity*. Westport, CT: Bergin and Garvey, 1997.

Irving, Washington. "The Legend of Sleepy Hollow." *The Complete Tales of Washington Irving*. Ed. Charles Neider. New York: Da Capo, 1998.

Irwin, John T. *American Hieroglyphics: The Symbol of the Egyptian Hieroglyphics in the American Renaissance*. New Haven: Yale UP, 1980.

———. *Doubling and Incest/Repetition and Revenge: A Speculative Reading of Faulkner*. Exp. ed. Baltimore: Johns Hopkins UP, 1996.

Jehlen, Myra. *Class and Character in Faulkner's South*. New York: Columbia UP, 1976.

Johnson, Marta Paul. "'I Have Decided Now': Laverne's Transformation in *Pylon*." *Mississippi Quarterly: The Journal of Southern Culture* 36 (1983): 289–300.

Johnson, Susie Paul. *Pylon. William Faulkner: Annotations to the Novels*. Ed. James B. Meriwether. New York: Garland, 1989.

Jones, Suzanne W., and Sharon Monteith, eds. *South to a New Place: Region, Literature, Culture*. Baton Rouge: Louisiana State UP, 2002.

Jordan, Winthrop D. *The White Man's Burden: Historical Origins of Racism in the United States*. London: Oxford UP, 1974.

Karl, Frederick R. *William Faulkner, American Writer: A Biography*. New York: Weidenfeld and Nicolson, 1989.

Kartiganer, Donald. *The Fragile Thread: The Meaning of Form in Faulkner's Novels*. Amherst: U of Massachusetts P, 1979.

Kawin, Bruce F. *Faulkner and Film*. New York: Ungar, 1977.

Keats, John. *Selected Poems*. Ed. Elizabeth Cook. Oxford: Oxford UP, 1996.

Keely, Karen A. "Marriage Plots and National Reunion: The Trope of Romantic Reconciliation in Postbellum Literature." *Mississippi Quarterly: The Journal of Southern Culture* 51 (1998): 621–48.

Kennedy, Beverly. "The Re-emergence of Tragedy in Late Medieval England:

Sir Thomas Malory's *Morte Darthur.*" *The Existential Coordinates of the Human Condition: Poetic—Epic—Tragic; The Literary Genre.* Ed. Anna-Teresa Tymieniecka. Analecta Husserliana 18. Dordrecht: Reidel, 1984. 363–78.
Kennedy, John Pendleton. *Swallow Barn; or, A Sojourn in the Old Dominion.* Baton Rouge: Louisiana State UP, 1986.
Kennedy, Richard S., ed. *Literary New Orleans: Essays and Meditations.* Baton Rouge: Louisiana State UP, 1992.
———. *Literary New Orleans in the Modern World.* Baton Rouge: Louisiana State UP, 1998.
Kerr, Elizabeth M. *Yoknapatawpha: Faulkner's "Little Postage Stamp of Native Soil."* New York: Fordham UP, 1969.
Kestner, Joseph A. *The Spatiality of the Novel.* Detroit: Wayne State UP, 1978.
King, Grace. *Balcony Stories.* New York: Macmillan, 1925.
———. *New Orleans: The Place and the People.* New York: Macmillan, 1895.
"The Kingdom of the Negro, the Mule, and Cotton." *Cotton Trade Journal* (international ed.) 12.1 (1932): 49–50, 51–52.
Kodat, Catherine Gunther. "Posting Yoknapatawpha." *Mississippi Quarterly: The Journal of Southern Cultures* 57 (2004): 593–618.
Kort, Wesley A. *Place and Space in Modern Fiction.* Gainesville: UP of Florida, 2004.
Kowalewski, Michael. "Writing in Place: The New American Regionalism." *American Literary History* 6.1 (1994): 171–83.
Kreyling, Michael. *Inventing Southern Literature.* Jackson: UP of Mississippi, 1998.
Labatt, Blair. *Faulkner the Storyteller.* Tuscaloosa: U of Alabama P, 2005.
Ladd, Barbara. "Dismantling the Monolith: Southern Places—Past, Present, and Future." *South to a New Place.* Ed. Suzanne W. Jones and Sharon Monteith. Baton Rouge: Louisiana State UP, 2002. 44–57.
———. "William Faulkner, Edouard Glissant, and a Creole Poetics of History and Body in *Absalom, Absalom!* and *A Fable.*" *Faulkner in the Twenty-first Century: Faulkner and Yoknapatawpha, 2000.* Ed. Robert W. Hamblin and Ann J. Abadie. Jackson: UP of Mississippi, 2003. 31–49.
Land of the Pharaohs. Dir. Howard Hawks. Writ. Harold Jack Bloom, William Faulkner, and Harry Kurnitz. Perf. Jack Hawkins, Joan Collins, Dewey Martin, Alex Minotis, and James Robertson Justice. Warner Bros., 1955.
Lane, Mills. *Architecture of the Old South.* Savannah: Beehive Foundation, 1996.
Lears, Jackson. *Fables of Abundance: A Cultural History of Advertising in America.* New York: Basic Books, 1994.
Leary, Lewis. *William Faulkner of Yoknapatawpha County.* New York: Crowell, 1973.
Leavitt, Mel. *A Short History of New Orleans.* San Francisco: Lexikos, 1982.

Lefebvre, Henri. *The Production of Space*. Trans. Donald Nicholson-Smith. Oxford: Blackwell, 1991.

Levins, Lynn Gartrell. *Faulkner's Heroic Design: The Yoknapatawpha Novels*. Athens: U of Georgia P, 1976.

Lévi-Strauss, Claude. *The Savage Mind*. Trans. George Weidenfeld. Chicago: U of Chicago P, 1966.

Limerick, Patricia Nelson. *The Legacy of Conquest: The Unbroken Past of the American West*. New York: Norton, 1987.

Lincoln, Bruce. *Theorizing Myth: Narrative, Ideology, and Scholarship*. Chicago: U of Chicago P, 1999.

Lively, Adam. *Masks: Blackness, Race, and the Imagination*. Oxford: Oxford UP, 2000.

"A Look at Paul Rainey—The Man." *News and Journal of the Tippah County Historical and Genealogical Society* 3.12 (1978): 1–2, 4.

López, Alfred J. *Posts and Pasts: A Theory of Postcolonialism*. Albany: State U of New York P, 2001.

Lupack, Alan, and Barbara Tepa Lupack. *King Arthur in America*. Cambridge, UK: Brewer, 1999.

Lutwack, Leonard. *The Role of Place in Literature*. Syracuse: Syracuse UP, 1984.

Lynen, John F. "The Design of Puritan Experience." *Theories of American Literature*. Ed. Donald M. Kartiganer and Malcolm A. Griffith. New York: Macmillan, 1972. 302–23.

MacKethan, Lucinda. *The Dream of Arcady: Place and Time in Southern Literature*. Baton Rouge: Louisiana State UP, 1980.

———. "Plantation Fiction, 1865–1900." *The History of Southern Literature*. Ed. Louis D. Rubin Jr. Baton Rouge: Louisiana State UP, 1985. 209–18.

Mackey, Albert G. *An Encyclopedia of Freemasonry and Its Kindred Sciences, Comprising the Whole Range of Arts, Sciences and Literature as Connected with the Institution*. Vol. 1. New and rev. ed. New York: Masonic History Company, 1919.

Malory, Sir Thomas. *The Birth Life and Acts of King Arthur of his Noble Knights of the Round Table their Marvellous Enquests and Adventures the Achieving of the San Greal and in the End Le Morte Darthur with the Dolorous Death and Departing out of this World of Them All*. London: Dent, 1927.

———. *Le Morte Darthur: The Winchester Manuscript*. Oxford: Oxford UP, 1998.

Malpas, J. E. *Place and Experience: A Philosophical Topography*. Cambridge: Cambridge UP, 1999.

Marx, Karl, and Frederick Engels. "Manifesto of the Communist Party." *Karl*

Marx and Frederick Engels: Selected Works, in One Volume. New York: International Publishers, 1968. 31–96.

Matthews, John T. "The Autograph of Violence in Faulkner's *Pylon.*" *Southern Literature and Literary Theory.* Ed. Jefferson Humphries. Athens: U of Georgia P, 1990. 247–69.

———. *The Play of Faulkner's Language.* Ithaca: Cornell UP, 1982.

Maynard, W. Barksdale. *Architecture in the United States, 1800–1850.* New Haven: Yale UP, 2002.

McClintock, Anne. *Imperial Leather: Race, Gender, and Sexuality in the Colonial Contest.* New York: Routledge, 1995.

McDowell, Linda, ed. *Undoing Place? A Geographical Reader.* London: Arnold, 1997.

McDowell, Peggy, and Richard E. Meyer. *The Revival Styles in American Memorial Art.* Bowling Green, OH: Bowling Green State U Popular P, 1994.

McGowan, Joseph Clarence. *History of Extra-Long Staple Cottons.* El Paso: Hill, 1961.

McHaney, Thomas L. "First Is Jefferson: Faulkner Shapes His Domain." *Mississippi Quarterly: The Journal of Southern Cultures* 57 (2004): 511–34.

McIlwaine, Shields. *Memphis: Down in Dixie.* New York: Dutton, 1948.

McPherson, Tara. *Reconstructing Dixie: Race, Gender, and Nostalgia in the Imagined South.* Durham, NC: Duke UP, 2003.

Melville, Herman. *The Confidence-Man: His Masquerade.* New York: Holt, Rinehart, and Winston, 1964.

Mencken, H. L. "The Sahara of the Bozart." *Prejudices: Second Series.* New York: Knopf, 1924. 136–54.

Meriwether, James B., and Michael Millgate, eds. *Lion in the Garden: Interviews with William Faulkner, 1926–1962.* New York: Random House, 1968.

Messadié, Gérald. *A History of the Devil.* Trans. Marc Romano. New York: Kodansha, 1996.

Millgate, Michael. *Faulkner's Place.* Athens: U of Georgia P, 1997.

Milum, Richard. "Faulkner and the Cavalier Tradition: The French Bequest." *American Literature* 45 (1974): 580–89.

Miner, Ward L. *The World of William Faulkner.* New York: Grove, 1952.

Minter, David. *Faulkner's Questioning Narratives: Fiction of His Major Phase, 1929–42.* Urbana: U of Illinois P, 2004.

———. *William Faulkner: His Life and Work.* Baltimore: Johns Hopkins UP, 1997.

Mixon, Wayne. *Southern Writers and the New South Movement, 1865–1913.* Chapel Hill: U of North Carolina P, 1980.

Morrison, Gail Moore. "Time, Tide, and Twilight": *Mayday* and Faulkner's Quest toward *The Sound and the Fury.*" *Mississippi Quarterly: The Journal of Southern Culture* 31 (1978): 337–57.

Murfree, Mary Noailles. *In the Tennessee Mountains*. Boston: Houghton, Mifflin, 1884.

Murray, Henry A. "Definitions of Myth." *The Making of Myth*. Ed. Richard M. Ohmann. New York: Putnam, 1962. 7–37.

New York Cotton Exchange. *Charters, By-Laws, and Rules of the New York Cotton Exchange*. 18th ed. New York, 1910.

Nietzsche, Friedrich. *"The Birth of Tragedy" and "The Case of Wagner."* Trans. Walter Kaufmann. New York: Vintage, 1967.

Norberg-Schulz, Christian. *Genius Loci: Towards a Phenomenology of Architecture*. New York: Rizzoli, 1980.

North, Michael. *The Dialect of Modernism: Race, Language, and Twentieth-Century Literature*. New York: Oxford UP, 1994.

O'Donnell, George Marion. "Faulkner's Mythology." *William Faulkner: Three Decades of Criticism*. Ed. Frederick J. Hoffman and Olga W. Vickery. New York: Harcourt, Brace, and World, 1960. 82–93.

Ohmann, Richard M., ed. *The Making of Myth*. New York: Putnam, 1962.

Oldenbourg, Zoe. *Massacre at Montsegur: A History of the Albigensian Crusade*. New York: Minerva, 1968.

Olien, Roger M., and Diana Davids Olien. *Oil and Ideology: The Cultural Creation of the American Petroleum Industry*. Chapel Hill: U of North Carolina P, 2000.

Owada, Eiko. "History and Memory in Faulkner's 'Carcassonne' and 'Black Music.'" *History and Memory in Faulkner's Novels*. Ed. Ikuko Fujihira, Noel Polk, and Hisao Tanaka. Tokyo: Shohakusha, 2005. 122–40.

Owen, Edward Roger John. *Cotton and the Egyptian Economy, 1820–1914: A Study in Trade and Development*. Oxford: Clarendon, 1969.

Page, Thomas Nelson. *Gordon Keith*. New York: Scribner's, 1903.

Parini, Jay. *One Matchless Time: A Life of William Faulkner*. New York: HarperCollins, 2004.

Parker, Robert Dale. *"Absalom, Absalom!" The Questioning of Fiction*. Boston: Twayne, 1991.

Paulding, James Kirk. *Westward Ho!* New York: Harper, 1832.

Polk, Noel. "'Polysyllabic and Verbless Patriotic Nonsense': Faulkner at Mid-century—His and Ours." *Faulkner and Ideology: Faulkner and Yoknapatawpha, 1992*. Ed. Donald M. Kartiganer and Ann J. Abadie. Jackson: UP of Mississippi, 1995.

———. "William Faulkner's 'Carcassonne.'" *Studies in American Fiction* 12 (1984): 29–43.

Railey, Kevin. "*Absalom, Absalom!* and the Southern Ideology of Race." *Faulkner Journal* 14.2 (1999): 41–55.

———. *Natural Aristocracy: History, Ideology, and the Production of William Faulkner.* Tuscaloosa: U of Alabama P, 1999.

Reinders, Robert C. *End of an Era: New Orleans, 1850–1860.* New Orleans: Pelican, 1964.

Relph, E. *Place and Placelessness.* London: Pion, 1976.

Richardson, H. Edward. *William Faulkner: The Journey to Self-Discovery.* Columbia: U of Missouri P, 1969.

Rigby, Peter. *African Images: Racism and the End of Anthropology.* Oxford: Berg, 1996.

Roach, Joseph. *Cities of the Dead: Circum-Atlantic Performance.* New York: Columbia UP, 1996.

Roberts, Diane. *Faulkner and Southern Womanhood.* Athens: U of Georgia P, 1994.

Roper, James. *The Founding of Memphis, 1818–1820.* Memphis: Memphis Sesquicentennial, 1970.

Rose, Maxine. "The Biblical Background of *Absalom, Absalom!*" *Critical Essays on William Faulkner: The Sutpen Family.* Ed. Arthur F. Kinney. New York: Hall, 1996. 259–67.

Ross, Stephen M. *Fiction's Inexhaustible Voice: Speech and Writing in Faulkner.* Athens: U of Georgia P, 1989.

———. "Oratory and the Dialogical in *Absalom, Absalom!*" *Intertextuality in Faulkner.* Ed. Michel Gresset and Noel Polk. Jackson: UP of Mississippi, 1985. 73–86.

Ruppersburg, Hugh M. *Voice and Eye in Faulkner's Fiction.* Athens: U of Georgia P, 1983.

Russell, Jeffrey Burton. *Lucifer: The Devil in the Middle Ages.* Ithaca: Cornell UP, 1984.

Ruzicka, William T. *Faulkner's Fictive Architecture: The Meaning of Place in the Yoknapatawpha Novels.* Ann Arbor: UMI Research, 1987.

Said, Edward W. *Orientalism.* New York: Vintage, 1979.

Salda, Michael. "William Faulkner's Arthurian Tale: *Mayday.*" *Arthuriana* 4 (1994): 348–75.

Saldívar, Ramón. "Looking for a Master Plan: Faulkner, Paredes, and the Colonial and Postcolonial Subject." *The Cambridge Companion to William Faulkner.* Ed. Philip M. Weinstein. Cambridge: Cambridge UP, 1996. 96–120.

Saxon, Lyle. *Fabulous New Orleans.* New Orleans: Crager, 1947.

Schulz, William. "Just Like Father: Mr. Compson as Cavalier Romancer in *Absalom, Absalom!*" *Kansas Quarterly* 14.2 (1982): 115–23.

Schwartz, Lawrence H. *Creating Faulkner's Reputation: The Politics of Modern Literary Criticism.* Knoxville: U of Tennessee P, 1988.

Scott, Evelyn. *The Wave*. Baton Rouge: Louisiana State UP, 1996.

Sebeok, Thomas A., ed. *Myth: A Symposium*. Bloomington: Indiana UP, 1958.

Sensibar, Judith L. *The Origins of Faulkner's Art*. Austin: U of Texas P, 1984.

Serafin, Joan M. *Faulkner's Use of the Classics*. Ann Arbor: UMI Research, 1983.

Shoaf, R. A. "The Alliterative Morte Arthure: The Story of Britain's David." *Journal of English and Germanic Philology* 81.2 (1982): 204–26.

Silber, Nina. *The Romance of Reunion: Northerners and the South, 1865–1900*. Chapel Hill: U of North Carolina P, 1993.

Simms, William Gilmore. *Woodcraft; or, Hawks about the Dovecote: A Story of the South at the Close of the Revolution*. New York: Armstrong and Son, 1882.

Singal, Daniel J. *The War Within: From Victorian to Modernist Thought in the South, 1919–1945*. Chapel Hill: U of North Carolina P, 1982.

Sir Gawain and the Green Knight. Trans. Brian Stone. London: Penguin, 1974.

Skei, Hans. *William Faulkner: The Short Story Career; An Outline of Faulkner's Short Story Writing from 1919 to 1962*. Oslo: Universitetlforlaget, 1981.

Slatoff, Walter J. *Quest for Failure: A Study of William Faulkner*. Ithaca: Cornell UP, 1960.

Slotkin, Richard. *Gunfighter Nation: The Myth of the Frontier in Twentieth-Century America*. New York: Atheneum, 1992.

———. *Regeneration through Violence: The Mythology of the American Frontier, 1600–1860*. 1973. New York: Harper Perennial, 1996.

Smith, Jon, and Deborah Cohn, eds. *Look Away! The U.S. South in New World Studies*. Durham, NC: Duke UP, 2004.

Snell, Susan. *Phil Stone of Oxford: A Vicarious Life*. Athens: U of Georgia P, 1991.

Soja, Edward W. *Postmodern Geographies: The Reassertion of Space in Critical Social Theory*. London: Verso, 1989.

Southern, Eileen. *The Music of Black Americans: A History*. New York: Norton, 1983.

Spencer, Jon Michael. *Protest and Praise: Sacred Music of Black Religion*. Minneapolis: Fortress, 1990.

Spencer, Sharon. *Space, Time, and Structure in the Modern Novel*. New York: New York UP, 1971.

Spillers, Hortense J. "Topographical Topics: Faulknerian Space." *Mississippi Quarterly: The Journal of Southern Cultures* 57 (2004): 535–68.

Spivak, Gayatri Chakravorty. "Can the Subaltern Speak?" *Colonial Discourse and Post-Colonial Theory: A Reader*. Ed. Patrick Williams and Laura Chrisman. New York: Columbia UP, 1994. 66–111.

———. *A Critique of Postcolonial Reason: Toward a History of the Vanishing Present*. Cambridge, MA: Harvard UP, 1999.

———. *The Postcolonial Critic: Interviews, Strategies, Dialogues.* Ed. Sarah Harasym. New York: Routledge, 1990.

Spratling, William, and William Faulkner. *Sherwood Anderson and Other Famous Creoles.* 1926. Austin: U of Texas P, 1966.

Stanchich, Maritza. "The Hidden Caribbean 'Other' in William Faulkner's *Absalom, Absalom!* An Ideological Ancestry of U.S. Imperialism." *Mississippi Quarterly: The Journal of Southern Culture* 49 (1996): 603–17.

St. Clair, William. *Lord Elgin and the Marbles.* London: Oxford UP, 1967.

Stokes, Mason. *The Color of Sex: Whiteness, Heterosexuality, and the Fictions of White Supremacy.* Durham, NC: Duke UP, 2001.

Stone, Phil. Preface. *"The Marble Faun" and "A Green Bough."* By William Faulkner. New York: Random House, 1965. 6–8.

Stonum, Gary Lee. *Faulkner's Career: An Internal Literary History.* Ithaca: Cornell UP, 1979.

Stowe, Harriet Beecher. *Uncle Tom's Cabin; or, Life among the Lowly.* New York: Harper, 1965.

Straumann, Heinrich. "An American Interpretation of Existence: Faulkner's *A Fable.*" *William Faulkner: Three Decades of Criticism.* Ed. Frederick J. Hoffman and Olga W. Vickery. New York: Harcourt, Brace, and World, 1960. 349–72.

Sumption, Jonathan. *The Albigensian Crusade.* London: Faber, 1999.

Sundquist, Eric. *Faulkner: The House Divided.* Baltimore: Johns Hopkins UP, 1983.

Taylor, Walter. *Faulkner's Search for a South.* Urbana: U of Illinois P, 1983.

Taylor, William R. *Cavalier and Yankee: The Old South and American National Character.* Garden City, NY: Anchor Books, 1963.

Tennyson, Alfred Lord. *Idylls of the King.* London: Penguin, 1983.

Thompson, John B. *Ideology and Modern Culture: Critical Social Theory in the Era of Mass Communication.* Stanford: Stanford UP, 1990.

Trafton, Scott. *Egypt Land: Race and Nineteenth-Century American Egyptomania.* Durham, NC: Duke UP, 2004.

Trefzer, Annette. "Postcolonial Displacements in Faulkner's Indian Stories of the 1930s." *Faulkner in the Twenty-first Century: Faulkner and Yoknapatawpha, 2000.* Ed. Robert W. Hamblin and Ann J. Abadie. Jackson: UP of Mississippi, 2003. 68–88.

Tuan, Yi-Fu. *Space and Place: The Perspective of Experience.* Minneapolis: U of Minnesota P, 1977.

Tucker, Beverly. *George Balcombe.* New York: Harper, 1836.

———. *The Partisan Leader.* New York: Rudd and Carleton, 1861.

Tucker, George. *The Valley of the Shenandoah; or, Memoirs of the Graysons.* New York: Roorbach, 1828.

Twain, Mark. *Life on the Mississippi.* New York: Bantam, 1981.

Twelve Southerners. *I'll Take My Stand: The South and the Agrarian Tradition.* Baton Rouge: Louisiana State UP, 1977.

Urgo, Joseph R. *Faulkner's Apocrypha: "A Fable," Snopes, and the Spirit of Human Rebellion.* Jackson: UP of Mississippi, 1989.

———. Introduction. *Faulkner in America: Faulkner and Yoknapatawpha, 1998.* Ed. Joseph R. Urgo and Ann J. Abadie. Jackson: UP of Mississippi, 2001. ix–xxvii.

———. "Where Was That Bird? Thinking *America* through Faulkner." *Faulkner in America: Faulkner and Yoknapatawpha, 1998.* Ed. Joseph R. Urgo and Ann J. Abadie. Jackson: UP of Mississippi, 2001.

———. "The Yoknapatawpha Project: The Map of a Deeper Existence." *Mississippi Quarterly: The Journal of Southern Cultures* 57 (2004): 639–55.

van Baak, J. J. *The Place of Space in Narration: A Semiotic Approach to the Problem of Literary Space.* Amsterdam: Rodopi, 1983.

Van Devender, George W. "William Faulkner's Black Exodus: Multiple Narratives in *The Unvanquished.*" *South Central Bulletin* 42 (1982): 144–48.

Vrettos, Theodore. *The Elgin Affair: The Abduction of Antiquity's Greatest Treasures and the Passions It Aroused.* New York: Arcade, 1997.

Wace and Layamon. *The Life of King Arthur.* Trans. Judith Weiss and Rosamund Allen. London: Everyman, 1997.

Wadsworth, Alfred P., and Julia De Lacy Mann. *The Cotton Trade and Industrial Lancashire, 1600–1780.* Manchester: Manchester UP, 1931.

Watson, James Gray. *The Snopes Dilemma: Faulkner's Trilogy.* Coral Gables, FL: U of Miami P, 1968.

———. *William Faulkner: Self-Presentation and Performance.* Austin: U of Texas P, 2000.

Weinstein, Philip M. *Faulkner's Subject: A Cosmos No One Owns.* Cambridge: Cambridge UP, 1992.

West, Cornel. *Prophesy Deliverance! An Afro-American Revolutionary Christianity.* Philadelphia: Westminster, 1982.

Wheelwright, Philip. "Semantic Approach to Myth." *Myth: A Symposium.* Ed. Thomas A. Sebeok. Bloomington: Indiana UP, 1958. 95–103.

White, Richard. "Frederick Jackson Turner and Buffalo Bill." *The Frontier in American Culture: An Exhibition at the Newberry Library, August 26, 1994–January 7, 1995.* Ed. James R. Grossman. Berkeley and Los Angeles: U of California P, 1994.

Whitman, Walt. "Song of Myself." *Leaves of Grass: The First (1855) Edition.* Ed. Malcolm Cowley. New York: Penguin, 1959. 25–86.

Wilkinson, John G. *Manners and Customs of the Ancient Egyptians.* London: Murray, 1837.

"William Faulkner of Oxford." *Omnibus*. 1952. Prod. Robert Saudek. Perf. William Faulkner, Phil Mullins, Phil Stone. Ford Foundation Workshop. DVD transfer from original 35 mm negative. University, MS: U of Mississippi Media Production Services, 2005.

Williams, David. *Faulkner's Women: The Myth and the Muse*. Montreal: McGill-Queen's UP, 1977.

Williams, Raymond. *The Country and the City*. New York: Oxford UP, 1973.

Williamson, Joel. *William Faulkner and Southern History*. New York: Oxford UP, 1993.

Wilmore, Gayraud S. *Black Religion and Black Radicalism: An Interpretation of the Religious History of Afro-American People*. 2nd ed. Maryknoll, NY: Orbis Books, 1983.

Wilson, Charles Reagan. *Baptized in Blood: The Religion of the Lost Cause, 1865–1920*. Athens: U of Georgia P, 1983.

———. *Judgment and Grace in Dixie: Southern Faiths from Faulkner to Elvis*. Athens: U of Georgia P, 1995.

Wolff, Robert Lee. "The Three Romes: The Migration of an Ideology and the Making of an Autocrat." *The Making of Myth*. Ed. Richard M. Ohmann. New York: Putnam, 1962. 135–58.

Woods, William. *A History of the Devil*. New York: Putnam, 1973.

Wortham, John D. *The Genesis of British Egyptology, 1549–1906*. Norman: U of Oklahoma P, 1971.

Yafa, Stephen. *Cotton: The Biography of a Revolutionary Fiber*. New York: Penguin, 2005.

Zender, Karl F. *The Crossing of the Ways: William Faulkner, the South, and the Modern World*. New Brunswick, NJ: Rutgers UP, 1989.

INDEX

Abraham, 67, 115, 129
Absalom, 173, 216*n*12
Absalom, Absalom! (Faulkner), 13, 26, 33, 83–85, 109–11, 168–78, 182, 189, 214*nn*12–13, 214*n*16
"Address to the Graduating Class of Pine Manor Junior College" (Faulkner), 16
Advertising: and Faulkner's cosmos, 29; and New Orleans's founding, 74; of Monkey Brand soap, 85–86, 108; in *Pylon*, 103–5; and "hyperreality," 104; and ideology, 210–11*n*17; pastoral and technology in, 212*n*20
Aedes aegypti mosquito, 91, 126
Aerodynamics, 100
Agamemnon, 33, 158, 173–75
Airplanes: in "Mississippi," 28; Faulkner's experience with, 98–100, 210*n*11; in *Pylon*, 100–9, 210*n*12, 211*n*18, 214*n*11; in *A Fable*, 188–89, 197
Albigensian Crusade, 162, 215*n*5
Alliterative Morte Arthure, The, 155
Anderson, Sherwood, 18–19, 45, 50, 77, 78, 92, 109, 208*n*17
Apollonian, 38, 40–41, 64, 65
Arabian Nights, 83, 84
Arcady, southern, 30, 41
Architecture: classical revival, 33; Greek Revival, 33–34, 40; U.S. southern, 34; and Freemasonry, 212*n*1
Arthurian legend: in *If I Forget Thee, Jerusalem*, 114; development of, 154–57, 158–59, 215*n*2; southern uses of, 157–58; aristocratic uses of, 157–83 *passim;* in *Mayday*, 159–61, 174–75; and "Mirrors of Chartres Street," 160–61; and Christianity, 161; and questing motif, 161, 164, 166, 168, 175, 177, 178, 180, 188; in *Absalom, Absalom!* 161–62, 168–78; in "Carcassonne," 161–63; in *The Sound and the Fury*, 163–64; in *The Reivers*, 164–68; King Arthur as King David, 173; in *As I Lay Dying*, 177–78; in the Snopes novels, 178–82; in *Requiem for a Nun*, 182–83; in *A Fable*, 187–89; mentioned, 30–31
As I Lay Dying (Faulkner), 42, 139, 177–78
Atom bomb, 11
Aurelianus, Ambrosius, 154
Ayers, Major (in *Mosquitoes*), 93–94, 141

Bakhtin, Mikhail, 66, 76, 80, 167, 177, 212*n*21
Barthes, Roland, 3–4, 13–14, 204*n*10, 217*n*4
"Bear, The" (Faulkner), 66–69, 114, 146, 149, 216*n*14
Beardsley, Aubrey, 158–59, 160, 175
Beauchamp, Lucas, 147–51, 167
Beauchamp, Mollie, 146–51 *passim*
Beauchamp, Philip Manigault, 196
Bede, Venerable, 154
Belle (in *Sanctuary*), 142
Ben. *See* "Bear, The" (Faulkner)

240 Index

Benbow, Horace, 142, 209*n*25
Benjamin (biblical), 120, 128–29, 134, 146, 147
Bienville, Jean Baptiste Le Moyne, Sieur de, 72–73, 117, 126
"Black Music" (Faulkner), 33, 43–50, 53, 55, 59, 162, 208*nn*15–19
Blackbird, 37, 39
Blackness: goats as racist signifiers of, 40, 207*n*11; and marble faun, 41, 207*n*13; of Benjy Compson, 130, 140. *See also* Counterfeit Other; Hybridity; Marble faun; Whiteness
Bluebird Insurance Company, 37, 206*n*8
Bluegum, 129, 134
Boccaccio, 88
Bon, Charles, 18, 41, 83–85, 86, 87, 110, 116, 169, 171–74, 177, 190, 216*nn*12, 13
Bonaparte, Napoleon. *See* Napoleon (Bonaparte)
Bones, Brom, 53
Boone, Daniel, 114
Boston, 34, 44, 59, 137
Bourdieu, Pierre, 9, 203*n*8
Bricolage, 14, 67, 79, 98, 103, 154, 158
Bricoleur, 14, 207*n*10
British Empire. *See* England
Bundren, Addie, 139, 177
Bundren, Cash, 42, 139
Bundren, Darl, 42, 139, 214*n*18
Bundren, Jewel, 42, 139, 178
Burden, Joanna, 50, 64, 138
Butler, Gen. Benjamin "Beast," 75

Cabell, James Branch, 159–60
Caddy. *See* Compson, Caddy
Caesar, 17, 57, 66, 81, 82, 96, 186, 187, 189
Cairo, Egypt, 126
Cairo, Illinois, 122, 213*n*3
Cajuns, 112–15 *passim*
Camelot: as example of mythic place, 13, 183; the South as, 158, 164; as mythic imperial space of Christianity, 161, 164; similarity to Carcassonne, 162–63; Sutpen's Hundred as, 171–72, 176–77; Flem Snopes's Camelot, 178; and Lump Snopes, 179; and Clarence Snopes, 180; mentioned, 30, 153–57 *passim,* 160, 161, 162, 168. *See also* Arthurian legend
Campbell, Joseph, 1, 12, 212*n*1
Carcassonne, 161–63
"Carcassonne" (Faulkner), 162, 208*n*15, 215*n*6, 216*n*13
Caruthers, William Alexander, 157
Cecilia Farmer (name etched on glass), 143
Center, cultural, 10, 11, 13, 16, 17, 19, 35, 36, 38, 41, 44, 48, 49, 54, 57, 59, 68, 74, 76, 78, 81, 82, 83, 85, 87, 88, 92, 93, 102, 110, 115, 116, 120, 126, 128, 130, 131, 132, 133, 134, 137, 138, 139, 140, 142, 143, 145, 147, 155, 161, 162, 164, 177, 191, 192, 195, 196, 197, 198, 202*n*2, 202*n*6, 206*n*4. *See also* Periphery, cultural; Place; Space
Certeau, Michel de, 12
Charles III, 73
Charleston, 39, 43, 53, 55, 182
Charlestown, Ga., 53–56 *passim*
Chaucer, Geoffrey, 88–89
Choctaw, 27, 73–74, 83, 169
Christ, 18, 50, 107, 154, 161, 185–97 *passim*
Christian myth: and goat iconography, 40; and Greek mythic layer, 41, 46, 50–55; and Arthurian legend, 161–62, 187; mentioned, 21, 30, 80–81, 185, 190–92
Christmas, Joe, 41, 43, 50, 51, 190, 210*n*8
Churchill, Winston, 189
Cigar-store Indian, 42, 55, 65, 124
Cinderella, 53
Civil War, 23, 24, 26, 27, 38, 44, 49, 60, 62, 73, 74, 78, 122, 123, 124, 161, 171, 213*n*7
Classical revival architecture. *See* Architecture
Cleopatra, 135, 140–41, 143
Coca Cola, 117

Code duello, 80
Cold war politics, 4, 217
Colonel Confed (in *The White Rose of Memphis*), 89–90
Compson Appendix, 128–29, 140, 214*n*14
Compson, Benjy, 128–34, 140, 146
Compson, Caddy, 87, 128–30, 133, 135, 140–41, 164, 216*n*13
Compson, Jason, 36, 132–34, 137, 140, 141, 151, 216*n*13
Compson, Quentin (female), 133–34, 135, 140–41
Compson, Quentin (male), 23, 26, 83, 85–87, 99, 110–11, 128, 129, 135–38, 139–40, 149, 163–64, 169, 172–73, 175, 176, 177, 179, 183, 209*n*6, 216*n*13
Compson, Quentin MacLachan, 128, 140
Confederate States of America, 55, 73, 122; Confederate soldier statue, 55, 64–65
Consummatory stage, of myth development, 20, 21, 25, 26, 29, 62, 81, 105, 106, 107, 108, 141, 155, 158. *See also* Myth
Corporal (in *A Fable*), 186, 187, 190–93, 196–99
Cosmos: Faulkner's cosmos, 1–5 *passim,* 9, 10, 13, 15, 17, 19, 28–29, 30, 98, 109, 125, 126, 148, 153, 160, 161, 185, 198, 205*n*11; Faulkner's comments on, 19; general discussion of term, 205*n*16
Cotton: in "Mississippi," 25–26, 28; in *The Sound and the Fury,* 36, 132–33, 141; in "The Bear," 68–69; New Orleans cotton exchange, 74, 125; history of cotton/empire in Egypt and U.S. South, 121–26, 213–14*nn*6–10; and the Mississippi Delta, 121–26; and the Civil War, 122–23; in ancient Egypt, 122; long staple, 122; Egyptian exportation to Britain, 122; and rise of modern Egypt, 122–23; mixture of American and Egyptian strains of, 123–24; Extra-Long Staple, 123; Mitafifi, 124; Yuma, 124; Pima, 124, 125; as emblem of hybridity and empire, 124; and Native Americans of Southwest, 124; uses during World War II, 124; U.S. involvement in market after World War II, 125; and Hawley-Smoot Tariff Act, 125; Memphis Cotton Carnival, 125–26, 214*n*10; as the "golden fleece" (in Du Bois), 132; New York Cotton Exchange, 133; in *Sanctuary,* 142; in *Requiem for a Nun,* 143; in *Go Down, Moses,* 147; in *Flags in the Dust,* 148; "Cotton Kingdom" in *Absalom, Absalom!* 170; in *A Fable,* 195; and British Industrial Revolution, 213*n*5
Counterfeit Other: marble faun as, 41; Januarius Jones as, 51; Charles Bon as, 84; Al Jackson as, 92; Quentin Compson as, 140; white aristocrats as, 153; Christians in Carcassonne as, 162; military leaders in *A Fable* as, 189; mentioned, 87; source of term, 207*n*13. *See also* Faun
Counternarrative, 3
Cowley, Malcolm: introduction to *The Portable Faulkner,* 6–7, 12, 24, 29, 202*n*3; introduction to "Mississippi," 21, 23; and Faulkner's war experience, 99, 210*n*11
Coyle, Ray F., 159
Crane, Ichabod, 48–49, 53, 62, 63, 108
Crossing the river/sea motif. *See* Egypt
Crusade, 107, 161, 162, 164, 171, 187, 192, 215*n*5

Dark angel, 16–18
David, king of Israel: in *Absalom, Absalom!* 172–73, 216n12–13; in *Mayday,* 175; in *A Fable,* 188–89. *See also* Arthurian legend
Davis, Jefferson, 158
De Spain, Manfred, 63–64, 179
Deacon (in *The Sound and the Fury*), 136–37
Delta, Mississippi, 25, 30, 31, 112, 121, 122, 123, 126, 132, 142, 145, 146, 147, 194, 208*n*23, 213*n*4
Delta, Nile, 30, 121, 132. *See also* Egypt

242 Index

Dent, J. M., 158–60. See also Arthurian legend
Dilsey (in *The Sound and the Fury*), 128–36 passim
Dionysian, 38–64 passim. See also Greek/Roman myth
Dixon, Thomas, 158, 180
Donatello, 40
Drake, Temple, 141–43, 164, 168, 182–83
"Dream of Arcady." See Arcady, southern
Du Bois, W. E. B., 132
Du Pre, Virginia, 163

Easter Sunday, 130–32
Edison, Thomas, 124
Edmonds, McCaslin, 66
Egypt: as imperial precedent, 119; and Orientalism, 119–21; in U.S. and British iconography, 119–21; Egyptomania, 119–29 passim; mummy-unwrapping motif, 120, 131, 141, 150, 191; and Freemasonry, 120, 165, 188, 192–93, 212n1, 214n16, 214n18; in southern iconography, 121–26; Mississippi Delta as Nile Delta, 121–22, 123, 126; connections between South and Egypt, 122–26; in "Mirrors of Chartres Street," 126; in *Mosquitoes*, 126; in *Pylon*, 127; in *If I Forget Thee, Jerusalem*, 127–28; punctured earth/lost Egyptian civilization motif, 127, 133, 150; in *The Sound and the Fury*, 128–41; tomb-raiding, 133, 141, 149–50, 191; in *Light in August*, 138; in *The Unvanquished*, 138–39; Jordan River/Red Sea crossing trope, 138–40, 142, 146, 151; in *As I Lay Dying* 139; Cleopatra iconography, 140–41, 143; in *Sanctuary*, 141–42; in *Requiem for a Nun*, 142–43; in *Go Down, Moses*, 143–49; in University of Virginia interview, 144–46; in *Intruder in the Dust*, 149–51; in *A Fable*, 191–93; mentioned, 21, 24, 25, 30, 161, 166
Egyptomania. See Egypt
El Dorado myth, 72, 80, 82, 114

Elgin Marbles, 38, 206n9
England: British Empire, 33–34; and cotton trade, 123–124, 213n5; and Arthurian legend, 154–63; in *A Fable* (racehorse/sentry), 193
Everbe (in *Sanctuary*), 164–68 passim
Exodus, 138. See also Egypt
Extra-Long Staple cotton. See Cotton

Fable, A (Faulkner), 30–31, 185–99, 204n8, 208n20, 216–17nn1–4
Faerie Queene, The (Spenser), 156
Fairchild, Dawson, 88, 91–94, 96–98, 109–10
Falkner, Col. William, 88–91, 163
Farmer, Cecilia. See Cecilia Farmer
Father Abraham (Faulkner), 58, 208n22
Fathers, Sam, 66–69, 209n2, 214n15
Faulkner, John, 53, 99, 101, 202n4, 206n8, 210n11
Faulkner, William: motion and stasis in art of, 3; as center of intertext, 4–5; literary reputation, 6–8; comments on being relieved of duty at UM post office, 20, 205n13; and television program, 22; as portrait/icon, 22; as myth-maker, 25; comments to Phil Stone on ambition, 35–36; balance of romanticism and irony in youth, 36–37, 207n7; and performance, 37, 206n8, 210n11; regionalist inheritance of, 44, 109, 212n23; early depiction of blacks, 45; ideas about conflict in fiction, 53; in New Orleans's French Quarter, 71–72; shooting BB gun, 76–78; description of Victor's, 78; developing Al Jackson stories with Sherwood Anderson, 92; flying experiences in the RAF, 98–100, 210n11; alleged ideas about the sky and imperialism, 101; as scriptwriter for *Land of the Pharaohs*, 134; at the University of Virginia, 144–45, 174; problematic depiction of race relations, 151; drawings for *Mayday*, 160, 175; knowledge of/reading in Arthurian legend, 169, 215n3;

Malorylike conflation of myth, 173, 216*n*13; description of tragedy in *Absalom, Absalom!* 174; work resisting notion of center, 202*n*2; "performance" instead of "use" of source material, 204*n*8; high school graduation speech, 205*n*15; with Clark Gable, 206*n*6; understanding of African Americans as "Negroes," 207*n*12; short story sending list, 208*n*14; referring to self as "black," 208*n*19; and hunting in Delta, 208*n*23; and Shushan Airport, 210*n*12; and removal of conventional punctuation in *Pylon*, 210*n*14; and picture of World War I soldier on *Pylon* manuscript, 210*n*15; unused blurb for *A Fable*, 216–17*n*3. *See also titles of works*

Faun: as racially hybrid, 40–41; and Jewel Bundren, 42; and cigar-store Indian, 42, 55; and Wilfred Midgleston, 43–50; as "farm"/"foreign," 49–50; and Januarius Jones, 51, 54; and Donald Mahon, 52–53, 54, 57; in *The Hamlet*, 58–66; and Eula Snopes, 62; Will Varner as, 63; Labove as, 63; Tug Nightingale as, 64; Bayard Sartoris as, 65; and Ike Snopes, 65; in "The Bear," 66–69; Sam Fathers as, 66; Ike McCaslin as, 67; in "Mirrors of Chartres," 80–81; Quentin Compson as, 140; Lucas Beauchamp as, 147–49; the corporal as, 190–91; centaur as, 208*n*24; mentioned, 159. *See also* Marble faun; *Marble Faun, The* (Faulkner); *Marble Faun, The* (Hawthorne)

Fetishization of Other, 86–87, 142
Fisk Jubilee Singers, 135
Fitzgerald, F. Scott, 39
Flags in the Dust (Faulkner), 56, 148, 153, 163, 177, 203*n*7, 209*n*25
"Flea, The," 91
Flying. *See* Aerodynamics; Airplanes
Foreigners, 50, 60, 133, 190, 192
Foucault, Michel, 14, 202*n*1
Fragmented space, 8–9, 10, 13, 18, 24, 28, 29
France, 4, 31, 57, 72–82 *passim*, 155–56, 162–63, 171, 189–98 *passim*
Franklin, Benjamin, 24, 112, 120, 134
Freemasonry, 120, 165, 188, 192–93, 212*n*1, 214*nn*16, 18. *See also* Egypt
Frenchman's Bend, 58, 60, 63

Gable, Clark, 37, 206*n*6
Galahad, Sir, 157, 163, 175
Galwyn of Arthgyl, 159–60, 163, 175
Gawain, Sir, 155–56, 164, 166, 171, 174, 178–79, 216*n*14
General Camphollower (in *The White Rose of Memphis*), 89–90
Generalissimo (in *A Fable*), 186–87, 189, 190
Gens de couleur libre, 74
Geoffrey of Monmouth, 155–56, 170
Gibbons (*History of Rome*), 56–57
Gildas (monk), 154
Gilligan, Joe, 51, 54–55, 56–57
Global North, 8–9, 76, 82, 193
Global South, 8–9, 44, 49, 60, 75–76, 82, 110–11, 193
Go Down, Moses (Faulkner), 66, 68, 120, 143–50, 205*n*12
Goats: racial iconography of, 40–41, 42, 207*n*11; in "Black Music," 45–47; and Joe Christmas, 50; and Januarius Jones, 51; as unit of currency in *The Hamlet*, 58–61; goat rancher, 58–61; Flem Snopes as Pan, 61–62; Snopeses as tribe of goatpeople, 65, 67; in "Mirrors of Chartres," 80; Uncle Parsham's imperial as goat whisker, 167; mentioned, 48, 94, 115, 209*n*5. *See also* Greek/Roman myth; Marble faun; *Marble Faun, The* (Faulkner)
Golden Octopus, the, 75
Gone with the Wind (Mitchell), 27
Gordon (in *Mosquitoes*), 87, 94, 95, 97
Gragnon, General (in *A Fable*), 187–89, 191, 195
Grecian urn. *See* Greek/Roman myth
Greece, 33–34, 38, 47, 207*n*9

Greek Revival architecture. *See* Architecture
Greek/Roman myth: influences on the South, 33–34; influences on Faulkner, 33–35, 37–39, 40; in *The Marble Faun* (Faulkner), 34–35, 38–43; Grecian urn imagery, 37–38, 47–48, 51, 57, 65–67, 199, 207*n*10, 209*n*25; in *As I Lay Dying*, 42; in "Black Music," 43–50; in *Light in August*, 50; in *Soldiers' Pay*, 50–57; in *The Hamlet*, 58–63, 65–66; in *The Town*, 63–64; in *The Mansion*, 64–65; in "The Bear," 66–69; in *The Sound and the Fury*, 132; in "Mirrors of Chartres Street," 161; in *Absalom, Absalom!* 172–74; in *Mayday*, 175; in *A Fable*, 187; in *Jurgen*, 216*n*13; mentioned, 13, 21, 30, 141, 160. *See also* Architecture
Groom (in *A Fable*), 192–94
Guinevere, 155–56, 159, 172–79 *passim*

Habitus, 9, 87, 114, 136, 143, 163, 164, 180
Hagood (in *Pylon*), 101, 105–7
Hamlet, The (Faulkner), 37, 58–63, 65–66, 77, 149
Handy, W. C., 43
Harvard College, 137, 169, 172
Hawley-Smoot Tariff Act, 125
Hawthorne, Nathaniel, 35, 40
Helen of Troy, 65, 159, 179
Heterotopia, 14, 187
Hieroglyphics, 104, 122, 127, 130, 134, 192
Hightower, Gail, 50, 163
History of Rome (Gibbons), 56–57
Hogganbeck, Boon, 67, 114, 164–68, 215*n*7
Holiday (magazine), 21–22 *passim*, 205*n*14
Holmes, Jack, 101, 212*n*22
Horizontal transcendence, 174
Horizontal-vertical planes (of mythic places), 3, 13, 16, 68
Huckleberry Finn, 194
Hybridity: centrality to Faulkner's art, 17–18, 28, 29; of speech, 29; of spaces, 30, 34; of marble faun, 34; of Wilfred Midgleston, 45–49; of Joe Christmas, 50; of Joanna Burden, 50; of Gail Hightower, 50; of Margaret Powers, 54, 57; of written law (in *The Hamlet*), 61; in *The Town*, 63; of Tug Nightingale, 64; of Sam Fathers, 66; of Isaac McCaslin, 67; of Charles Bon, 83–85; of white men in *Absalom, Absalom!* 85–86, 214*n*12; of monkey/Monkey Brand Soap imagery, 85–86; yellow fever/the color yellow and, 91; Al Jackson stories and, 93; of characters in *Mosquitoes*, 94–97; in *Pylon*, 98–107 *passim*, 210*n*14, 211*n*18; of men in *If I Forget Thee, Jerusalem*, 112–16, 128; of American-Egyptian cotton, 123; of cotton as emblem of imperialism, 124; Egypt as trope of, 125; of Moses, 128, 214*n*13; of Benjy, 128–32; of Reverend Shegog, 131–32; of Jordan River/Red Sea crossing motif, 138–39; of Temple Drake and Nancy Mannigo together, 143; of the McCaslin-Edmonds-Beauchamp family, 144; of Lucas Beauchamp, 147–48; mule as example of, 148–49; of Thomas Sutpen, 175; of Paul (apostle), 187; of the corporal, 190; and the old general, 198; of South, 202–3*n*6; cosmos and, 205–6*n*16; and Faulkner's Native Americans, 208*n*14; in "Centaur in Brass," 208–9*n*24; inescapability of (descendants of Old Bailey), 209*n*6; in *A Fable*, 216*n*2. *See also* Blackness; Counterfeit Other; Marble faun; Whiteness

Iberville, Pierre Le Moyne, Sieur de, 72
Idylls of the King (Tennyson), 156
If I Forget Thee, Jerusalem (Faulkner), 87, 111–17, 127–28, 216*n*13
I'll Take My Stand (Twelve Southerners), 7
Imagined community, 8, 9, 204*n*10
Imperial impulse: explanation of, 9, 204*n*11; mentioned, 3, 10, 16, 18, 25, 28,

46, 58, 71, 72, 101, 104, 120, 123, 157, 183, 185, 186, 188, 189, 197, 206n16, 208n23
Imperial space: explanation of, 10–11; mentioned, 5, 13, 16, 18, 21, 29, 30, 34, 67, 72, 73, 76, 93, 96, 97, 120, 121, 130, 151, 175, 185, 210n10. *See also* Place; Space
Imperialism, 2, 10, 18, 21, 24, 30, 33, 38, 44, 49, 56, 57, 58, 72, 98, 101, 117, 119, 122, 125, 135, 168, 191, 205n11, 208n18, 210n16
Ingomar (barbarian chief), 88–89, 210n10
Intertext/intertextuality, 3–4, 5, 6, 15
Intruder in the Dust (Faulkner), 143, 149–51
Italians, 50, 65, 74, 78–80, 95–96, 137, 141
Ivanhoe, 88

Jackson, Al, 91–93, 98, 117
Jackson, Andrew, 117, 128
Jacob (biblical), 129, 134
Jazz, 39, 43, 53, 55, 69
"Jealousy" (Faulkner), 79–80
Jefferson, Thomas, 34, 41, 73, 208n18
Jefferson, Miss.: layered history of, 142–43; layout of downtown, 161; mentioned, 13, 15, 23, 36, 64, 65, 84, 87, 130, 139, 140, 146, 147, 168, 170, 177, 180, 181
Jeffersonian ideal, 46, 49–50. *See also* Arcady, southern
Jews: recovery of Jewish voices, 18; Jason Compson's comments on, 36, 133; Ike McCaslin's comments on, 69; Jewish story of Jesus, 80–81, 161; in "New Orleans" (Faulkner), 82; mentioned, 147
Jiggs (in *Pylon*), 101–10 *passim*, 210–11n17–18
Jones, Januarius, 50–57 *passim*, 63
Jones, Wash, 86, 172n12
Jordan River. *See* Egypt
Jumel, Louis Alexis, 122–23
Jurgen (Cabell), 159, 160, 169, 216n13

Keats, John, 35–48 *passim*, 64–65, 121, 209n25. *See also* Greek/Roman myth
Kennedy, John Pendleton, 157
Keystone, Faulkner's cosmos as, 5, 15, 20
King, Grace, 73, 76, 126, 209n1
Knight of the Black Plume. *See* Falkner, Col. William
Knight's Gambit (Faulkner), 178, 216n
Knights of Temperance, 163
Kohl, Linda Snopes, 64–65, 179, 181–83
Kosciusko, 24–25
Ku Klux Klan, 158, 180

La Salle, René Robert Cavalier, Sieur de, 72, 126
Lancelot, 155, 156, 171, 172, 174
Land of the Pharaohs (film), 134–35, 214nn16–17
"Landing in Luck" (Faulkner), 100
Laverne (in *Pylon*), 101, 107, 108, 109, 211n17, 212n21–22
Law, John, 72, 74, 94
Le Blond de la Tour, Chevalier, 73
Le Morte Darthur (Malory), 155–74 *passim*, 215n3
Lee, Robert E., 64
"Legend of Sleepy Hollow, The" (Irving), 48–49
Lévi-Strauss, Claude, 14–15, 207n10
Levine, Gerald David, 188–89, 195, 197
Light in August (Faulkner), 43, 50, 138, 163, 185, 214n16
Lincoln, Abraham, 121, 138
Lion, 67–69
Little Sister Death, 23, 139
Littlejohn, Mrs., 66
Local color, 44, 49, 92–93
Long, Huey, 17, 74
Long, Robert Cary, 34
Lost Cause, 158, 163, 215n1
Lost race of Egyptians. *See* Egypt
Louisiana, 72–75 *passim*, 112–16 *passim*, 195. *See also* New Orleans
Louisiana Hayride, 75

Louisiana Lottery, 74
Louisiana Purchase, 73
Luster (in *The Sound and the Fury*), 130

Maestri, Robert, 74
Magda (in *A Fable*), 198
Mahon, Donald, 52–57, 130, 208n21
Mallison, Charles "Chick," 64–65, 149–50, 179, 181, 209n24
Malory, Sir Thomas. See *Le Morte Darthur* (Malory)
Mannigo, Nancy, 143, 182–83
Mansion, The (Faulkner), 64–65, 179–82
Marble faun: in *The Marble Faun*, 34–43; Wilfred Migleston as, 48; Joe Christmas as, 50; Joanna Burden as, 50; Gail Hightower as, 50; and cigar-store Indian, 55; Donald Mahon as, 57; Flem Snopes as, 61; Eula Varner as, 62; Tug Nightingale as, 64; Bayard Sartoris as, 65; Sam Fathers as, 66; Ike McCaslin as, 67; protagonist of "Mirrors of Chartres Street," 81; Charles Bon as, 84; marble statue as, 87; Patricia as, 97; and Jiggs, 101; Lucas Beauchamp as, 147–48, 149; the corporal as, 190–91; Tom Tom and Tomey's Turl as, 208n24; mentioned, 53, 66, 69, 96, 140. See also Faun; Goats; Hybridity
Marble Faun, The (Faulkner), 34–43, 44, 50, 55, 69, 206
Marble Faun, The (Hawthorne), 40
Mary Queen of Scots, 88
Masons. See Freemasonry
Material/materiality: and this book's model of reading Faulkner, 5; and incarnations of space, 11, 203n7; and power, 11, 204n9; relationship to myth, 12, 14; materiality of Greek/Roman myth in Faulkner, 33, 37, 69; Patricia's abrogation of, 97; and toy airplane in *Pylon*, 109; in tall convict's life, 116; oppression of true Others, 140; in *Sanctuary*, 142; mentioned, 13
Mayday (Faulkner), 37, 58, 159–60, 163, 169, 174–75, 215n4, 216n14
McCannon, Shreve, 83, 85, 86, 110–11, 137, 169, 172, 176–77, 209n6
McCaslin, Isaac (Ike), 66–69, 149–50
McCaslin ledgers, 68–69
Mediterranean, 38, 75, 123
Memphis, Egypt, 126
Memphis, Tenn., 23, 25, 28, 88–89, 122, 125–26, 141–42, 147, 164, 166–68, 213n3–4, 214n10
Merlin, 155–56, 170, 173
Midgleston, Wilfred, 44–50, 51, 53, 55, 59, 63, 69, 162, 194, 208n17, 19
Midsummer Night's Dream, A (Shakespeare), 53
Miller, Glen, 43
"Mirrors of Chartres Street" (Faulkner), 80–81, 126, 160–61
Miscegenation, 41, 209n6
Miss Corrie. See Everbe
"Mississippi" (Faulkner), 21–28, 38, 164, 206n4
Mississippi Bubble. See New Orleans
Mississippi Delta. See Delta, Mississippi
Mitafifi. See Cotton
Monkey Brand Soap, 85–86, 108
Monkeys, 55, 85–86, 108, 131
Monticello, 34, 46, 49, 208n18
Mordred, 154–56, 171–73
Mormon religion, 127
Moses, 120, 127, 128, 138, 142, 144–45, 151, 195, 214n13. See also Egypt; Hybridity
Mosquitoes (Faulkner), 87–97, 101, 109, 110, 116, 126, 141, 208n19, 216n13
Mules, 24, 54, 64, 68, 86, 136, 148–49, 167, 215n20
Mummy-unwrapping motif. See Egypt
Myth: fundamental to Faulkner, 6–7; and imperial space, 11; as heterogeneous linguistic economy, 11–12; and materiality, 12; former treatments of in Faulkner, 12–13; as mode of speaking for oppressor and oppressed, 16–17; temporal di-

mension of, 20; stages of development, 20–21; and value of industriousness, 24; definition/application of term in this book, 205n10. *See also* Arthurian legend; Christian myth; Consummatory stage, of myth development; Egypt; Greek/Roman myth; Mythic place; New Orleans; Primary stage, of myth development; Romantic stage, of myth development

Mythic place: definition/discussion of, 13–15, 20; mentioned, 5, 16–18, 21, 24, 25, 27, 29, 30, 33, 34, 43, 46, 47, 50, 53, 55, 57, 61, 62, 67, 68, 72, 76, 81, 96, 97, 98, 120, 132, 143, 151, 154, 157, 160–62, 174, 175, 180, 183, 185, 210n10. *See also* Imperial space; Myth; Place

Napoleon (Bonaparte), 57, 73, 82, 88, 117, 119, 213n3

Native Americans: linked to demonic iconography, 40; cigar-store Indian, 42–43; goats as, 59; Sam Fathers as, 66; Boon Hogganbeck as, 67; in New Orleans, 74, 78; Pete as, 96, 141; and cotton, 124–25, 213n8; mentioned, 12, 18, 21, 24, 27, 103, 147, 149, 151, 208n14

Native informant, 71, 108

Nausikaa, 87, 92

Nennius, 154

New Orleans: history of, 71–76, 209n1–2; founding of, 71, 72; disasters in, 71; "Mississippi Bubble," 72; on French maps, 72; gifted to and rebuilt by Spanish, 73; regained by Napoleon, 73; and Louisiana Purchase, 73; racial/ethnic complexity, 74; opulence of, 74; corruption of, 74–75; Oriental aspect of, 75, 209n3; liminality of, 76; literary treatment of, 76, 209n4; Faulkner's experiences/impressions of, 76–78; in "Jealousy," 79–80; in "Mirrors of Chartres Street," 80–81; in additional sketches, 81–82; as Scythia, 82–83; and Charles Bon, 83–85; in *Mosquitoes*, 87–97; as basis for New Valois in *Pylon*, 97–110; in *If I Forget Thee, Jerusalem*, 111–17; New Orleans Cotton Exchange, 125; similarities to Delta, 126, 213n4; in *A Fable*, 193–95; mentioned, 25, 29–31, 48–49, 154, 160–63, 171, 177, 210n12

New Orleans Times-Picayune, 72, 79, 81

New Valois. *See* New Orleans; *Pylon*

New York, 34, 36, 44, 48, 49, 56, 133

New York Cotton Exchange. *See* Cotton

Nightingale, Tug, 64–65

Nile Delta. *See* Delta, Nile

Nobel Prize, 7, 21, 29, 36, 106

Noble savage, 42

"Ode on a Grecian Urn" (Keats), 37–38, 67

Ohio, 19, 24, 56, 59, 107, 109, 195, 211n17

Omnibus television program. *See* "William Faulkner of Oxford" television program

O'Reilly, Don Alexander "Bloody," 73

Orientalism, 75, 83, 103, 119

Page, Thomas Nelson, 49, 91, 158

Palimpsest, 15, 154, 175, 216n12

Pan, 38–63 *passim*, 160, 175

Paris, 78, 195, 197

Passive recalcitrance of topography, 1–2, 28, 46, 67, 187, 202n2

Pastoral. *See* Arcady, southern

Pauger, Adrien de, 73

Paulding, James Kirk, 157

Periphery, cultural, 2, 10, 11, 12, 13, 16, 17, 19, 35, 36, 38, 44, 48, 49, 52, 54, 57, 59, 68, 76, 77, 83, 87, 88, 92, 93, 95, 97, 110, 115, 116, 120, 128, 130–33, 137–40, 142, 157, 161, 164, 168, 177, 180, 192, 194–98, 206n4. *See also* Center, cultural; Place; Space

Pete (in *Mosquitoes*), 94–96, 141

Pharaoh, 119, 134–35, 146–47, 191, 214n17

Philippe, Duke of Orleans, 72

Pima. *See* Cotton
Place: as pause in movement, 3; interaction with space, 3, 13–14, 201–2*n*1, 202*n*5, 203*n*7; recent critical treatments of, 203*n*7. *See also* Imperial space; Mythic place; Plot; Space
Plot: Faulkner's tactics in construction of, 4; of mythic-material ground, 14–15, 18, 33, 46, 62, 67, 170; mentioned, 98, 134, 160, 169, 173
Pontchartrain, Lake, 87, 91–92, 94, 97
Popeye, 141–42, 208*n*19
Portable Faulkner, The, 6–7, 12, 29, 202*n*3, 214*n*14
Postage stamp, 19–20
Powers, Margaret, 51–57, 208*n*19
Pre-Raphaelites, 157, 172
Priest, Lucius, 164–68, 216*nn*8, 10
Primary stage, of myth development, 20–21, 25, 26, 29, 62, 104–6, 114, 155. *See also* Myth
Protean nature of spaces, 3, 9–10, 16
Punctured-earth motif. *See* Egypt
Pylon (Faulkner), 87, 97–109, 110, 113, 115, 117, 127, 150, 188, 210*n*15, 211*n*19, 212*n*21–22, 214*n*11

Quest: tall convict's, 114; for the Golden Fleece, 132. *See also* Arthurian legend

Rainey, Paul, 59–60, 208*n*23
Ratliff, V. K., 3, 58–62, 63–66, 149, 179, 181, 214*n*16
Reba (in *Sanctuary*), 141–42, 164, 168
Reconstruction (post–Civil War U.S.), 44, 49, 50, 74, 78, 148
Reporter (in *Pylon*), 98–102, 105–9, 113, 127, 212*nn*21–22
Requiem for a Nun (Faulkner), 15, 141, 142–43, 149, 182–83
Rincon, 44–45, 49, 162
Rittenmeyer, Charlotte, 111–16, 127–28, 216*n*13
Roman myth. *See* Greek/Roman myth

Romantic stage, of myth development, 20–21, 25, 26, 29, 62, 98, 106–8, 141, 155. *See also* Myth
"Rose for Emily, A" (Faulkner), 149–50
Roskus (*The Sound and the Fury*), 136–37
Rowan Oak, 21, 23
Royal Air Force (RAF), 99, 188, 210*n*11. *See also* Faulkner, William
Runner (in *A Fable*), 190, 193–97 *passim*
Ruth, Babe, 35–36, 60, 208*n*23

Said, Edward, 75, 119
Sanctuary (Faulkner), 36, 141–42, 164, 178, 206*n*5, 208*n*19
Sander, Aleck, 150
Sanskrit, 84, 169
Sartoris, Bayard, 1–2, 26–27, 65, 168, 177
Sartoris, Carolina Bayard, 163
Sartoris, Col. John, 56, 65, 139, 163, 177
Satan, 40–43, 50, 51, 58, 61, 77, 90, 207*n*11. *See also* Faun; Goats; Marble faun
Saxon, Lyle, 71, 76, 209*n*1
Saxons (Anglo-Saxons), 28, 74, 154–56, 171
Schwartz, Lawrence, 6–8
Scott, Sir Walter, 90, 157–58, 163
Scythia, 82–84
Sea Islands, 124. *See also* Cotton
Sentry. *See* Groom (in *A Fable*)
Shegog, Reverend (in *The Sound and the Fury*), 131–32, 151
Sherwood Anderson and Other Famous Creoles (Spratling and Faulkner), 76–77
Shumann, Jack, 101–15, 150
Shumann, Roger, 101–9, 211*n*17, 212*n*21
Simms, William Gilmore, 157
Simulacra, 104, 211*n*17
Sir Gawain and the Green Knight, 155, 216*n*14
Smith, Joseph, 127
Snopes, Clarence Egglestone, 180, 183
Snopes, Eck, 65–66, 181, 214*n*16
Snopes, Eula Varner, 62–64, 65, 140, 179, 209*n*25

Snopes, Flem, 3, 58–66, 77, 178, 181, 183, 208*n*24, 216*n*15
Snopes, I. O., 66
Snopes, Isaac (Ike), 60–61, 65, 67
Snopes, Launcelot (Lump), 66, 179
Snopes, Mink, 60, 179
Soldiers' Pay (Faulkner), 19, 50–57, 58, 97, 130, 215*n*20
South America, 60, 124, 193, 197
Southern space, reevaluations of, 8–9, 202*n*6
Space: and narrative, 2; Faulkner's treatment of, 3; interaction with place, 2, 201–2*n*1; intertextuality as channeled through space, 6; and power/strategies of performance, 9–10; fragmentation of, 10–11; and narrative/myth, 11–12, 18; Faulkner's space as fragmented and imperial, 13; Foucault and, 14; space of opacity, 15. *See also* Center, cultural; Imperial space; Periphery, cultural; Place; Southern space, reevaluations of
Spain, 73, 75
Speaking (of groups): Spivak and "Can the Subaltern Speak?" 11–12; use of myth as linguistic economy to "speak," 16
Spratling, William, 77–78, 102
"St. Louis Blues March," 43
Standard Oil Company, 44, 208*n*16
Stevens, Gavin, 63–65, 141–50, 178–82, 216*n*14
Stone, Phil, 35–36, 206*n*7
Stowe, Harriet Beecher, 76, 212*n*24
Subaltern, 11, 48, 57, 96, 108, 186, 192, 197
Sut Lovingood, 92
Sutpen, Henry, 83–87, 169, 171–74, 216*n*12
Sutpen, Judith, 84, 87, 171–75, 216*n*12–13
Sutpen, Thomas, 18, 80, 84–87, 92, 134, 161–62, 168–83, 214*n*12, 216, 216*n*12
Sutterfield, Rev. Tobe, 190, 193–96, 198

Tall convict (in *If I Forget Thee, Jerusalem*), 111–17 *passim*

Talliafero (in *Mosquitoes*), 87, 95
Tarzan, 102–3
Television program. *See* "William Faulkner of Oxford" television program
Tennyson, Alfred Lord, 156–58 *passim*, 160, 172
Third World, 197, 203*n*6
"To the Graduating Class, University High School, 1951" (Faulkner), 11
Tomb of the Unknown Soldier, 191–92, 197
Tomb-raiding motif. *See* Egypt
Tooleyman, Monsieur (in *A Fable*), 195
Topography, passive recalcitrance of. *See* Passive recalcitrance of topography
Town, The (Faulkner), 3, 63–64, 178–79, 181, 214*n*16
Trace, of former mythic-imperial layers, 14–16, 20, 38, 40, 46, 52, 55, 57, 62, 65, 66, 79, 87, 94, 97, 140, 143, 149, 187, 191, 196, 198, 209*nn*24, 25
Treaty of San Ildefonso, 73
Trojan Horse, 109, 174
Troyes, Chrétien de, 155, 164
Tucker, Beverly, 157
Tucker, George, 157
Twain, Mark, 19, 157

Ulloa, Don Antonia de, 73
Uncle Parsham (in *The Reivers*), 167
Uncle Tom's Cabin (Stowe), 76, 136
Universal Oil Company, 44, 162. *See also* Standard Oil Company
Unvanquished, The (Faulkner), 1–2, 26, 138–39, 140, 163, 168, 206*n*4
Utah, 113–16, 127. *See also* Mormon religion

Van Dymings, Mr. and Mrs., 46–51 *passim*, 208*n*18
Van Tassel, Katrina, 49, 53, 63
Varner, Eula. *See* Snopes, Eula Varner
Varner, Will, 60, 66
Vaundreuil, Pierre-Cavagnal de Rigaud, Marquis de, 73

Vertical-horizontal plane. *See* Mythic place
Vertical transcendence, 174
Vieux Carré, 71, 74
Virginia, University of, 144

Wace, 155, 170
Washington, George, 120, 127, 214n12
"Wealthy Jew" (Faulkner), 82
White Rose of Memphis, The (Falkner), 88–91, 93, 157
Whiteness: and marble faun, 41; whitening of black forms (music), 43; and Joe Christmas, 50; and Confederate soldier statues, 56; transformation from blackness into (in New Orleans), 78; Thomas Sutpen's poor whiteness, 85; of statue in *Mosquitoes*, 87; Benjy Compson's racial hybridity, 130, 140; of Reverend Shegog, 131; Jason Compson's championing of, 133; and Quentin Compson, 135–40; mentioned, 27. *See also* Blackness; Counterfeit Other; Hybridity; Marble faun
Whitman, Walt, 6, 69
Wilbourne, Harry, 111–17 *passim*, 127–28
"William Faulkner of Oxford" television program, 22, 205n15
William Nichols streetcar incident (New Orleans), 77
Wooden Indian. *See* Cigar-store Indian

Yankees (baseball team), 36
Yazoo Delta. *See* Delta, Mississippi
Yellow fever, 74, 88, 91, 126
Yoknapatawpha County: West-Yoknapatawpha Company, 59; recent treatments of space in, 203n7; mentioned, 1, 7, 15, 18, 20, 26, 29, 58, 62, 128, 140, 142, 147, 151, 178, 180, 196, 202n4,
Yuma. *See* Cotton

www.ingramcontent.com/pod-product-compliance
Lightning Source LLC
Chambersburg PA
CBHW070303240426
43661CB00057B/2636